SOUTH AMERICA
UNCENSORED

SOUTH AMERICA
UNCENSORED

Jungles of Fascism
Genuine Good-Neighborliness
Portrait of a Continent
In Search of Frontiers

By

Roland Hall Sharp

Docteur ès Sciences Politiques, Graduate Institute of International Studies,
Geneva, and the University of Geneva
Staff Correspondent on Latin-American Affairs for
The Christian Science Monitor

Longmans, Green and Co.
NEW YORK • TORONTO
1945

Dedicated to the silenced liberals in
South America who represent
the democratic yearnings
of oppressed millions

CONTENTS

viii CONTENTS

IN SEARCH OF FRONTIERS

Illustrated with 32 pages of photographs, charts, and maps.

WHEREIN WE MEET

At the end of 1937 I set forth to range the length and breadth of Latin America in search of information on that region's peoples, resources, and significance for the rest of the world. Since then I have seen the South American continent from end to end and side to side and right down through the middle. As the journeys multiplied to seven, the mileage grew to 110,000. Much of it was the hard way, overland, instead of in the air.

Always these primary questions were before me:

How serious is the fascist tinge of government, especially in Argentina and Brazil?

What lines of policy by the United States will promote genuine friendship and security in the Western Hemisphere?

Where do interests of Europe and Asia affect South America?

Are South American resources actually as promising as we have been told?

Do modern pioneers have opportunities here, and if so, where are the best locations as well as the pitfalls?

What are South America's cultural values?

Above all—for people are the indispensable resource in any country—who are the residents of South America? How do they think and live? What are their special talents, aspirations, needs, and possibilities?

In search of answers to these and other questions, I have set aside preconceived notions and allowed South America to tell me its own story. Whenever possible I have stayed with the people and traveled on their stern-paddle river steamers, their wood-burning trains, modern silver streamliners, busses ranging from jalopies to "Pullmans," trucks, mules, dugout canoes, horseback, and afoot.

The latest trip took me 28,500 miles through the deep interior from the Amazon Basin to Magellan's Strait. Airplanes were used only where no other transportation was available, or when the air-view gave a broader comprehension of land formations. On earlier trips I had crisscrossed the continent to reach nearly every remote place that is worth seeing. Many of the interior landmarks have been revisited at intervals during the past seven years, in contrasting seasons of excessive heat, cold, rain, or drought.

Offsetting South America's developed and potential resources, I have found, is a generally unsuspected poverty of soils, as well as severe handicaps of jungles, deserts, misplaced mountains, and human elements that go far toward explaining the continent's retarded progress.

These journeys of observation in human relations, economics, political science, and diplomacy, were made in my position as Staff Correspondent on Latin-American Affairs for *The Christian Science Monitor*. It is a roving assignment admirably suited to special needs of the Latin-American news field. For fifteen years I have been trained in that international daily newspaper's standards of truthfulness, accuracy, dependability, fearlessness, fair play, thoroughness, independence, depth, objectivity, and constructiveness.

A natural interest in Latin America gradually shaped my writing in that direction. My doctoral thesis at the Graduate Institute of International Studies and the University of Geneva dealt with nonrecognition of territorial or other gains brought about by force. This doctrine, lifted to world stature by former Secretary of State Henry L. Stimson, had some of its origins in Latin America. While the thesis was in preparation I went to Japan, Manchuria, and China to observe effects of the Stimson Doctrine on Japanese aggression, completing a trip around the world from Geneva. Returning to Boston in 1934, I served in the home office, in the Washington Bureau, and on various trips in the United States before being assigned to Latin America late in 1937. I soon began to pile up those 110,000 miles.

In preparation I started to study both Portuguese and Spanish. En route I found German useful in several parts of Latin

America. French served many times among the well-traveled ruling classes, until my South American languages became stronger. That first trip was the grand tour by air. Early in 1938 it was still somewhat of a novelty for a North American news and radio correspondent to visit all of the Latin-American countries. Since then, hundreds have made the usual round, and it has become a well-beaten track.

Yet the South American continent cannot be understood solely on the basis of aerial grand tours to the coastal cities. Unfortunately, much of the writing to reach the public in recent years has not penetrated behind the façade of Buenos Aires and Rio de Janeiro, Santiago de Chile and the other capitals. One reason I have not previously undertaken a book on South America is that I had not crossed certain horizons of the interior. Like most people, I tended to fill in those unknown areas with scenes and resources, opportunities and possibilities, beyond what they actually hold. Suspecting myself somewhat of this tendency, I hesitated to draw conclusions on some of the most vital questions about South America until I had seen every characteristic region. Meanwhile a steady flow of news and special reporting deepened my knowledge, corrected some of the more flagrant and pervasive illusions about South America, and prepared me for the crystallization that took place during the last trip.

Something broke through in me out there alone in jungle camps. It deepened when Brazilian and Argentinian secret police picked up my trail for no reason other than my mission as a reporter of the free press. On river boats loaded with needless disease I saw that the people could be spared so much by so little wholesome education. Then I stood in tin-kingdom palaces of Simón I. Patiño at Cochabamba, Bolivia. He has never seen two of these although his total spending in and around this remote Andean city is reliably estimated at $30,000,000!

Insight came through. A light played on bits of information that had not seemed to make sense but now were seen as parts of South America as it is, rather than as it has been imagined. Week after week the interior hammered into me the facts of its poverty even in soils and other basic resources.

Reluctantly I revised my estimates downward.

With genuine democrats and liberals of South America I felt the weight of dictatorial and fascist repression in unexpected places. It squeezed popular liberties into a tighter corner than ever before during my experience. This was the more surprising since it was not confined to Argentina, Paraguay, and Bolivia, but was clearly apparent even in Brazil, one of the United Nations fighting supposedly for more democracy in the world.

Out of such inescapable findings, at times startling, came the conviction that the true story of South America must be told— as far as it can be uncovered and published through the dark obscurities of propaganda and political censorship. What the free press means was literally burned into me in the mesmeric atmosphere of Brazil, where even qualified foreign correspondents are lulled into voluntary compliance with some of the most fascist press controls in the world. I expected in advance to have trouble sending political news out of Argentina, and did. I was not prepared to be followed in Brazil by secret police who made it plain by their actions that the discreet political reporter should not try to see too much. Knowing my own friendly regard for Brazil as a whole, and my affection for its lovable people, I found this surveillance by police of the Vargas regime far harder to endure than similar mistrust of my motives in Argentina and elsewhere. The Vargas regime seeks to impose a blackout of the free press. So do other military dictatorships in South America. By political censorships of that kind the free press is not obligated under any law. To them the free press is not required to pay respect. With every rightful restriction of wartime military censorship in any country I willingly comply. Against attempts of political censorship anywhere to silence the free press I act under a sober responsibility to inform my particular segment of the public.

That, in brief sketch, is the background of this writing. My aim is to present a matured report on what South America means to me after seven years of intensive firsthand observation. I know that is a short time and make no claim of having done more than perceive some of the main outlines in this complex, obscure, and widely misunderstood continent. The following pages, except for historical data, are based on my own field experiences. Throughout, the purpose is to awaken a more realistic point of view toward South America. Anyone who is looking from more highly developed countries toward this area as a field for pioneering, investments, or a new home will find here surveys and comments specifically designed to answer his main questions.

While references will be made to Latin America as a whole, and to inter-American relations in the large, I want at the outset to emphasize that this book is no encyclopedia, no impossible attempt to cover the twenty Latin-American nations, or even the ten nations of the South American continent, in one easy volume. Attention is focused on a few of the most important currents in South America which must be understood as a basis for intelligent action during many years to come. Some of the facts and events hitherto hidden or thrown out of focus by censorship and propaganda are dark. Wherever possible within the space available I have balanced the picture with some of the fine reports that can accurately be rendered about South America. The critical passages are constructive in purpose, not aimed against any person even when acts of public figures are opposed by name.

Controversial terms such as fascist, totalitarian, and others used in the text are defined, as I understand them, at the end of the book. My aim is never to apply these key words loosely to individuals or governments. What I mean by them in any given context may be checked by reference to my small glossary, under the heading, *A Few Definitions*.

Events and personages of the political scene will change, but the soils of the Amazon Basin and other misleading horizons of the interior—as well as promising ones—will be there until time and technical skills transform them. South America's actual riches come into truer perspective when we candidly face the continent's difficulties of geography, climate, limited resources (they are not boundless as is frequently stated), faulty transportation, shortsighted politics, and a confused social equation.

Also, our sympathies for the South American peoples are deepened by knowledge of their hardships on a continent that in many ways is antihuman, yet strangely beckons from afar to the uninformed as some overlooked land of promise.

Many of the acknowledgments that spring to thought for information and insight cannot be made here. South American liberals to whom such credit is due have already tasted bitter reprisals—on counts other than any aid they extended to me—by fascist regimes. To name them here might only add to dangers faced by themselves and their families. I have dedicated the book to all of them; to my friends and to unknown democrats who work, as they find means, for the inevitable emancipation of South America from its own, as well as foreign, oppressors. Running over in memory the thousands of individuals who have extended generous aid leaves me at a loss to begin naming them. The omissions would shout at me from between the scanty lines of specific acknowledgments.

To the Carnegie Endowment for International Peace a word of thanks is offered. When I accompanied a group sent to South America in 1941 by the Endowment for a "no-strings-attached" tour of observation, my first major break-through occurred into the limitations of South America's reputed wealth in several vital fields. In the company of men who know soils, including Dean Harlow L. Walster of the North Dakota College of Agriculture, I changed some basic views. I saw these experts look at South America's best tropical or semitropical earth—even the famous *terra roxa* in the Brazilian State of São Paulo—and shake their heads. On the Argentine *pampa* they were enthusiastic as we rolled through rich acres of Buenos Aires Province. Yet these lands are, in ratio to the whole continental area, as two finger tips placed to touch the center of the other palm.

It has also been valuable to accompany former Secretary of State Cordell Hull or the former Undersecretary of State, Sumner Welles, on diplomatic voyages to Lima, Panama, Havana, and Rio de Janeiro. Other governmental officials, including those of the United States Rubber Development Corporation, at times facilitated my entry into remote areas. One of my most enjoyable trips into the jungle came with Peruvian engineers early in 1939 as they drove their highway through from Lima at the Pacific

Ocean to Pucalpa on the Ucayali River, where ocean-going ships can sail via the Amazon to the Atlantic, and on to Europe.

Only the unselfish desire of my wife, Elizabeth Guy Sharp, gracious and stalwart life partner that she is, causes me to dedicate this book to South America's forgotten liberals instead of to her. A few voyages with me, one all the way to Chile, and her constant support from the home base, have inspired and sped the work.

Even such scanty acknowledgments show how impossible is the payment here of my impounded thanks. The pages to follow, while entirely on my own responsibility, will strive to even the balance.

ROLAND HALL SHARP

Williamstown

Argentine Fascism: Parade of July 9, 1944, in Buenos Aires.

A

Trophies Seized from Nazis in Southern Brazil
The Hitlerian uniform draped on a dummy in the police museum at Pôrto Alegre was worn by Ernst Dorsch, regional Nazi leader.

Brazilian Soldiers in Armies of the United Nations

Secret Police Examining Weapons Taken from Brazilian Nazis
Dum-dum bullets were molded secretly to fit the bore of rifles used by the Brazilian Army as Nazis in 1937-40 planned a *putsch*.

C

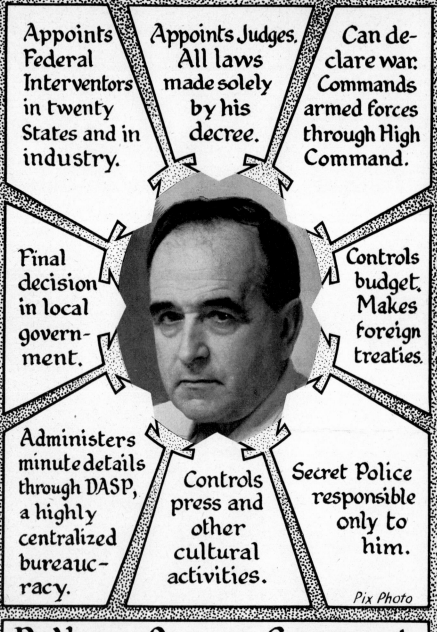

Appoints Federal Interventors in twenty States and in industry.

Appoints Judges. All laws made solely by his decree.

Can declare war. Commands armed forces through High Command.

Final decision in local government.

Controls budget. Makes foreign treaties.

Administers minute details through DASP, a highly centralized bureaucracy.

Controls press and other cultural activities.

Secret Police responsible only to him.

Pix Photo

Dr. Vargas: One-man Government.

JUNGLES OF FASCISM

Brazil: Fascist United Nation

GAGGED WITH HANDKERCHIEFS they have tied across their own mouths, a thin line of São Paulo University students advances through downtown streets of Brazil's commercial metropolis. They are headed toward the city's central plaza, called Praça do Patriarcha. It is the evening rush hour. Office workers jam into busses and overloaded streetcars.

As the students approach, military police of the Vargas dictatorship quickly mass.

Tense silence spreads through the crowd.

Unwavering, grim, on come the students. The whole content of their protest is summed up in those self-imposed gags.

The police know what they mean.

So does the crowd.

They mean that after more than thirteen years of dictatorial power the regime of Dr. Getulio Vargas holds a democratic, orderly, kindly people in the vise of a hypocritical fascism.

They mean that Brazilian soldiers—their own brothers—were making the supreme sacrifice in vain on battlefields of Europe during the war against Hitlerism, if Brazilians at home could not once more enjoy their normal human rights.

This act of silent defiance is the culmination of a long and bitter dispute. When police raided the traditionally immune Eleventh of August Academy, a fair hearing was requested by the students—and denied. Then they marched. Unseen at their side move millions of Brazilians who rise up inwardly against their clever fascist overlords, but do not find organization or a voice.

The Vargas secret police see to that.

Brazilian liberals long ago discovered that the reputed mildness and benevolence of the Vargas regime are an empty smile. The

3

pleasantness easily turns cold and vicious when anyone presumes to insist on his human rights in defiance of the dictatorship. The smile is there only as long as unquestioning obedience is paid to a fascist system.

Young as they are, the students realize they may be facing imprisonment, torture, or execution at the hands of the *Tribunal de Segurança Nacional*. Since its establishment in 1936, this Tribunal of National Security has sentenced thousands of persons on political grounds. There are concentration camps on islands off the Brazilian coast. The *Secção do Esculache* of the Political and Social Police specializes in torture.

Still the students march.

From an upper window in an office building a member of the State Cabinet notices the commotion. He rushes down to remonstrate with the police, who by this time menace the students with their guns. At pistol point he is prodded back into the building and told to stay there. So a fascist machine overrides one of its own officials and crashes toward tragedy.

The students hold their ground under repeated orders to disband. Revolt smolders among aroused Paulistas who confront the police and watch the set faces of those gagged students. São Paulo is democratic to the core. Paulistas detest fascism—especially when it cloaks itself in the stolen name of democracy. São Paulo has seldom been deceived by tricks of Vargas manipulators.

Circling the crowded Praça do Patriarcha once, the students return to the Largo São Francisco outside their Law School patio. Mounted police close all street exits. A leader of the students attempts to reason with the police and is cut by a saber stroke. Behind come other students trying to enter the Law School gate where menacing guards wait for them.

Suddenly, with needless force, the blow falls. Tear bombs would be enough. Instead, the police either don't have any, or choose more intimidating means. The order is given to fire, not at the oncoming line, but at the pavement. Bullets ricochet. Students and innocent bystanders are hit. No one outside the police knows how many were killed that evening of November 9, 1943. The most reliable reports I have been able to obtain set the figure between three and eight. Some estimates range up to twenty-one. Many more were injured, twenty-six seriously. The number is not the decisive point. Neither does the subsequent shakeup of the São Paulo Cabinet wipe the slate clean. The point is that those students dared to come into the open with the central fact about political conditions inside Brazil under Vargas dictation. In this regard they showed more character and more courage than the Department of State in Washington. "Be nice to Brazil" is the way a State Department spokesman summed up official policy when I laid some of these facts before him. I love Brazil, but for that very reason I do not confuse so tolerant a nation with harsh and alien methods temporarily imposed upon it. Neither can a writer remain silent on such things without betraying the Brazilian people and ignoring his responsibilities under the free press.

Those São Paulo students defied one of the most fascist press censorships in the world. They defied it to hide the flame ignited by their brave young lives. They, not the sleek purveyors of Vargas propaganda, are Brazil. . . . Brazil of Tiradentes the martyr of freedom. . . . Brazil whose heart rises to the new dawn of democracy in the world. . . . Brazil determined to throw off a subtle and absolute dictatorship.

With jaguar alertness, the regime's intimidators crushed this student protest. Then press falsifiers in the *Departamento de Imprensa e Propaganda,* or DIP, set out to hide its traces in the jungle of their facist deception. They almost obliterated the trail. Not a word about what happened to those students has ever passed Brazilian censors. So far as I know, the first detailed news story to reach the world was the one I brought out and wrote from memory. Notes and names on paper were out of the question. Secret police camped on my trail in São Paulo. One false move, one attempt to talk with families or friends of those students, and I would have been seized. I have been held incommunicado by Brazilian police three times with less reason.

The free press does not exist in Brazil under Vargas. Any writer who does not conform to official propaganda could not stay in the country.

Popular revolt came close in São Paulo that November evening. The students were only part of a political challenge that reminded Dr. Vargas of his unfulfilled promises. This time in Brazil I heard a stronger undercurrent than ever before of dissatisfaction with the long stifling of democratic liberties. Brazil's people reasonably expected to find themselves in an atmosphere more congenial to the democratic way of living, after Dr. Vargas cast his lot with the United Nations and began training troops for service in Europe. Instead, the clamps were screwed down harder than ever on the press and on every slightest expression of opposition to governmental policies. Critics, however constructive, exposed themselves to being labeled as suspicious characters, if not fifth columnists.

So the war against world fascism was used in such instances as an oppressive denial of Brazilian popular rights, instead of releasing them. Brazilians could not help an inner revolt. Unnecessary bondage goes against their temperament. Within the narrow limits of a political strait jacket, this deeply tolerant and tenderhearted people makes its weight felt. Despite an administration that wobbled on the issue of world freemen versus Nazi enslavement, Brazilians in their millions never missed a heartbeat on the side of world democracy. Eventually the regime subordinated its pro-Nazis, or rather, changed their hats. Most of the same men are still in office at this writing. There has been no basic shift in the Vargas staff since days when Germanophile Brazilian Generals expected a Nazi triumph and held Brazil in line to benefit from Hitler's "New Order." Brazilians who had been asked to send their sons to fight for human freedom from fascism of the Nazi brand, could not understand why the simplest of democratic rights were denied to them at home.

Dr. Vargas, of himself, had made no move toward bringing his fascist domestic policy in line with his democratic foreign policy. Vargas propagandists assert that he has the overwhelming support of the country. His social legislation is said to have bound labor to him. For whatever reason, he has consistently shied away from going to the country with the test of elections in any form. Influential members of the Vargas Cabinet coun-

seled as early as June of 1943 that elections be called. This I
have on the authority of Dr. Oswaldo Aranha, at that time
Foreign Minister. The six-year term set by the Vargas Constitution of 1937 would have terminated November 10. As
the date neared, political tension mounted. In the State of
Minas Gerais, source of Brazil's major mineral contributions to
the war, seventy-six prominent citizens issued a public manifesto on October 24. More than a hundred added their names.
Signers included former President Arthur da Silva Bernardes, and
two sons of the late Dr. Afranio de Melo Franco, onetime President of the Geneva League of Nations. Virgilio de Melo Franco,
whose idealism and sincerity caused Dr. Aranha to call him the
Ariel of the 1930 Revolution that brought Dr. Vargas to power,
has since been arrested with several liberals. I read the entire
manifesto in Minas Gerais. It is as mild and scholarly a document
as could be phrased. Addressed to the people of Minas Gerais, it
was circulated in mimeographed form until the secret police cut
it off. No cry to revolt was raised. Deep intellectual yearning
for a breath of fresh air animated the manifesto's eleven brave
pages. Its legality and moderation, contrasted with the lawless
expediency used by Dr. Vargas—man of action—must have
amused as well as angered him. His retaliation was typical.

"These people are my friends," Dr. Vargas said to a colleague who gave me this intimate detail. "Why did they not
come to me?"

After enduring many cynical years of increasing Vargas
fascism in the name of patriotism and friendship, possibly the
signers felt their only recourse lay with the people. Their manifesto could not be more than a faint candle, quickly snuffed.
Dr. Vargas spurned this reminder of his repeated promises to call
elections. In 1942, on entering the war, he had annulled Article
80 of his 1937 Constitution which would have ended his "presidential term." The Constitution itself has never been submitted
to the national plebiscite specified in Article 187, and so remains
in force by decree of Dr. Vargas himself.

One by one, every signer of the manifesto who held a position that could be shut off by official action or pressure, lost it.

The long Vargas arm reached into banks and universities. São Paulo rose to the Minas Gerais initiative. The students were in the thick of this political unrest. Dr. Vargas prides himself on not using force. He substitutes cleverness, as Hitler did during his earliest diplomatic triumphs. Yet the threat of violence is always there, as São Paulo was reminded. After the student tragedy, Dr. Vargas staged a visit to São Paulo. He said in a public speech that no tolerance would be shown toward public disturbances. Earlier, when he extended his power by decree, he warned: "It would be criminal to agitate now on our internal front" for "a special form of internal stability."

Later, Dr. Vargas appointed Coriolano de Goes, Chief of Police in São Paulo when the students were shot, as highest police official of Brazil with headquarters in Rio de Janeiro. At the time Coriolano de Goes was on trial in São Paulo for his part in the student massacre. He promptly quashed his own trial.

Intelligent Paulistas, who tried in 1932 to stop Vargas by a revolt that did not succeed, knew that the dictator meant more than a delay in restoration of the promised elections. He was telling them they would be hammered into submission far faster than before if they should revolt against him again. São Paulo and the whole country is fully aware that the astute Getulio has armed himself, as a result of his pro-United Nations foreign policy, with the mightiest military machine in South American history.

Brazilians are tenderhearted people who dislike bloodshed. When goaded to it, they might revolt. They might even face machine guns and other weapons produced by Brazilian industry under the Vargas dictatorship. They could hardly revolt against tanks and warplanes sent to legions of Vargas from the United States—"Arsenal of Democracy."

So they are held in bitter silence.

They rejoice to be a United Nation.

They willingly sacrifice for the defeat of fascism abroad.

They grind inside over being ruled by a fascist dictator who uses any means—including pretenses of democracy—to impose his will and his way on Brazil.

Argentina: Fascist Spearhead

Someday men will marvel, when reading the story of these times, that a fascist wave should have swept through South America at the very moment when Mussolini and Hitler were sinking in the wreckage of their discredited "New Order." I came into South America again in time to see it happen. At first I began to feel it as something working in the dark, hiding its aims, pretending to be something else. I could not believe that any political leader would be so foolish as to ride with the burned-out star of fascism to its last plunge in the sea.

Coming down through the continent, I had to accept the evidence. Fascism in varying forms showed itself by unmistakable signs. It had been there all the time, but the surprise was to find it intensified rather than diminishing. Every country of South America had either broken diplomatic relations with the Axis or gone to war against it. Argentina, last in line, severed relations when I was on a boat in the Paraguay River headed south toward Buenos Aires. Earlier, in Brazil, I sat on the train beside a young man who guarded a sealed milk can between his knees with more care than a can of milk requires. It turned out to be vaccine for Brazil's Expeditionary Force, then entering final stages of training for service in Africa and Europe.

Outwardly, South America appeared to be united at last against the Axis. Why, then, the stiffening of fascist controls inside Brazil, the cooling of Paraguayan relations with the United States, the immediate deflation of Argentina's gesture toward the democracies, and a Bolivian *coup d'état* staged with the aid of notorious pro-Nazis? However illogical this course of events seemed, it soon began to make sense within the perverted logic of fascism. Stupid to the end, it still is dangerous in its lairs of jungle thinking. It banks on the continued existence of fascism in the world, for confirmed fascists are not changed by a crushing military defeat. Stubborn, unteachable, blinded by illusions, fascists plot again to hurl their mechanized hordes on a world of slumbering freemen.

South American fascists, especially in Argentina, clung with fanatical zeal to their expectations of a world in which democracy would have had no place. For them, Hitler is still a hero, defeated in a cause that was their own. Not until the fact was inescapable would some German-trained Argentine Army officers admit that Hitler and the *Wehrmacht* could be driven to their knees by the "decadent" democracies. Fascism took its first definitive modern form in Rome under Mussolini and spread to Munich. Long before that, all of its essentials had been ingrained in the fiber of South American politics. Nothing was lacking except the superficial trappings of colored shirts, arm bands, streamlined devices for public opinion control, mass meetings, mystical symbols, and techniques for welding the nation into one fighting whole behind a fanatical leader.

Such trappings are alien to the South American temperament. Basic fascism, however, is native among sections of the ruling classes. They found in Hitler someone who spoke their language, when allowance had been made for superficial differences. He essentially was attacking democracy. His totalitarian system developed subtle methods for holding a people in subjection—even willing subjection. His crusade against Communism made him their champion. His diplomacy and promises found ready acceptance in many quarters which had no love for the United States or Great Britain. Viewpoints of this kind were so marked in South America from 1938 to 1941 that I found many editors, writers, government officials, intellectuals, and other members of the conservative classes openly pro-Hitler. South American liberals and the overwhelming majority of the people were instinctively on the side of the democracies.

For the United States and for Europe, the extent of fascism in South America is a continuing and primary concern. Unquestionably the fascist forces that came so close to dominating the world will continue to seek every possible refuge, every available base of future operations. The aim is to perpetuate a false ideology and prepare for the next battle in an agelong effort to reverse humanity's forward motion toward freedom. What refuge could be more attractive than the soil of a continent where basic fascism is native—especially when military rulers of a country as large and powerful as Argentina have shown themselves ready and willing to play the game? Also, the fact that over this continent fly flags dedicated to human liberty would serve to deepen fascist camouflage.

Sources which cannot be disclosed, yet penetrate into inner circles of secret information in Argentina, report that since early 1944 the Nazis have been sending the embryo of their future war-making power into Argentina for safekeeping. Spanish ships and German U-boats have been the carriers. Faced with certain defeat in Europe, Germany this time cannot count on preserving its inventions, technicians, and indispensable military experts at home to prepare for World War III. The Kilgore subcommittee of the United States Senate Committee on Military Affairs stated in a report issued November 13, 1944, that German economic reserves are being deployed throughout the world in preparation for the next war.

Argentina under the current military dictatorship has offered the Nazis their most secure refuge, for several reasons. Nowhere else in the world could Germany find a country outside the area of coming Allied military control and ruled by a government sympathetic to the Nazis. Careful observers of events in Argentina agree that internal conflicts have resulted in giving power temporarily to officers of totalitarian and pro-Nazi outlook. The fact can be read in actions, quite apart from statements and maneuvers designed to deceive the United Nations.

As the sands run out for Nazi armies in Europe, Argentina has become the largest single escape corridor still open to the future. A few months at most are left to the German military caste and industrialists, at this time of writing, for removing whatever can be salvaged of the German war potential for transfer to a temporary new base. There is no possibility that Argentina ever could be converted into the main base for renewed German aggression a generation from now. Germany's aim is to use Argentina's fascist regime as a means of tiding over the immediate future when the aroused Allies will exercise strict surveillance inside Germany. The Prussian military mentality counts on a gradual relaxing of Allied vigilance in years to come. Working drawings of secret war inventions that might be lost if left in Germany, can be saved in Argentina for later return to the *Vaterland*. Inventors and technicians who might be kept from preparing for the next war in Germany, can carry on in Argentina. The arms-hungry military in Buenos Aires welcome German armament skills. Fritz Mandl, former Austrian producer whose bicycle factories were quickly converted to arms manufacture when war began in Europe, has been in Argentina some time, managing four factories.

Totalitarian controls hide the flight of Nazi capital to Argentina, but the Central Bank of Argentina admitted late in 1944 that European refugee funds valued at a billion dollars were clogging local financial channels in Buenos Aires. German firms with branches in Argentina have enjoyed the protection of the regime. The amount of German refugee capital is kept secret, but its existence in substantial amounts is unquestioned. The few measures taken to discipline Nazi firms and agents have been designed to deceive the Allies and win diplomatic recognition for the regime.

In a clever maneuver that appears to have been repulsed at this time of writing, Argentina sought to capitalize on Latin-American dissatisfaction with the policy pursued by Washington. Preoccupied with the war and postwar organization, the State Department for many months had declined Latin-American requests for a fourth meeting of American Foreign Ministers. Argentina, utilizing its seat in the Pan American Union, took the initiative in calling for a conference to consider its case. The bid carefully exempted Argentine internal affairs from scrutiny. It also specified that in the international field Argentina would allow its acts to be discussed, but not the implications of those acts. Washington's conviction that the regime nominally headed by Gen. Edelmiro J. Farrell was pro-Nazi was shown in a refusal to confer on those terms. Delaying tactics were adopted with the collaboration of most of the other American Governments. The aim both of the State Department and of the Argentine opposition was to force the regime out, not allow it to make a few concessions and then go ahead with its fascist program inside Argentina and in collaboration with fascist forces abroad.

Britain's position in the Argentine crisis has been complicated by British investments totaling £350,000,000 which weighed against any action that might have provoked revolution or other disturbances. The fascist regime exerted pressure against British firms. Downing Street at times associated itself with Washington, but the application of economic sanctions was hindered by Britain's wartime need for Argentine meat and other foodstuffs.

Argentina's fascist connections with Nazi Germany and Franco Spain were being guarded behind a censorship that sought to intimidate correspondents as well as suppress information when I entered the country. Some of my colleagues had been arrested for no reason other than efforts to obtain news. I reached Buenos Aires at the height of that controversy. With other correspondents, I used every available device for getting past the censorship because it was political and illegitimate. I found it far easier to elude than the older and more experienced Brazilian censorship. At one dramatic point during the short-lived revolt led by Lieut. Col. Tomás Duco, I was headed toward the Strait of Magellan by bus. When I was more than halfway down the coast from Buenos Aires, the police came to my hotel in Comodoro Rivadavia and questioned me. My cameras especially aroused their suspicions.

That session ended well. Possibly the holiday mood of the city smoothed my path. It was the first evening of Carnival. The two agents who knocked at my door went away and returned with their local commander. He finally allowed me to continue my trip, and even invited me to attend the Carnival parade as his guest. After dinner his deputy came for me. We rode in the commander's car up and down the main street through the crowd of merrymakers. Perhaps the police thought that was as good a way as any to keep me out of mischief. The next morning I was stopped at the bus station by an armed guard who took considerable convincing before he would let me travel.

It was a surcharged moment in South American affairs to be

on such an assignment. Gen. Pedro P. Ramírez had just been replaced by Gen. Edelmiro J. Farrell as President of Argentina, and the United States had refused to recognize General Farrell. The Argentine Government was confused, divided, irrational. It closed the Chilean border in an effort to prevent the crossing of automobiles to be sold in Chile at higher prices than the Argentine market was allowed to pay. So poorly conceived was this restriction that the bus on which I was traveling could not pass the frontier between Gallegos and Punta Arenas until a cash deposit equal to the value of the bus had been paid in distant Buenos Aires! The Army officers turned politicians had not thought to exempt public conveyances from their automobile ban. This oversight cost me two days before I was able to reach Chile in a Chilean car that came through from Punta Arenas.

Later, at every step northward from Magellan's Strait, a blank wall rose in my path of travel, only to break and let me through. Time could not be spared, since more than 4000 miles ahead of me loomed the expiration date of my Brazilian *Carteira d'Identidade,* or document of permission to remain six months in that country. The itinerary called for overland travel all the way, with planes to be used only in emergency. The end of the trip would be in the Amazon Basin, and I could not run the risk of being caught there with expired papers in wartime.

All the way in my overland journey it had been impossible to make reservations far ahead, or even to learn whether travel facilities were available. Boat sailings from Punta Arenas north through Chile's inland passages were not known even as close as in Gallegos, a few hours distant by car. When I arrived at the Chilean port, I learned a boat was due to sail at a time that suited my schedule—but the waiting list of passengers had been accumulating for weeks. I was willing to sit on top of the mast, if necessary, but was told another sea gull couldn't find footing on that ship. The U. S. Navy came to the rescue in the person of an amiable young naval liaison officer, Hugh T. Adams, Lieut. j.g., U.S.N.R., and a sea gull or two moved over.

Six days later I reached the end of the Chilean railways at Puerto Montt to be told that every seat on *La Flecha,* or *The*

Arrow, a streamline train then ready to leave, had been sold from there to Santiago. The station master finally agreed to sell me a ticket as far as Temuco. Imagine my surprise, on entering the train, to find it almost empty! There were available seats all the way to Santiago. Before Temuco had been reached the conductor came and sold me a numbered seat through to the capital.

In Santiago I learned that the train across the Andes had been canceled that week end. Motorcars were running, but had long waiting lists. Toward evening a seat opened for me, and at four in the morning we were to be off. The only complication, apart from possible trouble with the Argentine censors, was that the various delays brought me into Santiago at a time when I could not present myself at the Argentine Consulate there. My visa was in order, but the unusual requirement of a preview personal appearance is one of the legislative extremes indulged by Argentina's military. I decided to go ahead. In a car filled with Argentines and Chileans I rode through predawn darkness toward Argentina. I was loaded with the luggage of my long and varied trip. Before me loomed the crest of the Andes—a cold and hard place to be turned back. I was told that the North American photographer Julien Bryan had been held at this border some time for having cameras with him. I had still and motion picture equipment, as well as large quantities of exposed and unexposed negatives.

Always that Brazilian deadline drew closer. To cheer me up the money to complete the trip was tied up at a bank in Buenos Aires! Argentina, as well as the highest Andes and deepest Amazon Basin, had to be surmounted. This was one of the tensest moments of the entire trip. I had been sending cabled articles from Chile which, although unsigned, might have been traced to me and used to prevent me from re-entering Argentina.

So I rode the zigzag road through Uspallata Pass.

We drew up at the border station. The car was Argentine, and that no doubt helped me. Also, the Farrell regime was trying to win diplomatic recognition by Washington, and so may have given orders not to embarrass United States citizens unduly. I stood in line while a sleepy boy entered the number of my passport among those of the other passengers, and we went on. I was back in Argentina, but still had to get out with my photographs and notes for most of the trip. It had been impossible to send them home. Carefully safeguarded by omission of names of people who might be endangered by being found there, the notes had been carried through jungles and deserts, past Brazilian secret police, into Argentina, past Argentine police as I went out to Chile, and I had them in the country again.

I found Buenos Aires tremendously changed during those few weeks of my absence. Every day the fascist tinge of government deepened. News correspondents lived under the tightening strictures of a regime determined to absorb the press and convert it into a powerful instrument for nationalistic propaganda. The same process was under way that had begun to throttle the free press in Brazil thirteen years earlier. Argentina still lagged more than seven years behind the Vargas regime in cajoling or crushing opposition writers and publications. The Associated Press and United Press in Buenos Aires had been subjected to severe sanctions, including stoppage for a time of cable facilities.

The most glorious expressions of Argentine journalism, *La Prensa* and *La Nación,* had not yet bowed their heads during that valiant month of March, 1944. Yet they stood in the twilight of a brilliant tradition. The fascist dictatorship was winning an unequal battle. My friends of the foreign press resident in Buenos Aires were still using every device their fertile imaginations could invent to bypass the censorship. Editors and writers of the Argentine press greeted me with the courageous sadness of men facing an oppressive legion they could not defeat with their broken pens. Argentina had almost caught up with Brazil in its blackout of the free press.

In education, local government, industry and diplomacy, Argentina was being driven furiously along the discredited path that even then had plunged Mussolini into disgrace and defeat, and was closing toward a dead end for Hitler and the Japanese. Argentines of nationalistic bent insisted they were acting under their own impetus, not in response to alien ideologies. It reminded me of Brazilian nationalists in 1938, who said the Vargas *Estado Novo* was entirely Brazilian, a Brazilian variation on the democratic theme. Nazis say their system is all German, and claim it is superior to democracy. The fact, of course, is that fascism may assume national variations, yet is recognizable anywhere by well-defined features. In the definitions at the end of this book I have stated my standard for judging whether a regime is fascist or not, and to what degree.

Taking democracy as one pole of government, dictatorship becomes the other pole. Dictatorships of the conservative Right are fascist in many varying degrees, while Communism is the dictatorship of the Left. Nazi Germany stands for the extreme example in modern times of full-blown aggressive fascism bent on world conquest. Fascist Italy, Japan, Hungary and other willing Axis satellites have presented similar extremes with local variations. Franco Spain has ranged itself in the same camp, although the force of events prevented fulfillment of imperial designs outlined in the Falangist program, including reconquest of Hispanic America. Portugal under Dr. Oliveira Salazar leans to the fascist outlook in some ways, although not in an aggressive or virulent form. Brazil, Paraguay, Bolivia, and several other Latin-American countries are fascist in varying degrees. Chile retains a working democracy, and leans Left. So does Mexico. A few smaller countries, notably Uruguay and Costa Rica, are operating democracies, as is the large nation of Colombia.

Always before in my writing on Argentina I had avoided the term fascist as characterizing the government, although I applied it to individuals in high position. During early 1944 Argentina's drift to fascism was unmistakable. The most startling single phase was not the open siege of a once free press, nor rivalries of Army politicians. It was public apathy and the door this opened to reviving fascist ambitions throughout the Americas. A costly price was paid by Argentina's people in the dwindling currency of their own democratic liberties. Even more costly has been the price exacted from America as a whole. From the growth of fascist thinking and diplomacy in Buenos Aires—unchecked at this writing—subversive roots spread into surrounding countries.

Basically democratic, the Argentine people at last are awake to the danger. Many of them responded at first to the military revolution of June 4, 1943, in its attack against corruption. As fascist aims of the regime became unmistakable through arrest of more than 2000 democrats and friends of the United Nations while pro-Nazis were given high positions, alarm spread among the people. Their liberal leaders went into enforced or voluntary exile. Even the Conservative Party, which had supported the former reactionary and ultraconservative Government under Dr. Ramón S. Castillo, joined the opposition. Dr. Rodolfo Moreno, a principal Conservative, is in Montevideo, Uruguay, united with Dr. Nicolas Repetto of the Socialists and Rodolfo Ghioldi of the extreme Left. The Argentine Underground is organized under the name of Patria Libre. Some twenty clandestine newspapers are widely circulated.

Dr. Moreno, writing in the opposition newspaper *Pueblo Argentino* at Montevideo, speaks as a Conservative to whom the military dictatorship in Buenos Aires has become intolerable. Spokesmen of the people label it "a government of Nazi invasion," and they mean German Nazi influence rather than fascism in general. Dr. Moreno writes:

"We Argentines who, without distinction of political orientation, do not tolerate the Nazi dictatorship now in power at Buenos Aires, appeal for comprehension by the nations of America, and especially our near neighbors. Two points should be made known at this moment, repeated, and made objects of daily insistence. They are:

"1. The Argentine people and the existing Argentine Government are not only different manifestations but antipodes.

"2. The Nazi dictatorship in Argentina represents a menace for the whole Western Hemisphere, and in particular for the neighboring democracies."

Whirlpools of Power Politics

The resurgence of Argentine diplomacy stood out easily as the most significant political current in South America during late 1943 and early 1944. Two years before when I went through Asunción, Paraguay, and La Paz, Bolivia, those cities were making a public display of their cordiality for Brazil. They were not entirely enthusiastic over results to that point of their decision to go along with the United States, which they had done to the extent of breaking relations with the Axis. But they still were hopeful of receiving promised military weapons and equipment. Argentina came back, and the reason is evident. South American fascists of Paraguay, Bolivia, and other countries staged a strategic retreat at the Rio de Janiero consultations of American Foreign Ministers in January, 1942. They did not in any sense abandon their own liking for the fascist way of doing things.

Argentina resisted at Rio de Janeiro despite the combined pressures of the United States and most of the other American countries. By its refusal to break with the Axis, and by forcing the other governments to accept an Argentine formula that greatly weakened the determined wording favored by nearly everyone else, Buenos Aires loudly trumpeted that it had won a resounding diplomatic victory. Throughout the democratic world it was generally agreed that Argentina had lost not only a moral opportunity, but prestige and possibilities for economic development. During the years immediately following, Buenos Aires had to take a back seat while the honors and money and fighting planes poured liberally into Brazil. By every available test of Argentine public opinion, the people did not like what Dr. Enrique Ruiz-Guiñazú had done at Rio. They went to the polls, as soon as they had an opportunity, and prevented the Castillo Government from bludgeoning through its project for control in the Chamber of Deputies. Commanding a slender majority in the Chamber after the election of March 1, 1942, the liberal forces in Argentine politics hammered as hard as they could against entrenched fascists. A congressional committee kept up its investigation of Nazi espionage and other subversive activities.

During the same formative years, when the present test of hemisphere solidarity became explosive, Argentina's conservatives didn't like what was going on any more than did the Argentine people, but their reasons were different. The people felt they had been betrayed. The ruling classes, and especially the Army, showed no signs of moral disquietude over what they had done. Yet they were keenly aware that gigantic Brazil next door was growing stronger every day. The United States was spending hundreds of millions of dollars on air bases, ports, steel mills, railways, military roads, planes, warships, tanks, and anything else Brazil needed as a fighting ally.

The head of steam generated in the Argentine Army gradually lifted the safety valve and then exploded in the swift *coup d'état* on June 4, 1943, led by Generals Arturo Rawson and Pedro Ramírez. Since then the Army has been supreme. Moderate officers rapidly were shoved aside. Pro-Nazis and fascists who most admired German military methods, and had counted on a Nazi victory in the war, seized control over foreign and domestic policy of the most highly developed South American country. While Brazil is larger, and even more advanced in some areas, such as industrial and intellectual São Paulo, Argentina is years ahead of all other Latin-American countries in the general level of its material culture. Only in politics, and in certain unfortunate national traits, does Argentina lag behind.

As soon as the Argentine military took over, they found themselves marshaling fascist forces which began to crawl out of hiding places not only in Argentina, but throughout Latin America. Fascists and their sympathizers rallied to this new spark of leadership in a world of growing darkness for their lost cause. Evidence of the fact had been accumulating earlier as I came through Paraguay, where Argentine diplomatic influence was again prominent after a period of eclipse by Brazil and the United States. There was no single leader of marked political talent among the fascists either in Paraguay or Argentina. The movement was rather an instinctive alliance of conservatives banded together to hold their economic and political privileges against the rising tide of world democracy. Spearheading this reaction were the military. They had a long tradition of German training. Some of them were enraged against the democracies for toppling the fascist "New Order" before its dark foundations had been laid. In several countries the Army struck to keep democracy at bay.

Argentina took the lead in this fascist surge. As a result, Argentine diplomatic fortunes in South America changed almost overnight from treadmill gloom to a sparkling era of sword-rattling and fascist plots. The tentacles of fascism closed in on an already prostrate Argentine Republic. They reached out in an effort to draw Paraguay, Bolivia, Peru, Chile, and even democratic Uruguay, into a fascist bloc. Advances were made to Brazil. Fascism in Brazil is so widespread that ready support for Argentina's initiative came from many influential Brazilians. In Rio de Janeiro I had been amazed, before entering Argentina, to find members of the Brazilian Government professing unconcern over the course of Argentina's growing fascism. Even Dr. Oswaldo Aranha, then Foreign Minister, had only kind words for the truculent neighbor next door. Possibly he was reflecting an official policy with which he later was to break.

"The custom of the world, and of men, is to forget," Dr. Aranha told me in his most urbane, smiling, and intimate manner. We were in his private office on the second floor of Itamarity Palace. While he did not elaborate, the implication was that Argentina would again be accepted among the American nations, and that this interlude of obstructive diplomacy in Buenos Aires would be forgotten. Recalling how Dr. Aranha had struggled as chairman of the Rio de Janeiro consultations in 1942 to bring Argentina along, and how he publicly embraced Dr. Ruiz-Guiñazú even after Argentina had tried to torpedo the meetings, I felt this might be Brazilian moderation at work. On the other hand, Dr. Aranha's attitude evidently carried deeper implications.

If he meant to pour oil on troubled waters, this gave indirect confirmation to the delicacy of Brazil's relations with the Argentine.

If his professed lack of concern over Argentina's fascist swing indicated a basic understanding between Rio de Janeiro and Buenos Aires, far more serious questions arose.

For the immediate issue in South America is not one of peace or war in the foreseeable future. The burning issue is how far the fascist reaction inside South America will go, and what forms it will take. The present Brazilian Government has yet to prove itself opposed to essential fascism as an instrument of administration in Brazil itself. This is the point that too often and too easily slips out of the equation when praise is heaped on the Vargas regime for its war against Nazis in Europe and in Brazil. So the core of South American diplomacy is found in these paradoxical questions:

1. Is Brazil's foreign policy inside South America as democratic as its foreign policy outside South America?

2. If so, does this intensify diplomatic tension with the openly fascist managers of Argentina's foreign policy?

3. If not, does the specter arise on the southern horizon of potential secret accords between fascist elements in the Armies of Brazil and Argentina, with various smaller satellites drawn in? This would be a supreme effort of military fascism to dig itself in against the postwar tidal wave of world democracy. It also would thrust before the United States a disarmingly subtle and widespread test of inter-American relations. Fascists of South America would be operating at least in part under the banner of democracy, and would be armed with many weapons from the United States.

Argentina's apparently irrational actions might have been explained by fascist support from other countries of South America. Proud as the young Argentine military are, it is not likely they would go as far as they have with no other driving impetus than illusions of their own power in a nation of 13,700,000 people. What they have done has the tangible or tacit support of forces far more powerful than themselves in South America and in Europe.

Berlin's long-range interest in keeping open any possible refuge for Germans, for capital they might smuggle out of Europe, and for efforts to regain the Reich's shattered world position, has been noted. While the Argentine dictatorship formally assured the United Nations on September 29, 1944, that no refuge would be extended to Axis war criminals or their funds, this is a field in which Argentina's past record is not clean. Axis spies operated there long after Argentina had formally agreed at Pan-American meetings to take measures for defense of the Western Hemisphere against such subversive elements.

Franco Spain has been a springboard in this attempted fascist drive from Europe to the Americas.

The position of the Roman Catholic hierarchy is controversial as regards fascism. A pattern made familiar in Spain during the Civil War has been partly repeated in Argentina. The ultraconservative hierarchy in Spain supported General Francisco Franco, the fascist dictator, in his destruction of the Spanish Republic, because of concessions he made to the clergy. The present Argentine military dictatorship and the hierarchy in that country also have found meeting grounds of mutual advantage.

Under the Argentine Republic a clerical campaign sought for many years to restore the traditional teaching of Roman Catholicism in the schools. The Republic steadily refused to undo a reform instituted by democratic forces intent on separating Church and State. The new Argentine dictatorship on December 31, 1943, made the teaching of Roman Catholicism compulsory in most of the educational system. The decree applies to "all public schools of primary, elementary, secondary, and special education . . . high schools and special subsidiaries of the National Universities . . . and common schools administered by the National Council of Education." The only exception is that parents who desire to have their children excused from regular religious classes may do so, but these children are given "moral instruction." Since teachers of these classes are subject to approval by ecclesiastical authorities, the hierarchy has regained educational ascendancy. This decree has been described as a reversal of the Argentine Republic's fixed policies toward religious instruction in the schools. Textbooks also are subject to clerical and governmental approval.

Accompanying the fascist reaction in Latin-American government is an upsurge of clerical activity noted by many qualified observers. It has been marred by intolerance that is reported by Protestant missionaries as more intense than in several decades. Much of the conservative reaction undoubtedly is a direct result of a potentially powerful inrush of democratic forces that had been kept at arm's length by dictatorial regimes.

Instructions issued by Dr. Alberto Baldrich, when he was the Argentine military regime's Minister of Education, subjected every school in the country to intensive propaganda along the following lines:

First the country, which endures; afterward the institutions, which change.

The country is always right.

One who is not a patriot is a traitor.

Argentina is for the Argentines because only they made it, defend it and deserve it.

There cannot be free men in a subjected country. While the country is not completely sovereign, individual liberty is a lie.

The June 4 revolution is an historical and definite fact and it was aimed not against any Argentine, but only against the enemies of the country.

Our country exists by the free determination of its people and by the victorious strength of its sword.

We are a liberating and instituting country. For this reason we have the right to perform a great role in America.

You must not only be an Argentine; you must know how to show it.

We must cultivate and maintain our different personality, based on the *criollo* [Creole] trunk—Spanish and (Roman) Catholic.

Argentina is an historic reality with its own and heroic style. To deserve the honor of sovereignty it is incumbent to live according to this, our own and heroic style.

Do not permit anyone to say that the *criollo* is lazy. When the authors of this lie arrived the country already existed and was respected because of the capacity and activity of the *criollo.*

The honor of being an Argentine does not carry advantages; it demands sacrifices.

Argentinism implies the most serious obligations.

To be an Argentine does not mean pacifism, speculation or anything literary. It means one must be dynamic.

Every additional child means another sentinel of sovereignty. The new Argentina requires healthy and heroic women.

Evidence also has accumulated to show that the military clique ruling Argentina responds to aggressive designs. Argentine fascism has gone beyond oppression of the people inside that country. The purpose of attacking the free press, of destroying political freedom, of regimenting industry, and of hectic arming is revealed in warlike statements by high Argentine officials. The exaltation of war went so far that the United States took the unusual step of issuing a press release about the speech by War Minister Juan D. Perón at La Plata University, noted later in these pages with more details. While a belligerent Argentine speech might not of itself constitute a menace to the peace of the Western Hemisphere, the whole explosive situation that has been developing in South America makes any spark worth watching. At the outset of a thoroughgoing analysis it is essential to lift the whole inquiry out of the realm of mere personalities. Neither Colonel Perón nor Argentina is more than a small digit in a much larger multiplication of figures. If the answers are not coming out as they should, responsibility rests on more than a single nation.

Why, for instance, is Argentina so intent on arming?

Also, why are the Army diplomats in Buenos Aires trying to draw allies to themselves? They claim to have Paraguay. Chile has been wooed, but apparently without success. President Rios categorically denied that Chile would join an Argentine military bloc. Bolivia was under visible Argentine influence for a time. When Washington finally extended diplomatic recognition to the Revolutionary Junta headed by Major Gualberto Villarroel, this action indicated a belief that Bolivia had been maneuvered outside the plottings of Buenos Aires. Some measure of Argentine diplomatic success was registered by recognition of General Farrell on the part of Ecuador, joining Chile, Bolivia, and Paraguay. The small Andean country of Ecuador, however, would be at best a remote and weak ally, even if it could be drawn away from recent cordiality toward the United States. Peru has a strong tradition of friendship for Argentina, dating back to the wars of independence from Spain when San Martín and Sucre and the other liberators forged a lasting bond. Such traditions do not necessarily sweep a country into the kind of military adventures offered by Buenos Aires fascists.

Outside of barracks where Argentine colonels dreamed again the discredited dream of conquest, the whole thing appeared little short of madness. Yet Argentine fascists know that many of the Latin-American Governments secretly admire them. They also know that the State Department in Washington sometimes enters into deals of convenience with fascist regimes. Was not Marcel B. Peyrouton, notorious in Buenos Aires for his profascist views when he served there as Vichy's Ambassador, called to high position in North Africa during a period of tortuous Washingtonian diplomacy? Had not similar acts of expediency marked State Department dealings with Franco Spain, known to be the Axis bridge to the Americas? Was not Brazil handily evading the stigma of its fascist dictatorship, and at the same time arming itself by a foreign policy that drew to it from the United States not only adulation but millions of dollars worth of industrial capital and weapons?

The main point at which Argentine fascism has caught up with its Brazilian forerunner and passed it is in the field of apparent plans for external aggression. Actually, little is known about Brazil's plans, if any, in the same direction. Over in the back country of Bolivia I heard serious remarks that large portions of the Beni region "really belong with Brazil." One long-time resident said he expected Brazil to expand in that area, opposite Mato Grosso. There is no visible reason for Brazil to want more jungles, but there is oil in these parts of Bolivia. So, as facts encountered, these bits of information are reported for whatever they may be worth. Whether Brazil develops aggressive tendencies or not, the fact remains that United States millions have raised Brazil to a military stature that causes Argentine Army officers to arm frantically in an effort to overtake their rival.

United States diplomacy in South America these past few years must bear a major share of responsibility for the present menacing unbalance. Argentine belligerence is only one symptom of deep dislocations. Washington's inconsistencies help to explain why the Argentine people, normally democratic, have so easily been persuaded, forced, or cajoled by fascist rulers into accepting the loss of their liberties without revolting. It is inevitable that a North American policy which favors a fascist regime in Brazil will arouse the exceedingly proud and patriotic Argentines. Such a policy will foment alarms, and even wars, in South America.

That Washington has consciously strengthened Dr. Vargas is common knowledge to those who have been close enough to the inside to see what was going on. When I talked about Brazil with officials in the State Department I found them accepting to a dangerous degree the specious propaganda of the Vargas regime. The United States Embassy in Rio de Janeiro since the Vargas coup of 1937 had done so to such an extent that no one could possibly obtain a balanced picture of Brazilian complexities by accepting uncritically what Embassy spokesmen said. Their outlook and attitude too closely paralleled the official Brazilian viewpoint.

Sumner Welles served as U. S. Undersecretary of State with special responsibility for Latin-American affairs during the critically formative Vargas years. He continues, out of office, an attitude toward Brazil that is comprehensible as well as widely held just now, but raises serious questions because of its omissions. The Vargas regime is given an almost clean slate in Mr. Welles' book, *The Time for Decision*. Although he admits the suspensions of constitutional guarantees, he interprets them in much the same way Vargas propagandists long have done. In a syndicated newspaper column dated April 26, 1944, Mr. Welles gave an impres-

sion against which most of his readers had no means of defense.
Quoting a public statement by Dr. Vargas, Mr. Welles omitted,
by inadequate documentation, words that make all the difference. This is the text from Mr. Welles' article:

> A few days ago President Vargas made this public statement:
> "When we are again fully in possession of the benefits to be
> derived from peace we will complete what our governmental in-
> stitutions lack. The Brazilian people will then, through the fullest
> and freest methods and without fear of any kind, make their
> decision known and choose their representatives within democracy,
> within law and order. . . . Brazil in peace will be governed in
> accordance with national desires."
> Thus the solemn assurance has now been given to the people of
> Brazil that they will once more enjoy popular self-government.

That sounds fine, but the words rendered "law and order" are
more accurately translated "laws and provisions." Mr. Welles
knows, as anyone does who has lived in Latin-American countries,
that a loophole of that size is large enough to transit a complete
reversal of any electoral law, however self-governing its provisions may appear on the surface. Thus, whether for diplomatic
reasons or by oversight, the North American public has been
misled on a vital subject. This is typical of what the State Department has done and continues to do. Quite apart from the
refinements of translating a Vargas statement into English, it is
known that the coming Brazilian elections are to be hedged
about with numerous "provisions" designed to perpetuate Vargas
policies in Brazil.

Before even going that far, the dictator is expected to resort
to new emergencies. Faced with prospects of war's-end in Europe,
his spokesmen emphasized Allied use of Brazilian air and naval
bases for the war against Japan. Brazil has never declared war on
Japan, but presumably would aid the Allies in any event. The
test will be whether or not Dr. Vargas uses this remote argument
to postpone elections that he had previously promised after the
war. As far as Brazil is concerned directly, the war ends with
defeat of Germany. There is no visible reason why the passage

of Allied planes through Natal to the Far East should make elections dangerous in Brazil—except possibly for the Vargas regime.

While the United States is committed under Pan-American agreements not to intervene in the internal politics of any other American country, it is not required to go out of its way to tighten the grip of an undemocratic regime because that regime is in power. Brazil's collaboration was indispensable during the war. A price had to be paid. Yet Brazil also stood to gain, and did gain, by assisting the Allies. Washington did not have to go beyond a bargaining position that would have given Brazil full value received for use of air base sites, without sacrificing democratic principles through open support of a fascist dictator.

Those are a few of the considerations that do not appear on the surface of the Argentine crisis, but exert tremendous influence on the volatile young fascists led by Colonel Perón. The Argentine colonels will have to face the consequences of their belligerence. Washington and Rio de Janeiro also should face themselves in the mirror and see what they see. Two-faced expediency on issues of democracy versus fascism cannot build or maintain lasting peace in the Western Hemisphere or in the world. The only consistent democratic diplomacy, as President Roosevelt has said, is to oppose fascism in all its forms, not merely in its end product—external aggression.

A shallow compromise which has not dignified Brazilian-United States relations is a limited definition of fascism as trying to take someone else's country. That definition was given to me in so many words in the State Department. It is a line on which Brazilian propaganda can and does attack fascism abroad, while hugging fascism tight at home. It is a divided line, not the straight path of enduring principles that lead to peace.

By arming Brazil, the State Department is known to have sought to counterbalance Argentine influence in South America. Exactly the opposite effect has resulted. The net outcome may even be to increase ties between Argentina and Brazil in a fascist bloc, necessarily secret. A diametrically opposed consequence may be to plunge the two largest South American countries into war. I have watched the Argentine fascist crisis develop in depth and scope. A factor not to be left out of account is the existence in Brazil, since 1930, of an increasingly successful fascist dictatorship. This point did not escape Buenos Aires, even if Vargas propaganda was successful in diverting attention from it in many other capitals, notably Washington. The diplomatic tug of war between Argentina and Brazil goes on constantly for influence over smaller neighbors—Uruguay, Paraguay, Bolivia, Chile, Peru. Dr. Carlos Saavedra Lamas, former Argentine Foreign Minister and author of a famous peace plan, was in office during some devious diplomacy in the Chaco War between Paraguay and Bolivia. One reason the doughty Paraguayans won is that they had Argentine backing in such tangible forms as rifles and ammunition. Argentina's duplicity occurred in the early 1930's, and ended in 1938 with a mediated settlement by which Paraguay gained the better part of the *Chaco*. Dr. Saavedra Lamas, with his high stiff collars, aquiline nose, and somber expression of a Spanish Don, represented a proud Argentina that still retained its republican form of government and was generally indifferent rather than hostile toward the United States. Despite fascist aspects of the brief Uriburu dictatorship in 1930-31, and Argentina's subsequent electoral frauds, its government assuredly could not be classified as fascist.

Brazil, on the other hand, had moved for seven years along a fascist path when Dr. Vargas on November 10, 1937, took the final plunge to his *Estado Novo,* or "New State." The extent to which Argentine meddling in the Chaco War was due to an aim of offsetting Brazil's growing power may never be fully disclosed. Unquestionably this element exerted a far more harmful effect than is generally known.

By December of 1938 when the Eighth Pan-American Conference met at Lima, Peru, Argentine diplomacy had taken a visible turn toward obstructive tactics. The reasons were deeper than petulance. Argentina aspires to leadership in Latin America. This is a settled aim, based on a conviction of national superiority. Sometimes, as at Lima, the attempt to assert leadership takes aggressive forms. For many years now it has collided almost constantly with a more powerful leadership exerted by Washington in Latin America.

Brazil has also increasingly disturbed Argentine complacency. There was a time when Argentina did not consider Brazil worth a second thought as a rival. Peaceful, huge, sprawling in the tropical sun, Brazil amused Argentina more than it aroused diplomatic jealousy. This attitude had begun to change as soon as Dr. Vargas whipped the sleeping giant into action, organized his secret police, dispensed with the checks and balances of democracy, and increased Brazil's armed might.

A marked characteristic of national psychology in Argentina, as in Chile, is to become self-assertive in geometric reverse ratio to the decline of actual position or power. Chile had its day on the crest of a nitrate boom from the 1880's to 1913. The Chilean Army and Navy, educational systems, and wealth, set it apart in South America. Argentina gradually forged ahead, and leaped into first place when the bottom was knocked from Chile's prosperity by the development of synthetic nitrates. Chileans do not forget their golden era. They are commanding in retrospect. Argentina, faced with gradual eclipse by gigantic Brazil, began showing signs of the same reaction as early as 1938. The Argentine delegates came to Lima with a flourish, and soon had the conference struggling to meet its "formulas." In contrast with this proud display, there was an amusing sidelight on faulty navigation in the Argentine Navy. The cruiser *Almirante Brown*, bearing Foreign Minister José María Cantilo for a brief visit, missed Callao, seaport of Lima, by fifty miles!

At Lima the delegates spent most of their time writing a Declaration of Constitutional Solidarity that would be accepted by Argentina. Long on legal technicalities, the Argentines usually have a formula up their sleeves. More than legal niceties were involved, for already a storm was gathering over the Rio de la Plata.

At Panama in the autumn of 1939, with war actually raging in Europe, the Argentines proved far more tractable at the First Consultative Meeting of American Foreign Ministers. This was only a respite.

To Havana for the second set of consultations in July, 1940, just after France had fallen, came an Argentine delegation headed by Dr. Leopoldo Melo. Himself experienced in international meetings from the era of the Hague Conferences in the first decade of this century, he spoke at Havana for a conservative Argentine oligarchy. Newsmen found it hard to retain an attitude of respect as Dr. Melo gave them interviews filled with bland assertions that everyone was taking this Nazi business too seriously. He insisted there was no danger for the Americas, and if there ever should be, Argentina would do its part.

Such evasive tactics reached their showdown at the third consultation of Foreign Ministers in Rio de Janeiro soon after the Japanese attack on Pearl Harbor. Dr. Ruiz-Guiñazú early proved that Buenos Aires at that time had no intention of breaking diplomatic relations with the Axis. Argentina and Chile refused to take a stand against Nazi Germany. The other American countries, instead of going ahead with their strong wording, watered it down so that the two dissidents could sign. They did.

One year later Chile broke with the Axis.

Argentina steadily became more conservative, more "prudently neutral," less inclined to offend Germany. Confidential reports were arriving from Argentine military observers in Europe to the effect that Hitler could not be defeated and was in fact winning the war. On that primary expectation of an Axis triumph the makers of foreign policy in Buenos Aires based their actions. The teeth of Pan-American resolutions never bit into Nazi newspapers such as *El Pampero,* or into Nazi spy rings. So flagrant was Argentina's disregard for hemisphere safety that the United States published evidence gathered by its own intelligence officers, giving names and addresses of Nazi spies in Argentina.

During those last months of the Castillo Government, a courageous band of Argentine democrats kept up their losing battle. Toward the end, Dr. Ramón S. Castillo tightened his grip on Argentina under his "state of siege" until anything seemed preferable. When the Rawson-Ramírez coup drove Dr. Castillo into flight on a river gunboat, the sun seemed to have broken through dark clouds over the Rio de la Plata. Soon it became plain that Argentina actually had slipped into a fascist reaction severe enough to make Dr. Castillo's harshest days seem mild by comparison. The rapidity with which Dr. Castillo returned to Argentina showed that no fundamental change for the better had occurred.

How to deal with Argentine fascism became the question. Points to keep in view are these elements of Argentine strength as seen in Buenos Aires:

1. The United Nations need Argentine meat, wheat, corn, wool, hides, and general foodstuffs not only during the war, but during world reconstruction. This need would render application of economic sanctions as hard on the Allies, especially Britain, as they would be on the Argentine.

2. Military fascists in Argentina have secret support of their kind in many of the other Latin-American countries. None of these native fascists wants to see the Argentine refuge for world fascism actually broken up.

What could Washington and its collaborators do that would not violate the general rule of nonintervention, and yet would help restore Argentina to its own democratic people? For the Americas this is one of the hardest diplomatic decisions of the war. When it has been made, a harder one looms ahead. For Washington appears not to have begun facing the inconsistency of a diplomacy that is largely responsible for bringing the Americas to this warlike pass. That diplomacy consists in building up the wrong people in South America, giving them unexampled power, condoning dictators, bringing them to Washington and parading them on Pennsylvania Avenue, loading them with honors, winking at their practice of fascism inside their own countries, and otherwise discouraging South America's real democrats. Argentina would not have become such a problem if years ago Washington had adopted a diplomacy based on principles favorable to the growth of democracy in South America, instead of playing into the hands of fascist dictators.

Traveling through the deep interior of South America I saw that even the most remote regions were being drawn into whirl-

pools of fascist power politics. Pôrto Velho on the Madeira
River seems, at first glance, to be far beyond any effective par-
ticipation in the diplomatic and military crisis now spreading
through South America. Yet this is the capital of the Territory
of Guaporé, one of five new strategic Brazilian border zones
established on October 1, 1943. In all directions from Pôrto
Velho extends jungle with only a scratching here and there of
human habitation. The sole means of modern travel available are
the airplane and slow river boats. When you can get a boat it is
piloted through tortuous channels to the far-off Amazon. Even
more distant are some of the other new territories. They have
been carved from older States and placed under special Governors
appointed by Dr. Vargas.

The Territory of Rio Branco, for example, is wedged in jungles
and savannas between British Guiana and Venezuela on the
borders of mountainous country that inspired A. Conan Doyle's
book *Lost World*.

The Territory of Amapá fronts on the Atlantic Ocean, but
extends inland through almost unbroken jungle between French
Guiana and the northern channel of the Amazon.

Next in order southward is the Territory of Guaporé. Cut
from the States of Amazonas and Mato Grosso, this territory
embraces several towns, as well as wild tribes whose domain is
seldom entered by white men. The region is nearly as remote as
any on the continent. The last two strategic zones have been
placed as buffers along the entire line of Brazil's frontiers with
Paraguay and Argentina.

The Territory of Ponta Porã extends between the Paraguay
and Paraná Rivers.

The Territory of Iguassú incidentally includes two of South
America's most magnificent waterfalls. Its main purpose is to
protect Brazil's border at a point of potential friction with
Argentina. In this district a concentration of Nazi sympathizers
extends from the southern Brazilian States of Santa Catarina
and Rio Grande do Sul into Argentina's Misiones Territory.

Brazil does not classify the new border zones as military
reservations. Official announcements stress greater administrative

efficiency and border control as primary aims. At least one Army troop is to be stationed in each territory at points designated by the Governor. As all of Brazil's twenty States and the older Territory of Acre were already under Interventors or Governors responsible only to Dr. Vargas, the change is one of detail rather than of fundamental policy. Yet it indicates special interest by Brazil in critical points of a long and poorly defended frontier. In addition, Brazil has established a new division of Maritime, Air, and Frontier Police. These Vargas police will centralize border controls formerly entrusted to governments of frontier States. Brazil's coastline comes to the sizable total of 4500 miles. On land, the line crosses jungles, rivers, mountains, and plains for 7500 miles. Brazil touches every country and colony on the South American continent except Chile and Ecuador. The diplomatic and military consequences of such a geographic position would be great anywhere in the world. Dense tropical jungle and other barriers reduce some of the impact on Brazil. Much of its long border is beyond the reach of any probable attacker.

Another factor that adds to Brazil's unique position in South America is its Portuguese origins and language. All of the surrounding countries were colonized by Spaniards, and still speak Spanish. The three European colonies on the mainland—British, French, and Dutch Guiana—are relatively small and do not enter into major moves of South American diplomacy. As Brazil rises to new stature under arms, the long-range currents of continental power politics receive an increasing and explosive stimulus. Brazil has more land and resources than any of its neighbors, except that Argentina's soils in the temperate *pampa* region are much richer. Mammoth Brazil has no visible need, and no outlined foreign policy, of doing more than to have and to hold its own. Yet in Brazil itself to some extent, and more acutely elsewhere in the continent, there are pinching and grinding economic shortages, poverty of peoples and nations, military ambitions, discontented minorities, and ramifications of the world-wide but battered fascist fifth column.

Also, elsewhere in the continent, is Argentina.

Far richer per square mile and per inhabitant than all other

South American countries in terms of developed wealth, Argentina views itself as the natural leader of Latin America. Argentine pride knows few restraints. The attitude of some Argentine military men reminds me of the way General Sadao Araki, as Japan's War Minister in the summer of 1933, sat behind his desk in Tokyo and with coldly smoldering black eyes told me Japan deserved, and would have, naval parity with Britain and the United States. Even Argentine women of refinement occasionally allow their national pride to become socially unpleasant. One such lady of the conservative class startled several of us not long ago during conversation in the United States by beginning to compare her country with others. Stating without reservation that Argentina is one of the great nations of the world, she tossed off Brazil and the rest of Latin America as unworthy to be compared with the Argentine.

Another revealing and specific instance of Argentine attitudes came on a steamboat crossing Lake Titicaca from Bolivia into Peru. An Argentine of the *pampa* was on board in charge of a shipment of mules and horses for the Peruvian Army. He spent his time alone for the most part, striding the deck and humming *gaucho* ditties. The only concession he made to the biting air at 12,500 feet elevation was to wind a heavy wool scarf around his neck and toss the end jauntily over one shoulder.

When I engaged him in conversation, he referred almost at once, with flashing eyes, to "this horrible voyage."

"Why horrible, *señor*?"

"Because Bolivia is the end of the earth."

While it would be unfair to characterize a whole nation on the basis of these extremes, it would also be unsafe for outsiders to ignore the high and dangerous level of egotism in Argentina. The more so, since many tangible signs in Argentina point to an unwillingness of the ruling classes, or even of the people, to play second fiddle in an orchestra led by the United States, with Brazil as featured soloist. Now, even more than during the consultations at Rio de Janeiro, the words of Dr. Ruiz-Guiñazú have lively significance.

"Argentina," he said, "will not be herded into any backstage chorus."

Moving slowly through the interiors of Brazil and of Argentina in 1943-44 during a half year of momentous flux, I was struck by the extent to which Argentina is developed from one end to the other, in contrast with Brazil's vast areas of wilderness. Another impression was the initiative shown by Argentina in linking itself with smaller neighbors. Long-established railways and superlative river transport combine with other means to make travel and trade relatively easy between Buenos Aires and the capitals of Paraguay, Bolivia, and, to a lesser extent, Peru. Only in the air has Brazil so far matched this Argentine transport network. Direct rail and river connections have been possible for many years between Rio de Janeiro in Brazil and Asunción, Paraguay. But Lima in Peru and La Paz in Bolivia remain cut off from Brazil overland except by long and circuitous routes.

South America's central transport situation came into dramatic focus for me as I stood looking upstream from the little river port named Pôrto Esperança. It is the present terminus for the railway from São Paulo to the Paraguay River. A concrete span reaches westward toward Bolivia—but ends in mid-air. Beneath the unfinished bridge flows the Paraguay River. Tied up along the bank are cargo vessels. Although this is a Brazilian port, most of the boats fly the pale-blue-and-white ensign of Argentina. Southward pulls the river toward Argentina, and eastward pulls the bridge toward Brazil, in a tugging of natural forces that epitomize the hidden currents of South American diplomacy.

Argentina is well ahead of Brazil in the transportation race. Asunción in Paraguay is linked to Buenos Aires by rapid rail and river service, as well as by air. La Paz, Bolivia, has long had direct rail connections with the Argentine capital. Although the distance to Rio de Janeiro is no more and the geographical difficulties not as great in some particulars, Brazil is still reaching out to close a large gap and complete railway relations with Bolivia. To La Paz, Argentina had to build one of the world's most difficult railways. The rise from the *pampa* at nearly sea level to the Andean *altiplano* at 14,000 feet occurs in Argentina, not in Bolivia. A fact seldom remembered about the Argentine is that it includes the southern end of the high plateau where Indians of great chest capacity live in the rarefied air. Brazil, in its effort to build rail links with Bolivia, does not have to cope with such mountains. Bolivia has already done the worst of that part, from Oruro to Cochabamba on the way to Santa Cruz. Argentina is even trying to reach Santa Cruz and its near-by oil fields with a railway before Brazil does. The geographic odds are against Brazil, as well as the economic ones, in the long haul across from Corumbá on the Paraguay River to Santa Cruz. I flew it this time, and saw the farthest advance of railway construction in the wilderness. It is a region of uninhabited mesas and vast plains. Our ship swooped low over a village of Indians none of whom probably had ever been out of their remote environment. Work goes forward on Brazil's railway, but it, and the great bridge across the Paraguay, are delayed by shortages of materials. Not until the bridge has been completed and the rail line driven through to join this bridge with Bolivia's distant railways, will Brazil even begin to match Argentina in this field.

A further transport complication for Brazil that has immediate bearing on questions of national defense and industrial development, is the unfortunate mistake in the past of allowing railways to be built with differing gauges. It is impossible to travel continuously over some of the vital rail networks. Passengers and freight must frequently be transferred from one train to another, instead of rolling ahead without delay. Adoption of a standard gauge in Brazil is indispensable, but it will be a costly undertaking. Many of the existing locomotives and cars will have to be remodeled or scrapped.

An evident aim of the present military dictatorship in Argentina is to capitalize on a position that has been strengthened by transport advantages, as well as by purely diplomatic factors. Chief among favorable developments, from the standpoint of fascist Army diplomats, is their chance to gather up and lead the forces in South America which do not want more democracy in their countries. Unable to hold back the full tide of world democracy, these reactionary elements intend to keep as much as they can of their fascist ways inside South America. The great —and not yet fully answered—question is Brazil's attitude in this picture with its potentials of peace and war. How serious is the situation may be read in Argentina's desperate efforts to surpass Brazil's armed power. According to a reliable report, Argentina has secretly devoted at least one sum of 1,405,000,000 *pesos* to extraordinary arms budgets. This comes to $350,000,000 at current exchange rates. The nation's industry is being rapidly militarized. The total spent is a closely guarded secret.

More arresting than the South American arms race is the type of military thinking now increasingly open and assertive in Argentina. Col. Juan D. Perón, as Minister of War and of Labor, declared in his speech on June 6, 1944, when inaugurating the Chair of National Defense at La Plata University:

"War is an inevitable social phenomenon. If nations wish peace they must prepare for war. War is of total character, embracing all phases of national life."

With such language Hitler and Mussolini prepared their peoples for aggressive war. Such words in the mouth of Colonel Perón were portentous, for he has been the strong man of Argentina in the initial phase of the fascist movement.

An Argentine document purported to be a secret memorandum outlining aggressive intentions is reminiscent of the *Tanaka Memorial* wherein Japan's plans for conquest of Asia were outlined. It is customary for such documents to be officially denied. The Argentine one is dated May 3, 1943, a month before the Rawson-Ramírez *coup d'état*. While I cannot vouch for the authenticity of the text, most of its details have already been carried to the point of action, or attempted action, by the Argentine military dictatorship. Addressed to Argentine Army officers, the memorandum declares:

> Comrades: The war has shown that it is no longer possible for a country to defend itself alone. One of the consequences of this development is the policy of alliances which lessen but do not altogether eliminate the dangers inherent in such a situation. The

age of nations is being replaced by the age of continents. Yesterday provinces united to form the nation. Today nations must unite to form the continent. This is the ultimate end of the present war. Germany is making a titanic effort to unite the European continent. The biggest and best-equipped nation will guide the destinies of the newly united continent. That nation is Germany.

In the northern part of America the role of the leading country will fall for a certain time to the United States. In South America, there are only two nations sufficiently big and strong to undertake leadership—Argentina and Brazil. It is our mission to make the leadership of Argentina not only possible but indisputable.

This task is immense and full of sacrifices. But you cannot strengthen your fatherland without being ready to sacrifice everything. The heroes of our independence sacrificed all they had, including their lives. Germany, in our day, has given a new sense of heroism to life. These will be our examples.

The first step on the hard road toward a great and powerful Argentina will be to take over the government. No civilian will ever be able to understand the greatness of our ideals. It will therefore be necessary to eliminate them from the government, giving them only the mission for which they are fit—work and obedience.

Once we have won power, it will be our mission to be strong, stronger than all the other countries together. It will be necessary to arm ourselves constantly, overcoming whatever difficulties may confront us, fighting against internal and external circumstances. Hitler's fight in peace and during war will guide us.

Alliances will be the next step. Paraguay is already with us. We will get Bolivia and Chile. Together and united with these countries, it will be easy for us to exert pressure on Uruguay. These five nations will then easily attract Brazil, due to its type of government and to its important groups of Germans. Once Brazil has fallen, the South American continent will be ours. Our leadership will be an accomplished fact, a magnificent fact realized by the political genius and the heroism of the Argentine Army.

Utopian, visionary, some will say. Let us direct our looks again to Germany. In 1919, defeated, Germany signed the Treaty of Versailles, which would have meant fifty years of Allied yoke as a second-rate power. In less than twenty years Germany rose to dominate Europe. Before 1939 it was better armed than any other country. By peaceful means it had annexed Austria and Czechoslovakia.

With the war, the whole European continent had to bend its will to that of Germany.

This was not achieved without sacrifices. An iron dictatorship was necessary to force the people to accept the sacrifices demanded by such a program.

In Argentina it will be the same. Our Government will be an inflexible dictatorship, although at the beginning we will have to make concessions, necessary to entrench ourselves solidly in power. The masses will be attracted. But they will have to work, to obey, and to make sacrifices, work more and make more sacrifices than any other nation. Only by doing this will it be possible to fulfil our armament program for the conquest of the continent.

Following the German example, we will inculcate the masses with the spirit necessary to travel the heroic path on which they will be led. We will do that by controlling the press, motion pictures, radio, books, and education, and with the collaboration of the (Roman Catholic) Church. Only thus will the masses give up the comfortable life which they now lead.

Our generation will be sacrificed for our ideal, the Argentine fatherland. Its light will shine with an inextinguishable light for the best of the continent and of humanity.

Long live Argentina!

If the fascists ever consolidated a bloc of Spanish-speaking countries, South America would be split in two. These are some of the reasons for Brazil's new strategic border territories.

The South American arms race exerts its pressures both ways across frontiers, and in geometric progression. Crossing from Brazil into Argentina, I found Argentine Army officers making no effort to disguise their main military preoccupation. It is the skyrocketing military might of Brazil. President Farrell of Argentina, himself a General, brandished a sword when there was no apparent reason for such a gesture. In his speech on the first anniversary of the June 4 coup he spoke near a 35-ton tank on display in a public plaza. This kind of large tank was said by governmental spokesmen to be coming from Argentine factories "in great numbers." It is in the logic of things military that any Army in control of a Government will use its political power to build up armed force. In Argentina, the armament race is made imperative, from a strategic standpoint, by the rising of a new colossus on the northern frontier. Behind the Vargas dictatorship and keeping it in power is the Brazilian Army. Behind Brazil's Army stands the productive power of the United Nations war machine. Already Brazil is formidable on land, in the air, and at sea. Argentina has fallen far behind. This began when a short-sighted, reactionary Government took the wrong turn during the historic consultations of January, 1942. By banking on an Axis victory, Argentina's fascist-inclined nationalists lost leadership in Latin America. Brazil and Mexico became the new "great powers" of the southern lands. Argentina went into temporary eclipse. The same shadow that fell across Argentina moved away from Brazil, leaving that land in a sudden burst of sunshine. Many observers who had been harboring doubts about intentions of the Vargas dictatorship and saw in it unmistakable fascist tinges, adjourned their misgivings.

Had not Brazil cast its lot with the democracies?

Had not Brazilian secret police for years been breaking up Nazi *Bünde* in South Brazil?

Under the influence of such reasoning, the State Department in Washington, as well as nearly all agencies dealing publicly with Brazil, closed their eyes to the continuance of fascist techniques inside Brazil. How far this "be-nice-to-Brazil" attitude—to use a term coined in the State Department—has gone, is shown in a dispatch written from Mexico City by such a liberal news agency as Allied Labor News. It is an extraordinary document that can be deciphered only by applying to it a code based on knowledge of the Brazilian censorship, the relations of labor in Brazil to the Government, and Brazil's double-edged policy that is prodemocratic in foreign affairs and undemocratic in domestic affairs. The dispatch reported that Vicente Lombardo Toledano, President of the Confederation of Latin American Workers, made public messages that had been given to him in Brazil by the National Maritime Federation and a Rio de Janeiro industrial union. The messages were addressed to the workers of the Americas.

Leading off with a reference to Brazil's stand "in the fight of all liberty-loving peoples against Nazi-Fascist barbarism," the messages have much to say about "domestic fascist and reactionary groups who for some time controlled our country and still persist in certain circles, sabotaging our war effort." Throughout, these fascist elements are represented as outside the Vargas Government and trying to undermine it. In expressions which may have been heartfelt, but in any case were required of them by the whole tenor of the present Brazilian social structure and censorship, the Brazilian workers gave support to Dr. Vargas in his fight against fascism. Señor Lombardo Toledano, a Mexican under no compulsion except his own conscience and any rules of diplomacy laid down by himself or his labor organization, picked up this theme and dealt with it significantly.

The first part of Señor Lombardo Toledano's comments coincided with the officially inspired attitude of Brazilian labor that the Vargas regime "is menaced by a domestic reactionary conspiracy linked to the profascist dictatorship in Argentina." The Mexican labor leader then weighs into the scales other evidence, sifting it all through an attitude that is visibly giving to the Vargas regime the benefit of every possible doubt regarding its own apparently fascist actions. As factual reporting, Señor Lombardo Toledano discloses that labor in Brazil, to quote the dispatch, "has no organizational freedom and arrests of labor spokesmen who overstep the bounds set by the Vargas Government are frequent." He also notes that "Brazil's Constitution is literally fascist, modeled largely on Mussolini's *Carta di Lavoro*," as the dispatch puts it.

Against these points he weighs his own expectation that the fascist aspects of the Vargas regime may be set aside "by a complete revision" of the present Constitution "in the near future." That is the hope expressed by many friends of Brazil. Meanwhile, the existence in Brazil, as well as in Argentina, of a deeply entrenched fascist system, is the submerged reef responsible for many of South America's menacing whirlpools.

Getulio Dornellas Vargas

Whoever expects to understand Brazil since 1930, or unravel the puzzling fascist plots that swept through South America when Hitler was going down to defeat in Europe, must look upon one Brazilian and try to fathom him. He is Dr. Getulio Dornellas Vargas. Although he cherishes the title of President— a sacred title rightly worn only by those who accept the freely expressed will of the people—he has ridden roughshod over Brazilian democracy fourteen years. Never has this self-appointed Chief of State received supreme authority at the hands of Brazil's people in regularly constituted elections.

That in itself would not necessarily spell modern fascism. South American dictators for generations have abused the name of President and manipulated democratic forms of government to suit their whims. Actually, those dictatorships carried in themselves the seeds of streamlined fascism. Tyrants such as Juan Vicente Gómez, who held Venezuela in a steel grip from 1908 to 1935, learned the power of a controlled press. Juan Manuel de Rosas in Argentina and the López dynasty in Paraguay devised many fascist tricks in the nineteenth century. Francisco López climaxed his fascism with a mad attempt to conquer South America.

Whatever combination of letters we draw from the alphabet to represent this fungus growth of fascism in human society, it is despotic, tyrannical, a denial of man's inalienable rights to freedom under laws established by common consent of the governed. Unfortunately for humanity, basic fascism is not the product of any one person nor of any single nation. Fascism assumes devious forms in successive periods. It springs from deep-seated mortal emotions in the darkness of oppressive, undemocratic thinking. This reactionary psychosis cannot be destroyed on battlefields where the only weapons employed against it are guns, tanks, or other material weapons. Fascism is a way of looking at things. It may breed unseen and rise up to influence or even dominate governments. Defeat of Mussolini and Hitler freed the world from one specter of fascist enslavement. Fascism itself remains to be dealt with in many subtle forms.

South America has become a principal arena of this struggle. In the center of the arena, armed to the teeth by United States millions, stands Dr. Vargas. What he does with his power in the next few months or years probably will determine whether peace or war is to be the lot of South America in our time. Argentina— proud, technically advanced, backed by sinister forces abroad— has its own brand of fascism, its own ambitions, and a settled determination not to be surpassed by the "monkeys" of Brazil. I found war between Argentina and Brazil being freely discussed on both sides of the border. In Brazilian Mato Grosso I heard: "Now is the time to settle the Argentine question." An Argentine Army officer said to me: "All we need is fifty million more population." Argentina has 13,700,000; Brazil, 44,000,000. Yet war between these two most powerful South American nations is not necessarily indicated, at least for some time. The answer mostly depends on Dr. Vargas. He might prefer to form a South American fascist bloc with Argentina, instead of fighting it.

Consider the position worked out for himself by this astute dictator. By every test under the definition of fascism at the end of this book, except external aggression, his own regime is fascist within the national mildness of Brazil. It has become more fascist every year since he rode north from the *gaucho* State of Rio Grande do Sul in 1930 and seized supreme power. By attacking other forms of fascism in 1937 and later, Dr. Vargas diverted attention from his own fascism. Later he used the same early attack against Nazism as propaganda to build up his pose before the world as a champion of democracy. It is true that his secret police broke up Nazi concentrations in southern Brazil. The short-lived *Integralistas*, or Green Shirts, were tricked, and then eliminated as a national political force.

The key that unlocks this typical Vargas strategy is found in application of a fascist tenet:

> *No fascist regime can tolerate on its national terrain the existence of other fascists except during an alliance*

*for mutually guarded aims. Fascism by nature is in-
tolerant of any opposition. The total intolerance displayed by the Vargas regime toward any rival—fascist
or democratic—is one of its most fascist features.*

For the record, I am convinced after seven years of open-
minded observation that fascism of a dangerous kind—because
it pretends to be democratic—weighs at this time of writing on
the fair land and friendly people of Brazil. The Vargas regime
goes beyond authoritarian methods. It is totalitarian and fascist.
All may be changed by Dr. Vargas himself, but Brazil is not
likely to rip up soon the roots of a fascist growth nurtured by
years of urbane, deceptive, social-legislating, yet unbridled,
Vargas power. When his fascist system had been firmly established inside Brazil, Dr. Vargas was ready to consider where his
interests could best be served in the field of foreign policy.
Again for the record, he left no doubt that the decision would
be based on expediency rather than on undying devotion to
democracy.

In Vargas foreign policy not a trace is seen of the genuine
antifascism I found among the Uruguayan people and Government early in 1941 when France lay prostrate and the United
States was still only awakening from its confused slumber. I do
not presume to know or judge the inward sympathies of Dr.
Vargas. His former Foreign Minister and intimate associate,
Dr. Oswaldo Aranha, told me in Rio de Janeiro that Dr. Vargas
always wanted the democracies to win. Dr. Aranha also confirmed that when Dr. Vargas made his pro-Axis speech from
the deck of a warship on June 11, 1940, he thought the Axis
was winning. At that time Mussolini had just played the jackal
against France. President Roosevelt spoke for freemen everywhere when he accused the Italian dictator of stabbing France in
the back.

Hardly had the President's words rung around the world
before Dr. Vargas stood on the deck of a Brazilian warship and
used language that seemed to have been written in Rome or

Berlin. He said the future belonged to "vigorous young peoples" and that only "stubborn liberals" resisted the march away from "decadent systems." According to standard Vargas propaganda, representative democracy then was decidedly "decadent." Paid writers openly scoffed at it as a relic of the "weak and effeminate liberal era." With an error of judgment he later was to correct, Dr. Vargas in that speech had "thrown a few chunks of meat" to the Nazis and Fascists. So the speech was described to me by a diplomat who knows the Brazilian dictator well.

Such dismay was aroused in the United States that Vargas propagandists quickly tried to explain the speech away. It was said to refer only to internal Brazilian conditions as a clarion call to the Brazilian people for more vigorous support of the *Estado Novo*. They have disliked the unitary state which Dr. Vargas substituted in 1937 for the former Republic of the United States of Brazil. Whether written for domestic or foreign consumption, the speech still was fascist. Whenever Dr. Vargas has committed an act of this kind, his apologists explain that his heart was not in it. That may be. By the same token, his heart may not be in professions of allegiance to the cause of world democracy. Dr. Vargas belongs by position, rather than by family, in the tradition of South American ruling classes. No group of people in the world is more alarmed over prospects of having a powerful democratic wave beat across their own shores. Real democracy would topple nearly every Latin-American regime. The first groundswells of resurgent freedom washed away long-established dictatorships in Guatemala, Ecuador, and El Salvador, even before Hitler had fallen.

Regardless of where his personal sympathies lie, Dr. Vargas evidently decided at some well-defined point that his foreign policy should veer toward the Allies. I have been told on responsible authority in Washington that Dr. Vargas personally was collaborating with the United States some time before he could bring the Brazilian military to the point of admitting that Germany would lose the war. It is reasonably certain that all Brazilian bridges to Berlin were not burned until Dr. Vargas was sure of a Nazi defeat. Opponents assert he was prepared to go along with Europe's fascists, if they had won. Once his course was set toward the Allies, Dr. Vargas carried through with characteristic thoroughness. His controls over press, radio, industry, communications, transport, and every remote Brazilian town enabled him to turn a switch, and presto, Brazil was on the way to become a United Nation! Newspapers which had been under orders to delete from speeches of President Roosevelt words such as "democracy" or "anti-Nazi," now bathed in a sudden perfumed flood of pro-Allied propaganda. The same fascist press managers who had extolled "vigorous young peoples" of the Nazi "New Order" could as easily discover that the "decadent democracies" still showed signs of survival—glorious survival.

Brazil's people steadily had been prodemocratic and pro-Allied. For the record, Dr. Vargas did not lead Brazil into the war against Nazi-Fascism. He came along with Brazil. To do otherwise might have ended his public career. From the standpoint of expediency, apart from possible higher motives, he made a right decision in joining the United Nations. He released in his favor the pent-up democratic emotions of Brazilians who had been compelled to remain silent while rabid pro-Nazi sheets such as *Meio-Dia* were permitted to run rampant. He assured Brazil an inside track to the Arsenal of Democracy and to the United States Treasury. He raced ahead of Argentina in diplomacy, industry, finance, and armaments.

Befogged Buenos Aires still stumbled along under the leadership of conservatives who were fascist and pro-Nazi. Refusing to see German defeat written in the skies until it was too late to capitalize on this sound judgment, Argentina lost prestige while Brazil gained all along the line. To Rio de Janeiro, not Buenos Aires, came the Foreign Ministers of all the American Republics in January of 1942 for their decisive consultations. There Dr. Vargas and Dr. Aranha overlooked none of the dramatic possibilities in staging their announcement that Brazil was breaking diplomatic relations with the Axis. Entrance into the war was then only a question of time. The sending of a Brazilian Expeditionary Force to Africa and Europe completed a wartime foreign policy that earned for Dr. Vargas world renown and for Brazil a place at the peace table. Whether this foreign policy is to carry home to Brazil a restoration of operative democracy for itself, may well prove to be the final test for judging the public career of Dr. Vargas.

Few claim to know the inner motivations of this cool, soft-spoken, diminutive figure. Yet his name and influence exceed in Brazil that of any predecessor except the democratic Emperor Dom Pedro II. Dr. Vargas keeps his own counsel. He does not rule through a single political party in the manner of Mussolini and Hitler. He has abolished all parties. The reticent Brazilian dictator listens while men speak. He rules alone. In his path of political conquest he has swept aside two elections, two Congresses, and three Constitutions. All but one of the Constitutions were of his own making.

How lightly Dr. Vargas regards the safeguards of a written Constitution is humorously illustrated in a story my colleague Turner Catledge likes to tell. We were together in Rio de Janeiro shortly after the Vargas coup of November 10, 1937. One morning he found me practicing my Portuguese by reading the new Constitution on Copacabana Beach. Later he had an interview with Dr. Vargas and incidentally mentioned he had seen a stranger reading the Constitution.

"That is more than I have done!" quipped the dictator.

It was a joke, but the joke has been made serious by his repeated disregard of the only Constitution Brazil is permitted to have. Urbane, clever, unquestionably one of the most adroit politicians of this period, Dr. Vargas arouses extremes of adulation and of alarm.

"He is a great statesman," said a scholarly Brazilian Consul to me in a neighboring country.

"He is a gangster-in-government!"

That was the judgment rendered by a Brazilian woman of good family. She said it in Brazil, making sure no unfriendly ears were listening.

On March 24, 1936, the Pan-American Society presented its medal to Dr. Vargas in Rio de Janeiro. Yet on September 25 of the same year a dispatch in *The Christian Science Monitor*, datelined significantly from Buenos Aires instead of from Brazil, and not written by me, made this accurate and prophetic report a full year before the 1937 Vargas coup:

> BUENOS AIRES, Argentina—Day after day, it seems clearer that certain official and nonofficial elements in Brazil are preparing for a "white" revolution and dictatorship. Step by step, the way is being prepared for a bloodless *coup d'état* which will annul the Constitution altogether, dissolve the Congress, and establish a Fascist dictator of the Italian type.

This dispatch has been borne out by events, with only variations of detail in the form and some important differences in purpose between the Brazilian and Italian dictatorships.

Another view, from a recent letter:

"We must fight fascism within our continent. In Brazil fascism overwhelms the people by terror, corruption, and deteriorating propaganda."

Those are words of a Brazilian political refugee. He is one of many who do not sign their letters because, as one group writes: "We are constantly followed by the shadow of terrible persecution against ourselves and our families."

Former Foreign Minister Aranha said to me: "In his heart Dr. Vargas is not a fascist; he never could be." A few months later the Foreign Minister resigned in protest against a typical Vargas maneuver. The careers of these two Brazilians from the *gaucho* State of Rio Grande do Sul have been closely linked. Dr. Aranha rode in the forefront of the 1930 revolution that swept Vargas into power. For several years he served in Washington as a popular Brazilian Ambassador before becoming Foreign Minister and has stood out as an advocate of friendship with the United States. By naming him Foreign Minister in 1938, Dr. Vargas capitalized on this reputation and kept one of his strongest potential rivals where he could be watched. Neatly Getulian! It was natural that Dr. Aranha should be re-elected Vice-President of the Brazilian Society of Friends of America, an organization devoted to promoting friendship with the United States. In August of 1944 the Foreign Minister was scheduled to make his speech of acceptance. On August 12, the day before this publicized event, Vargas police closed the Society's premises. Publicly humiliated, Dr. Aranha submitted his resignation. It was accepted with a promptness that hinted the dictator had deeper reasons for making a change in the Foreign Ministry. Those who are familiar with Vargas methods had wondered when Dr. Aranha would become the latest potential rival to feel the sharp edge of a blade Dr. Vargas hides behind those smiling —yet unsmiling—eyes.

How ignominious a way to dismiss a talented Foreign Minister! The line of previously deflated rivals is long. The methods of their undoing resemble a collection of Oriental tales. For his own perpetuation in office he has skillfully trimmed sail to whatever prevailing winds. He has used the war against world fascism as a means for removing the stigma of fascism from himself. He has used the war against world fascism to deepen the grip of his own fascist system inside Brazil. He has used the war as another "national emergency" whereby he could delay restoration of democracy to the Brazilian people. These actions fit into the public career of Dr. Vargas with unvarying consistency. At different periods he has used different excuses for his rationalized assumption of power. By whatever device, the power itself goes on.

Always on top of the political heap emerges this enigmatic official who was reared on the Argentine border. Some Brazilians have told me they consider him as little Brazilian as Napoleon of Corsica was French. Unemotional, self-contained, calculating behind an external smile that comes and goes as stage setting without disclosing what he actually thinks, he is as unlike most Brazilians as a glacier is from a tropical night. His actions are there for anyone to see. First must be swept away the cloud of sweet vapor in which official propaganda in Rio de Janeiro and in Washington seeks to keep him wreathed. A politician of rare astuteness, he is disarmingly gentle toward opponents. When the decisive thrust comes, it is swift as a rapier. Usually the stroke is made to appear as though it came from someone else.

By such tactics Dr. Vargas not only revolted against the elections of 1930, but cast himself in the role of a liberating national hero. The "enemy" from which he delivered Brazil was representative democracy. The first political rival to feel his steel in the arena of supreme power was President Washington Luis, who now lives in New York, an exile. Then Governor of the southern cattle State of Rio Grande do Sul, Dr. Vargas ran for President as candidate of the Liberal Alliance. Election day was May 1 in a year of world depression that sent waves of revolution through Latin America. Washington Luis was forbidden by the Constitution of 1891 to become President a second time. In the Latin-American tradition he had designated a successor, Governor Julio Prestes of São Paulo, a Conservative. Dr. Vargas lost the election. Charging the result had been manipulated against him, he prepared to revolt. With powerful backing from sections of São Paulo and the second political State, Minas Gerais, he struck in the following October. Riding north with his *gaucho* supporters he seized the Presidency on October 26. President Washington Luis was forced to resign four days later.

Against many of those who had sped Vargas on his way he was to turn when the moment came. His career shouts: Beware an alliance with Vargas! Brazilians who turned to him in relief from an admittedly faulty application of democracy in Brazil soon discovered a sobering fact. They found themselves dealing with someone who showed no respect whatever for the hard-won safeguards of democracy itself, in principle or in practice. With one stroke he suspended the democratic Constitution of 1891 and substituted for it a decree placing legislative as well as executive authority in his own hands. That was on November 11, 1930.

São Paulo quickly saw how it had been deceived. Brazil as a whole learned more slowly the sharpness of his knife, and how deep it could cut. The rich and intelligent State of São Paulo still had enough strength of its own left in 1932 to challenge what its leaders called the rising black star of a fascist dictatorship. Paulistas fought bravely for three months but lost their armed revolt. They did not lose their mental integrity. They refused to climb on the Vargas bandwagon. Their thinkers kept a grip on the free press in the *Estado de São Paulo,* the best newspaper ever to appear in Brazil. Early in 1940 it was confiscated. Ever since, this former glory of Brazilian journalism has been a rag of Vargas propaganda.

Steadily, as he eliminated one opponent after another, this first full-fledged dictator in Brazilian history came into the open with fascist governmental practices. The drift to fascism was inevitable, once his political premises had been laid down. As a guiding landmark he assumed that the Brazilian Republic failed miserably between 1889 and 1930. Yet in one of the best-balanced, most authoritative, and impartial studies of the Vargas regime, Prof. Karl Loewenstein takes issue with this sweeping and unfair indictment.

"The 40 years of the liberal Republic," he writes in his book, *Brazil Under Vargas,* "were a definite and incontrovertible success."

Most of Brazil's troubles during those years were charged by Dr. Vargas against Ruy Barbosa and other liberals who imported to Brazil a constitutional system modeled on that of the United States. From this premise Dr. Vargas derived a self-appointed mission to save Brazil from the consequences of democracy. In the logic of things, no one could carry such reasoning through to the stage of practical action without adopting undemocratic methods. Since the period in which Dr. Vargas shaped his regime was strongly influenced by fascism of the Nazi, Italian, Portuguese, Spanish and other types, it is not surprising that he and his entourage absorbed some of their virus. Dr. Francisco Campos, as Minister of Justice and author of the 1937 Constitution, labored to explain to me at Rio de Janeiro in 1938 that the underlying motive of the *Estado Novo* was a new kind of democracy, with "executive power direct from the people." It recalled Hitler's specious theories of democracy in *Mein Kampf.*

The extent to which Dr. Vargas consciously uses fascist techniques is a subject for lively debate. In an apology that struck me as uncomplimentary, a United States diplomat who knows the Brazilian dictator intimately said he has not always realized that some of his actions were fascist.

Dr. Vargas understands what fascism means, all right.

It is standard practice for his person to be held above serious criticism. He cannot avoid a certain amount of popular joking about him, and takes part in it himself. This latitude falls within the official propaganda picture of him as a benevolent, kindly, humane President, a family man, scholar, member of the Brazilian Academy, and patriot. In its extreme form, official adulation at times paints him as a Washington and Lincoln rolled into one. He greatly admires Franklin D. Roosevelt.

Up to this time of writing, actions of Dr. Vargas heavily weight the balance against assertions that he is a democrat at heart. Such statements have frequently been made to me. I search the record without finding supporting evidence. On the contrary, his career is loaded with indications of basic fascist thinking.

After abolishing the 1891 charter on which Brazilian rights of popular self-government had been based for nearly a half century, he showed no inclination to bind himself by a new Constitution. The São Paulo revolution of 1932, although put down, stirred Brazil enough to force him to make concessions to demands of a still articulate democratic opinion. The first Vargas Constitution resulted. In its clauses appeared unmistakable signs of fascism. Vaguely worded phrases gave the Government power to suspend publications when they printed "false material," or even authenticated information that was held likely to "disturb public order" or "provoke social unrest." Steps were taken toward a corporative structure of industry and labor.

The title of President was conferred on Dr. Vargas at the same time by his hand-picked Constituent Assembly, not by vote of the people.

During the three years that followed, Dr. Vargas gave a new turn to his thesis that democracy would not work in Brazil. The Chamber of Deputies that sat again in Tiradentes Palace found itself exposed to a studied campaign designed to discredit it before the nation. Brazilians who went through that period have told me how Dr. Vargas compounded his case against Congress. He was laying the groundwork, with characteristic subtlety, for abolishing Congress altogether. Here emerges the portrait of a dictator who steadily destroyed representative government instead of strengthening it. He was still at work on his basic premise that democracy had failed in Brazil, was failing again, and that he, Vargas, would have to step in to save the country from the consequences. Always the central theme is the same: Vargas ruling, Vargas unencumbered by elections or the checks and balances of democracy, Vargas deciding what is best for Brazil and imposing it by persuasion, wit, guile, or raw force.

Next in the rutted ways of fascism came a series of Communist scares. Dr. Vargas utilized a revolt of 1935 in parts of the Army and Navy to equip himself with a constitutional amendment, voted by Congress, whereby he could suspend constitutional guarantees. This move was ostensibly aimed against Communists. Again it is the familiar pattern of a fascist dictator manipulating a Congress to vote itself out of existence—this time in the Americas. As the elections set under the Constitution for January 3, 1938, drew near, Dr. Vargas faced the prospect of early retirement. He was forbidden by the Constitution to enter the presidential lists himself.

On Brazil's horizon had risen several fascist organizations. Nazis were marching in southern Brazil among large German colonies in the States of Rio Grande do Sul and Santa Catarina. Green Shirts under the mystic name of Integralists were scrawling their Sigma sign across the map of Brazil. Taken from integral calculus, the Sigma stands for the "sum total of things." Dr. Plinio Salgado, founder and leader of the Integralists, organized the first national group of its kind in Brazilian history. Political parties under the Republic functioned in each State, not nationally. In the Federal Congress, representatives sat as delegations from São Paulo, Minas Gerais, Rio Grande do Sul, and the other seventeen States. The Integralists, with excess zeal, claimed hundreds of thousands of members. Their anti-Semitism and totalitarian trappings were the most Hitlerian phases of native Brazilian fascism. I still have the faded paper book of Integralist doctrines and rules which a furtive Brazilian farmer gave me. He called it his "Bible," and asked me mysteriously if I was awake to the world Jewish menace. Simple people like that were swept into ranks of *Integralismo*.

Dr. Vargas watched these fascist movements. They, unlike his own brand, displayed uniforms and arm bands, banners and parades. His is less obvious, subtler, and far more effective.

The Nazi *Schützenbünde* or Shooting Societies, and other typical Nazi agencies, were first to feel the weight of Brazil's nationalistic campaign. Vargas secret police under Major Filinto Mueller—themselves organized along lines of the German Gestapo —cut to ribbons a Nazi network in Brazil directly related to those then undermining a dozen countries in Europe. The story is told in reports issued by police of Rio Grande do Sul. At Pôrto Alegre, capital of the State, they have assembled a museum of trophies seized from Brazilian Nazis. Bullets to fit the bore of rifles used by the Brazilian Army show how far Nazi plans went. The Hitlerlike uniform of Ernst Dorsch, Chief of the National Socialist Party of Pôrto Alegre, is draped on a dummy. A significant fact about this destruction of the Nazi system in southern Brazil is the propaganda use made of it. The museum itself is a persuasive and colorful "proof" for visiting foreign journalists that Brazil has not gone fascist.

Brazilians in a position to brush aside such propaganda have given me this analysis:

German, Italian and Japanese colonial nuclei have never been a serious *political* problem in Brazil, nor did they ever threaten national integrity. The problem was merely one of *education*. The steps toward nationalization which were taken in the past few years had less of a patriotic significance than would appear at first sight. Whoever knows Brazilian political life intimately is aware that such measures are more often than not aimed at looting private property belonging to small businessmen and farmers—property which is taken forcibly from its owners and given away as gifts to friends and relatives of the police agents. Under the pretext of crushing fascism, these acts aim rather at publicity and at canvassing new servants and devoted friends of the Government. The same method was used against so-called Communists, during the dark period when anti-Communist reaction was rampant, immediately after the 1935 revolution.

Whoever has lived in Brazil during the years 1939 to 1942 is aware that the country was permanently threatened by a Nazi coup from within, by the Government itself, with the help and support of the German Reich. It was known that such maneuvers were clearly aimed against the United States. Brazilian democrats who viewed the United States with genuine friendliness were constantly threatened with persecution and reprisals. Any measures taken against fascism would, therefore, have to be aimed first at the Government men themselves, above all the Army General Staff, the police, and the Press and Propaganda Department.

How can anyone believe in the sincerity of anti-Nazi measures, when everyone knows that the highest posts are still held by those who set up in Brazil the machinery of terror and oppression, and who were decorated by Hitler for "Distinguished Service to Germany." Although war was declared on the Axis, and friendly words are constantly aimed at the United States, the dominating group did not alter in the least, where internal questions are concerned. The same regime of terror goes on, the same atmosphere of espionage and oppression, the same antidemocratic, fascist and personal propaganda spread to all corners of Brazil, the same absence of freedom of opinion.

Such tactics cannot be taken seriously as proofs of democratic sympathies; and one is amazed to see that they are taken seriously in the United States, most of all in official circles. Vargas' wish is to get as much as possible out of the United States, for his own benefit, although he is probably laughing surreptitiously at "American naïveté."

When will the United States understand?

The aim of Vargas propaganda is to put off as long as possible the day of North American reckoning with his own fascism. A revealing bit of such propaganda is an article that falls into logical difficulties and extricates itself by considerable wrenching of logic as well as of language. Apparently a thoroughgoing attack against fascism, the article appeared in an illustrated supplement of the newspaper *A Manhã*, dated October 12, 1943. The title is: *Brazil and the Extinction of Fascisms*. A linoleum-block print of Dr. Vargas accompanies it. He is portrayed as determined and democratic. The article opens with a statement that the United Nations have a task before them larger than merely "beating the material power of a ferocious enemy." It adds:

"More important than that is the destruction of the totalitarian idealism which created that power, to the end of conquering the world and reducing it to slavery, in the old dream that ever lived in the morbid German imagination."

A speech by President Roosevelt is then quoted in which he said, ". . . it is not possible to obtain total victory in this war if there be permitted the survival of any vestige of fascism in any of its malignant forms."

There follows a passage of Vargasian reasoning that needs to be read in full for an appreciation of how ideological terms are juggled. The following is the English translation as made and published in Brazil beside the original Portuguese.

"To be sure," it begins, "the Atlantic Charter guarantees the autonomy of the races, leaving to their judgment the political form each one would like to adopt. But it is not possible any more, even within the spirit of that great document, to consent to the formation in any part of the world of new foci of those corrosive doctrines that threw the universe in the tragic situation of this moment.

"Just as the inviolability of domicile sometimes suffers conditional restrictions when it has turned into a place of refuge for paid assassins who menace the collective tranquillity, so the political autonomy, recognized by the Atlantic Charter as due to all, will never more serve as immunity for the recomposition of any kind of fascisms.

"The experience of this war is too severe for the United Nations to let themselves be swayed anew by the almost suicidal romanticisms found in the old liberal democracies or in the open-door regimes."

It is a neat text, smooth, evasive, filled with logical contradictions. Its full impact can be felt only by weighing its words against the record of Brazil's own present fascism. Note particularly the implied definition of fascism as external aggression, with nothing said about the seedbeds of fascism itself. It is a more startling fact that the State Department in Washington applies the same shallow definition of fascism in its dealings with Brazil. This point has been made unmistakable to me by high officials. Effects of such unprincipled diplomacy are tragically apparent in South America. As long as the roots of fascism remain undisturbed inside any country, its devil's-grass will spread. Fascism breeds wars, directly or indirectly. The only way to deal with fascism is to dig it out, root and branch. The words of the Brazilian article under analysis said as much, but with typical Getulian slipperiness evaded the main issue of fascism inside Brazil. Note also that even in such an article the Vargas propagandists could not restrain themselves from blaming democracy for the world's troubles, including the Hitlerite war. Any advocate of democracy freely acknowledges the mistakes made by nations which fell short of their responsibilities under systems of self-government. It is another thing for the Vargas regime to set itself up as a critic of world democracy. Let the critics first give proof of democratic sympathies and democratic sincerity, inside their own country.

A high member of the Brazilian Government who, for obvious reasons, should not be named, told me that the present form of government in Brazil would be "terrible" in the hands of anyone except Dr. Vargas. Yet Dr. Vargas is architect and executor of the regime over which he rules in the unmerited name of President. That contradiction of terms—an official of benevolent reputation who has produced a governmental machine of terrible danger—sums up Brazil's political paradox of this decade.

Unfortunately the corrosive effect of the Vargas system is not confined to Brazil, or even to South America. Someday, present United States diplomacy will have to face its responsibility for arming in Brazil the oldest, subtlest, and most deeply entrenched fascist system in South America. While Washington fumes against Argentine fascism, it winks at Brazilian fascism. Argentina's clumsy barracks-room politicians are lagging years behind Dr. Vargas in their attempts to establish fascist controls over the press, education, industry, culture, and diplomacy. Unless the Brazilian dictator is prevented from carrying through his full program of deception, he will emerge from this war against fascism as the most successful of fascist dictators. Inside the camp of democracy and using its outward forms, he and his terrible system would breed new wars, for fascism is not the way chosen by men of peace.

There stands the Dr. Vargas who long since would have been paraded on Pennsylvania Avenue and loaded with honors by the United States Government, if certain diplomats had been given their way.

There stands the Dr. Vargas who aspires to vote at the peace table of a reborn democratic world.

O Estado Novo

The justification advanced by Dr. Vargas for his long assumption of dictatorial power in Brazil is that he had a program for breathing new life into a nation which he says had grown moribund under the Republic. Leaving aside for the moment any attempt to compare Brazil of the Republic with Brazil of Vargas, what are the life-giving methods on which he has relied?

Catchwords will not speed the inquiry. Dr. Vargas would be first to repudiate the name of *O Estado Novo* itself if any practical purpose could be served by such a step. Theorists who have surrounded him supply the slogans. He contents himself with the practical substance of power. If he could have maintained himself in office and kept his dictatorial rule under a system of free elections, he would have called them long ago. It is a truism of Brazilian politics that he never will permit elections until he is ready to retire, or has taken adequate precautions to prevent democracy from getting out of hand. As long as he wants to be President, the elections would be manipulated by devices familiar in South America. Only in his sixty-third year at this writing, he is said to have told President Roosevelt that he will be on the job in Brazil after his colleague from Hyde Park has had X terms in the White House.

An unfailing touchstone for judging any political regime is its attitude toward the press. In the definition of fascism that has been laid down for accurate use in these pages, public-opinion control is placed first among modern devices that set fascism apart from old-fashioned South American dictatorship. Another pertinent point in the definition is violation by a powerful minority of individual rights. It is a human right, recognized by democratic governments as valid after centuries of sacrifice and struggle, to have free access to all available sources of information. Long ago it was seen that if any special interest could control the printed page, it could go far toward dominating a people. The free press grew in response to demands of the people for an independent source of information. One of the most retrogressive currents in South America has been the education of whole nations away from a true sense of what the press means. In Brazil particularly, the Vargas regime has confused and darkened the thinking not only of millions of defenseless people on this issue but has broken down many former intellectual leaders. Not all Brazilians have been deceived. A few dare to say what they think about present misconceptions of the press in Brazil, but they won't say such things except to someone they trust. No Brazilian writer or editor could criticize press decrees, or any other phase of the Vargas Administration, without falling out of favor and possibly facing serious reprisals.

In Brazil the free press does not exist. It has not existed since November 10, 1937, when Dr. Vargas dissolved Congress and launched his *Estado Novo*. Before 1937, the press had been under increasing pressures ever since the revolution of 1930 that carried Dr. Vargas into power. The Constitution of 1934, in which Dr. Vargas compromised with the still active opposition, paid lip service to press freedom. Yet already the shadows were gathering and falling across the open book of public knowledge. When he had entrenched himself in power, Dr. Vargas moved ahead with his full program, including prostitution of the press. A Propaganda Department had been established in 1934. It later fell under the fascist influence of Dr. Francisco Campos in the Ministry of Justice, and became in 1939 the Department of Press and Propaganda, or DIP. To this day, DIP sits in the house that rightly belongs to a free Brazilian press. As if to symbolize its reversal of democracy, DIP occupies the building formerly used by the Chamber of Deputies. The other branch of Congress, the Senate, has been converted into offices for the Ministry of Justice.

DIP is an organization that goes as far as anything in the Western Hemisphere toward fascist conceptions of public information. It is not limited to the newspaper press, but embraces books, magazines, radio, the theater, and even tourism. When North American reporters arrive singly or in groups to see Brazil for themselves, they often are met by smiling emissaries of DIP. Limousines may be drawn up at the station curb. Every facility is offered—except the kind of information the Government wants to suppress.

A characteristic of DIP is its evident aim of inducing Brazilian and foreign correspondents into voluntary compliance with its betrayal of the free press. So conspicuous has been the success of DIP in this regard that foreign correspondents resident in Brazil make little effort to tell their readers the whole story. They have largely been lulled into forgetfulness of what the press must be in order to remain the press.

The instant public information becomes a function of government, to that degree the press ceases to exist. All that is left is propaganda in varying degrees.

The difference between Brazil's smooth press techniques and Argentina's awkward ones has been clearly evident in the actions of foreign correspondents. Those resident in Rio generally accept the one-sided official "news," while the men in Argentina use every available device to circumvent the censorship. The justly famed friendliness of Brazil does not entirely account for the restraint of foreign and national correspondents. Behind the smile of DIP is always the threat of force. No foreign correspondent could remain in Brazil if he tried to report with even moderate objectivity. This book, for instance—while as impartial and fair as I know how to make it—could not have been written from Brazil. When the magazine *Time* on May 29, 1944, picked up portions of an article I wrote on the Brazilian political situation, the edition of *Time* printed in Brazil had to omit my report. A large blank space gaped where the censor's pencil had fallen. *Time* the next week commented that Brazilian readers had another proof of the press blackout.

Brazilian writers and editors are as unhappy a lot of men as one could meet. Some have emasculated their profession, either under the influence of persuasive arguments or in order to feed their families. The great majority bitterly endure their enforced servitude. A few have stood up for their convictions and taken the consequences. Others have been unable to silence their consciences and have turned to different pursuits. Those who have come to the United States on good-will tours were not permitted to report their impressions freely when they returned to Brazil. The United States has spent millions of dollars on such good-will tours in recent years, only to have the fruitage blighted by Brazil's officious censorship. In such instances, it would be hard to prove that Brazil's press controls have been aimed solely against Nazis and Fascists or other subversive elements. The aim is clearly political, having nothing to do with national security—that is, unless national security is interpreted as being inseparable from viewpoints dictated by the Vargas regime.

An effective means for keeping editors in line is DIP's control over newsprint supplies. Every publisher is required to register with DIP at the start of each year. Those who have remained in line during the preceding twelve months receive a provisional permit to obtain newsprint through customs. If at any time during the year they publish articles displeasing to DIP, they face five progressive penalties. First they are warned. Next, publication is suspended for a few days. A third offense causes the provisional newsprint permit to be suspended. All paper used during the preceding period is then held to be contraband illegally imported. The fine doubles the original cost of the paper. Few publications could survive this confiscatory fine. If they do, they face on fourth offense a requirement of submitting all copy for censoring before publication. The censors can easily make an editor rewrite his entire edition two or three times—an unbearable cost and uncertainty. Finally, the paper can be closed definitively. When this occurs, the government usually appropriates the name for one of its own propaganda sheets. Such was the case with *A Manhã and A Tarde* in Rio de Janeiro years ago.

So the atmosphere of DIP and its branches in the twenty Brazilian States is fulsome and repellent to working reporters of the free press. DIP's elaborate quarters are replete with motion-picture studios, radio stations, and all the trimmings, while the real press has been starved in a dark corner. The regime does not willingly discuss such a question. When pressed for answers, officials resort to the standard excuse of dictators everywhere—that there is a national emergency calling for extraordinary measures.

Brazil has been under emergency conditions for many years, but much of the emergency has been exaggerated to serve aims of the regime. Neither the Brazilian people nor friendly outsiders see why the most fascist press in the Americas should deceive the only South American country that has sent an Expeditionary Force to Europe to help defeat Hitler. There may be some disagreement on the extent to which these instruments of press control are used to promote fascist ends. The mechanism itself is all that any fascist dictator could ask. Early in 1944 considerable alarm was expressed in the United States over attacks launched by military rulers at Buenos Aires against the Argentine press. *La Prensa* and *La Nación,* Argentina's two most powerful and independent daily newspapers, finally bowed to fascist edicts. The point not generally grasped is that Brazil's press several years ago fought—and lost—its battle for freedom.

The mere calling of limited postwar elections, which Dr. Vargas has been compelled to promise after insistent public demand, will not free Brazil's press unless the voting is genuinely representative of a democratic people. DIP would be swept away by the first clean wind of restored democracy in Brazil.

Another touchstone for judging the intentions of a political regime is its attitude toward education. The Vargas censorship determines the content of books as well as of newspapers. It has dominated Brazilian textbooks used in the schools. In the field of adult education and general reading, the same censorship has sought to hold national opinion in line with Vargas theories. The situation in Brazilian schools is brought vividly into focus by considering what would happen to any teacher who stood up and taught his pupils that the Brazilian Republic was "a definite and incontrovertible success," as Professor Loewenstein plainly writes in a passage previously quoted. That teacher probably would lose his position and might be summarily disciplined. However honest his teaching, he would be denying the basic dogma of the Vargas dictatorship. The existence of that dogma is well known by all teachers. Whether they agree with it or not, they make sure that nothing in their teaching exposes them to official reprisals. There is no essential difference between this imposition of a Brazilian dogma and the imposition of similar dogmas by Hitler. Race superiority is a more explosive doctrine than the teaching that Vargas dictation is superior to democracy, but both are equally deadening to intellectual integrity. At the fountainhead of knowledge, the entire Vargas program has struck subtle blows against democracy and the principles of educational freedom. This fact is evident among young Brazilians, many of whom believe Vargas propaganda because their powers of independent thought have been stultified.

Men whose contributions to Brazilian democracy will live and again be exalted in the schools, have been subordinated to the mystic conception of Dr. Vargas as a symbol of national awakening and unification. By official decree, his picture hangs in every school and public building. The standard portrait is repeated so often that it becomes one of the most monotonous aspects of the Brazilian scene. In addition, posters show him in more intimate poses. *Victory With Vargas* has appeared in numerous forms to identify the dictator with the deep United Nations sympathies of the Brazilian people. Broadly smiling, he and President Roosevelt are shown together as the two great democratic leaders of the Western Hemisphere.

The inconsistency between such professions and the daily experience of Brazil's people has steadily driven Dr. Vargas toward an eventual showdown. In keeping with his standard strategy, he yields to popular demand and then tries to make it appear that he has been leading. This, however, is not direct representation of a people by their Chief Executive. The difference is that concessions to popular demands for restoration of democratic rights are made, if at all, only when to do otherwise would imperil the dictatorship. To this date of writing, not one such right has actually been restored in Brazil. In the field of foreign affairs, Dr. Vargas aligned his policy with the wishes of the people, but not until long after Brazilians had shown themselves eager to support the democracies. In the field of domestic policy, Dr. Vargas has gone no farther than to make promises for fulfillment "after the war."

Brazil has learned that Dr. Vargas is a past master at producing political conditions that play into his hands. From the start of his tenure he has capitalized on actual national emergencies and manufactured others. Dictatorship, especially when it has adopted fascist techniques, thrives on crises. As a settled method of government since 1930, Dr. Vargas has resorted to decrees of national emergency. Early in his career he had to persuade Congress to do this for him. When he could dispense with this troublesome democratic procedure, he decreed whatever he needed to retain power. This liking for extralegal procedures is also a touchstone for judging the political motivation of a regime.

Entering the war as a United Nation probably was inevitable for Brazil and also supremely suited the purpose of having another reason for continuing the unbridled dictatorship. Earlier, the reasons advanced had been Brazil's need for unification and defense against various internal enemies. The sweeping and unfair indictment of the Republic by Dr. Vargas caused him to lump together as national enemies not only Nazis, Fascists, Communists, and fifth columnists generally, but democracy and even —in effect—the Brazilian people themselves.

Vargas propaganda stems from two broad falsities. The first is that, in order to deal effectively with subversive elements, the regime has to withhold all democratic liberties from the nation as a whole. The second is that Brazil's people are not ready for democracy even in its fundamentals such as free press, free speech, unbiased education, and a government of laws rather than of dictated decrees.

It is accepted by any nation, at peace or in war, that police measures must weigh heavily on lawbreakers and spies. Penalties directed against such elements can be concentrated on them, leaving maximum freedom to law-abiding citizens. This is not the case in Brazil under Vargas. Brazilians do not object when secret police attack subversive forces, but do inwardly rebel when normal political activity is also treated as though it were subversive.

To say that these people—kindly, intelligent, nonviolent, orderly—are not ready to have a free press and other normal democratic rights, is to distort plain facts. With familiar paternalism, the Vargas regime acts on the assumption that it knows what is best for Brazil. The people are permitted to make their wishes known, but only in ways that keep all authority and final decision in the hands of one man—Dr. Vargas. On my first trip to Brazil early in 1938, I found widows and simple country-people entering Catete Palace, with its glittering crystal chandeliers and marble staircase, to see the President. I was told that Brazil would be run as a big family. Six years later, I heard more details about the way this family runs, to buttress facts observed in visits during the intervening years. Most of the family is made up of lovable, livable, democratic, friendly people. Millions of them can't spell their own names, but they are nearly all well grounded in human values. Among them a sense of humor is spontaneous and contagious. The color of their skin makes little if any difference to them. They are naturally communal. When a Brazilian tells a story on a train or river boat, he does not limit it to his nearest companion. He instinctively broadens his circle until everyone within easy earshot has been drawn to share the fun, or to hear more serious affairs when such is the mood. I have found that among them are no strangers. Certainly they never treated me as one. Only the Vargas police did that.

Brazil, larger than the continental United States by five times the area of New York State, is awakening to discover new powers. The country towers among all other Latin-American countries in size and military might. It stirs, flexes expanding sinews, and feels throughout vast lands its growth toward world stature. As yet the South American giant gropes and stumbles, for this land of jungles, semideserts, faulty transportation, and racial mixtures has a long way to go before it can be fully integrated. Rulers of Brazil when it was a Portuguese colony, then an Empire, a Republic, and now a dictatorship under Vargas, have sought by differing methods to colonize and develop a stubborn terrain. Brazil has been greatly aided by the United States with military, industrial, and technical resources. Former Secretary of State Hull gave assurances that military bases built in Latin America at a cost of hundreds of millions of dollars will be handled in future for the mutual benefit of the co-operating powers. For Brazil, this means that some of the world's finest air bases—at Belém, Natal, and farther south—will serve every need of Brazil's growing air forces. The industrial foundation for Brazilian power also is being strengthened. At Volta Redonda near Rio de Janeiro a $65,000,000 steel mill is rising to begin heavy industry. The "Iron Mountain" at Itabira Mine in the State of Minas Gerais is being blasted apart to pour 69 per cent iron ore into new furnaces.

As Brazil awakens to itself, so the world devotes greater attention than ever to Brazil. Many people want to know whether it offers possibilities as a new frontier home for them. Industrialists are examining the country's resources and potential markets. Diplomats of the Americas and of Europe adjust their calculations to Brazil's growing power. No one has seen all of this mammoth land, but anyone who samples its typical regions is sure to come away with at least one clear impression—size, sheer magnitude, overpowering extension. Governing such a country would be difficult under any form of administration. A close parallel is China, although the differences equal or surpass the resemblances. Older and teeming, China has the same kind of distances to surmount, the same separation of large political units from the center of government, similar transport gaps, and other forces that tend to divide rather than unite.

Brazil achieved nationhood in days of the democratic and liberal Brazilian Emperors. Deep in the interior at a point such as Guajará-mirim, the most distant settlement of Mato Grosso, I felt at first as remote as on some lush green moon. Hardly had the river boat touched the sloping muddy bank when I forgot remoteness in marveling how Brazilian is the town. Somehow the Brazilian people and culture have stamped the tropical wilderness, as they have left their own imprint on the semiarid Northeast, on prosperous coastal midlands in the Rio de Janeiro-São Paulo area, and on open cattle country of the south. Already the Brazilian achievement in cultural unification on a difficult terrain stands high among the epics of world peoples. The cultural unity that so impresses a visitor to any part of Brazil had its origins in the family relationship whereby members of the Braganza dynasty identified themselves with their people. Theirs was an aristocracy and a nobility. Like such social systems anywhere, it had dark and oppressive features. In Brazil these have weathered with time to leave mostly pleasant memories of the Royal House. In Petrópolis the surviving scions of Brazilian royalty live near the carefully tended shrines of that gracious period. When Dr. Vargas goes to the cool mountain heights of Petrópolis, he pays taxes to the Royal House for use of a summer residence that belongs to them.

A fact seldom remembered outside Brazil is that one of the most democratic and enterprising periods in national development came during the independent Empire. That was from 1822 to 1889. Rio de Janeiro served as the seat of government for the Braganzas after Napoleon invaded Portugal in 1807. From 1807 to 1822, Brazil accordingly was a royal metropolis of a worldwide empire, instead of being merely a colony. Dom Pedro I sided with the Brazilian people against being reduced again to colonial status. As Regent, he proclaimed independence on September 7, 1822, in the *Grito de Ypiranga,* or "Cry of Ypiranga" —Brazil's Declaration of Independence. The Dom Pedros, I and II, ruled as constitutional monarchs. Their concessions to democratic evolution were such that by the end of the Empire in 1889 Brazil was a soundly liberal parliamentary democracy that compared favorably with similar monarchies of the day. Elections increased in importance with the steady broadening of the franchise.

Dom Pedro II for 58 years did not withhold freedom of press, of expression, of political activity, or any other human right on the ground that the Brazilian people were unready to use such liberties for the nation's benefit. While guiding Brazil in a political evolution that led toward the establishment of the Republic, Dom Pedro II drove railways into the interior. He sought to revive the São Francisco Valley in the Northeast by laying tracks around Paulo Afonso Waterfalls. In his reign the Amazon Basin reached the doorstep of its highest prosperity as supplier of wild rubber to a bicycling world. Even so, after nearly four centuries of settlement, Brazil had hardly been nibbled at the edges. The reason was not that men turned back halfheartedly. Most of the territory had already been explored in its broad outlines, and found to be harder to crack than a Brazil nut held in unaided human fingers.

The Republic took up the task in 1889 when the monarchy was abolished during Dom Pedro II's absence in Europe. What the Republic did for Brazil both in politics and in economics is a large and debatable question. A favorite argument of the Vargas regime is that the Republic held back Brazil's growth. Elaborating this theme, a prominent official told me that under the Republic there were four representatives in Congress for Amazonas, but they seldom came from the Amazon country, being "imposed by politicians" of Rio or São Paulo. In contrast, this official pointed to the steady stream of businessmen and others who come to Rio for consultations with Vargas officials on Amazonian affairs. These consultations take place in the Council of Economics, the Council of Commerce, and others. The official estimated that all of the councils working each day in the capital would outnumber three or four bodies such as the disbanded Brazilian House of Representatives.

"It would be far easier for President Vargas to handle a House of Representatives than to manage this kind of government," he added. The "kind of government" through which Dr. Vargas is grappling with Brazil's many economic, social, political, diplomatic, and other problems may be briefly summarized as follows:

1. A supreme executive, with final power of decision on any question. He is unhampered by elections or other democratic checks and balances.

2. Executive agencies dependent directly on the President. These include the ten Cabinet Departments: Justice; Foreign Affairs; War; Navy; Air; Agriculture; Labor, Commerce, and Industry; Public Health and Education; Transportation and Public Works; and Treasury. Full Cabinet meetings are infrequent. The President sees his Cabinet advisers singly or in pairs. He alone commands full information on governmental affairs. He alone is vested with sovereign power. Beyond the Cabinet, there are several other executive agencies. Prominent among them are the Tribunal of National Security, including secret police; the Department for Administration of Public Services, or DASP; the Department of Press and Propaganda, or DIP; the Commission for Defense of National Economy; the Council of Foreign Trade; Executive Commission of Steel and Iron; National Petroleum Council; and so on. All of these funnel directly to the desk of Dr. Vargas.

3. Industrial syndicates, with compulsory membership by employers and labor. The government holds final power in any dispute. Strikes and lockouts are forbidden.

4. Various other advisory councils.

The presidential powers, formidable as they are on paper, represent only a small part of the actual authority wielded by Dr. Vargas. In the absence of Congress, he legislates entirely by decree. He appoints Federal Interventors in the states and can do so in any industry, with powers subject only to his sanction. He names judges. It is doubtful if any Chief of State in the modern world has exceeded the one-man rule gradually built up for himself by Dr. Vargas. This is the type of three-in-one executive, legislator, and judge which an enthusiastic propagandist for Dr. Vargas summed up in this self-contradictory encomium:

"The discretionary President is, by his method of acting, the most constitutional of Presidents."

It is this attempt to clothe an absolute and at times brutal dictatorship in the shining raiment of democracy that exposes hypocrisy in the Vargas regime. The present unratified Constitution, issued by decree with the 1937 coup, opens with these words in Article 1:

> *Brazil is a Republic. Political power emanates from the people and is exercised in their name and in the interest of their well-being, their honor, their independence, and their prosperity.*

This apparently forthright statement of democracy, followed in the same paragraph by provisions for "exercise" of political power "in the name" of the people instead of by them through elected representatives, opens the door in practice to anything the dictator wants to do. Something new in political history would be registered if Dr. Vargas could prepare Brazil for democracy by the fascist methods he has used. Democracy will be restored in Brazil and will steadily deepen in effectiveness, but not because of the Vargas regime. The regime itself is being forced by world events to bow to resurgent democracy. Brazil's people will rise to the new day in grateful release from years of repression.

In Brazil are many capable people who feel that every right objective set forth as a justification for the present form of government could be achieved without resort to fascist methods. Such dissidents constitute the silenced political opposition—not as foreign underminers, but as sincere democrats. They are thinkers, well-educated, and know the rest of the world through travel. For many years persons of this type have had three alternatives. They can go into exile, as many have done. They can remain in Brazil and cease their democratic activities. Or, they may engage in secret efforts to restore political rights to their country. Against the last, Vargas secret police are constantly on the alert. In the Brazilian tradition, violence occurs rarely, yet there is no mistaking the temper of the regime. Anyone who doesn't agree becomes a marked man.

Constructive aims on which thinking Brazilians generally are in accord are these:

1. That the country needs economic development—especially transportation—to draw more closely together Brazil's scattered regions.

2. That the Brazilian masses must be educated more widely before they can make a more effective contribution to a democratic form of government.

3. That political unity on a national scale is desirable, without destroying the individuality of the States.

4. That actual subversive elements must be kept under control, by means that leave law-abiding Brazilians in possession of their full democratic rights.

5. That Brazil must keep pace with advancing social and labor practices.

The Vargas regime claims for itself a position of leadership in Brazilian history on most of these aims. The one conspicuous omission is anything related to democratic rights. The main complaint of Dr. Vargas against democracy, apart from his undeclared desire to avoid facing elections and other democratic restraints, is that the transfer of many provisions of the United States Constitution to Brazil in 1891 disunited the country. Under the Empire, Brazil had been united. In North America, the Constitution gradually welded the States into a Federal Union. Success was achieved only after a long and hard Civil War had failed to break the Union apart. In Brazil, the same principles of federal union released the States, giving them more freedom of action than they had before. São Paulo and Minas Gerais, the two most industrialized States, quickly rose to domination of national affairs. The Presidency alternated between them, with occasional inroads by a citizen from some other State. The result was that São Paulo and Minas Gerais easily led Brazil in politics, as they did in wealth, population, and schooling.

Whether the net balance sheet of the Brazilian Republic from 1889 to 1930 shows more gains for the nation than that of the Vargas regime from 1930 to date, is the point at issue. What dividends, that is, have the Brazilian people to show for their enforced surrender of democratic liberties? The Vargas regime points to many evidences of social, economic, and national progress—always omitting any reference to the price paid in currency of universal human rights. I have talked extensively with people whose memories run back over half a century of residence in Brazil. They freely admit faults of the Republic, but wish they had it back. They acknowledge that not enough attention was given to measures for ameliorating the lot of Brazil's laboring masses. A bourgeois oligarchy carried through the aristocratic and semifeudal tradition of an economy that had been freed from slavery only in 1888. Politicians in the Federal Congress abused their privileges and neglected their opportunities. These are old and familiar blights on the upward growth of genuine, operative self-government. They occur in the most advanced democracies. Dr. Vargas during his early political career had seen them from the inside as he rose through the State Legislature of Rio Grande do Sul to the Federal Congress. Later he became Federal Minister of Finance and Governor of Rio Grande do Sul before starting his dictatorial march.

As an advocate of labor legislation, Dr. Vargas stood for a larger measure of economic democracy than many of his colleagues in Brazilian politics. This fact sped his 1930 revolution to success. His sincerity need not be questioned. A capable administrator, patriotic, and dissatisfied with the course of events in Brazil, he may well have acted in full good faith. It is not my intention to pass final judgment for myself on this public figure until his record has been completed. It is unquestionable, however, that he has used dubious means in pursuit of objectives both worthy and unworthy. It is the old conundrum—whether evil means are justified by good ends. Dr. Vargas confirms by actions his evident belief that a democratic end can justify a fascist means.

Dispensing for the moment with theoretical discussions of democracy, as Dr. Vargas does by choice, I now want to come to grips with practical results of his governmental action. Examination of the *Estado Novo* leads me to the conclusion that every tangible gain claimed for Brazil is offset by a more serious loss.

Even the labor decrees deny to the workers all political rights. Strikes, the weapon whereby oppressed masses first compelled owners of sweatshops to ease the yoke of 16-hour days, have been forbidden to Brazilians ever since 1937. Lockouts, the counter-weapon of management, also are barred. The government emerges, with typical fascist economic reasoning, as the final dictator of labor-capital relationships. This is a far different thing in Brazil from governmental regulation of those vital social forces by a government actually representing the majority of the people, and made responsive to them through regular elections. The economic structure under Brazil's existing Constitution, itself only a decree, is forged into an instrument for furthering "the imperative interests of national production," in words of Article 139. In economic dominance, no fascist dictator could ask more. Whether Dr. Vargas has aggressive intentions or not, he holds totalitarian controls over the nation's productive effort. Few men could possess such power and not abuse it.

In the political field, Brazil under Vargas has lost even the embryonic democracy of the Republic. Dr. Vargas referred to this fact when making one of his promises to call elections after the war. "We shall restore," he said, "those organs of our national life which are not yet functioning." The fulfillment of this promise, and the way it is done, may write a new chapter in the career of Dr. Vargas. It could not erase the fact that previously for fourteen years the breath of political freedom had been choked off by stealth in Brazil.

In economics, the Brazilian dictatorship has been able to move more swiftly than a democracy could have done to institute desirable regulations of trade and production. Public works have multiplied. The city of Rio de Janiero has been transformed. Whether the modernistic skyline and the broad swath of Avenida Presidente Getulio Vargas are to the liking of Brazil's people doesn't make any difference in the visible result. There they are. The new avenue, typical of the dictator's aim to impose his name on Brazilian history, is a monument and a symbol. It is meant to impress on visitors for time to come that a man named Vargas galloped north from the plains of Rio Grande do Sul. It says in heroic measure that he has shaped Brazil more than any other ruler, with the exception—not yet entirely conceded by the regime's eulogists—of democratic Emperor Dom Pedro II. The Avenida Vargas cuts a wide and rubbled swath from Guanabara Bay near Santos Dumont Airport and the near-by naval base. A continuous block of buildings has been torn down between streets that now become sidewalks.

Crossing the Avenida Rio Branco—Fifth Avenue of the city— the new boulevard gathers up in its course the most cherished traditions of Brazil. Vargas the man, like the avenue bearing his name, is depicted as bisecting Brazilian history. From the Avenida Rio Branco, named for one of the statesmen who strengthened representative government in Brazil and served as a brilliant Foreign Minister, the Avenida Presidente Getulio Vargas meets the Plaza of the Republic. Just across from this tropical park are the modern Ministry of War, in its skyscraper, and the central railway station named for Dom Pedro II. Then the avenue replaces a historic canal lined with double rows of stately royal palms. Beyond, on the mountainous skyline, rises the rounded peak of Tijuca.

In São Paulo another Vargas public work, a large stadium built with characteristic fascist flourish, causes Paulistas to writhe over this evidence in their midst of the era of Vargas dictation.

Political favoritism in the economic field is reported as wasteful, or more so, than logrolling in the disbanded Congress. Then, at least, dissatisfied citizens had a recourse through elections. Under Vargas there is no way of knowing what is done with public funds. It is unreasonable to expect that even a benevolent dictator could prevent graft and corruption among his subordinates. The governmental task set by Dr. Vargas for himself is beyond human possibilities. It deprives him of any claim to fame as inventor of an effective system of government. The vaunted efficiency of dictatorship piles his desk with papers on the most minute details of national, state, and local administration. Only he has final power of decision on any issue, however small. Yet this huge nation could hardly be governed adequately by hundreds of the most talented and impartial public administrators. So aware are the humorous Brazilian people of what happens on the desk of Dr. Vargas that his propagandists have sought to allay public suspicions and jokes. With an obtuse news item that sent roars of suppressed laughter through Rio while I was there, the inept explainers gave assurance that the hard-working *Presidente* pays full attention to all of those piles of paper on his desk. Brazilians know it couldn't be done, not even by Getulio.

The closed corporation bureaucracy of this dictatorship is shut off from wholesome effects of a political opposition and the salutary influences of coming elections. Only the secret police, Army, Navy, and other indispensable agents of power are kept at top efficiency. Many qualified observers of Brazilian activities in the Amazonian wild-rubber program, and in the Itabira iron project, are not impressed by claims of economic efficiency in the *Estado Novo*. North American engineers of highest standing fought political interference as long as they could and then resigned. That story is told elsewhere in these pages. Even if Vargas contentions are correct that Brazil has derived material benefits from his reign, it will be long before political and intellectual damage inflicted during this period can be effaced.

The worst long-range political deficit of the Vargas regime is its failure to develop leaders to take over when the dictator is gone. So jealous of power is he that no other political figure is allowed to attain growing national stature. The school of democratic government in which he learned public administration no longer exists. In the place of elected State Governors he has substituted puppets. His Cabinet is a collection of yes-men. Strong leaders such as Oswaldo Aranha or João Alberto Lins de Barros have been permitted to hold prominent positions, but the dictator skillfully protects himself against them. Both of these leaders are no longer in the Cabinet. No friend of his would be safe from a devious downfall if that friend ever challenged the seat of power.

The forces against which Dr. Vargas has maintained his position fall into two broad categories. First are external ones—Nazis, Fascists, Japanese, and Communists (actual or imagined). For propaganda purposes these forces have been exaggerated. The more serious opposition to Dr. Vargas has come from inside Brazil. Paulistas of the State of São Paulo, who dominated national affairs for many years before Dr. Vargas, are still his principal adversaries. Similar elements exist in the mining State of Minas Gerais. Intellectuals and liberals who refused to fall in line with the *Estado Novo* are under constant surveillance. The secret police have silenced all public activities of such dissidents who remain in Brazil. Even so, underground resistance goes on. The semi-native fascist Integralists are used when it suits his purpose, although officially they are banned. Finally, an unknown number of Brazilians in all walks don't like what has been done, but remain unorganized and seldom dare to voice their deep feelings.

To deal with these and other opponents who from time to time have arisen in his path, Dr. Vargas has relied mainly on his own rare talents for political maneuvering. The Army and some other powerful segments of the nation have frequently supported him for their own ends. With shrewdly calculated strokes, he has kept even these giants divided when that served his purpose.

As Brazil enters a period of unprecedented economic growth and military power, these issues become vital not only to Brazil, but to the Western Hemisphere and all mankind.

Paraguay: Continental Cockpit

In the effort by South American fascists to stave off insistent democratic demands of the people and consolidate an oppressive military bloc across the continent, Paraguay holds a key position. Argentine Army fascists found in Paraguay some of their most willing allies.

So it was that when my latest journey took me again into Asunción, capital of Paraguay, revolution was rampant and being brutally suppressed. Outwardly the city was quiet by day. Few nights passed without sounds of gunfire somewhere. In basements of barracks the accused were being tortured in the attempt to exact incriminating confessions. The concentration camps of Peña Hermosa, Ingaví, Isla Poi, and others were filled with political prisoners. Most of these were guilty of nothing more than being liberals or of opposing the regime of Gen. Higinio Morinigo. Hundreds of the best people in Paraguay were rounded up and jailed while I was in the country.

Although such conditions are not new in South America, this time they formed an integral part of the fascist reaction which has swept through the continent. A strong indication of this fact came in the ousting of the Foreign Minister who, at the Rio de Janeiro consultations of 1942, had carried Paraguay to the decision of breaking with the Axis. He is Dr. Luis A. Argaña. When Argentina's "Colonels' Lodge" had established control in Buenos Aires, the younger officers of the Paraguayan Army became more aggressive in Asunción. By the time of the Bolivian coup on December 20, 1943, they felt sufficiently backed by Argentina to resist openly the United Nations foreign policy for which Dr. Argaña stood.

President Morinigo, being a general, faced the same type of rebellion that has pitted Argentine colonels against their military superiors. Dr. Argaña would not recognize the Bolivian Revolutionary Junta, headed by Major Gualberto Villarroel, which at that time had not removed from itself the stigma of pro-Nazi sympathies. It is significant that the Bolivian chieftain was also drawn from among the younger Army officers. The Paraguayan majors and colonels, in direct line with Argentina, were banded together in *El Frente de Guerra,* or the War Front. General Morinigo held them in check, and Bolivia was not recognized. Dr. Argaña stayed.

How the current was running became unmistakable when the next burning issue arose over recognition of Gen. Edelmiro Farrell as President of Argentina, replacing Gen. Pedro Ramírez. It was common knowledge that General Farrell, like President Ramírez—but more so—was a figurehead. Argentine politics still were dominated and manipulated by the young officers. They had not abandoned the substance, although they had been compelled to change the form, of their United Officers Group, or GOU. Stronger than ever in this group was Col. Juan D. Perón, then Minister of War as well as of Labor.

In Paraguay, the War Front forced recognition of General Farrell, and Dr. Argaña resigned.

It was, of course, denied by governmental officials in Buenos Aires, Asunción, and La Paz that Argentina played any direct part in the drastic cooling of Paraguayan and Bolivian relations with the United States. The diplomatic denial did not outweigh many signs by which diplomatic influence can be measured. In the controlled press, for instance, both Paraguay and Bolivia were quick to follow the Argentine line. They rose to defend the reactionary Argentine regime against criticism.

Some close observers of the Paraguayan scene hold that fascist forces are losing to advocates of friendship with democracies, and particularly the United States. Even the three most active pro-Nazis in high position have lately been showing signs of trying to shift their tack. They are Col. Victoriano Benitez Vera, Chief of Cavalry; Col. Bernardo Aranda, Chief of Staff; and Major Pablo Stagni, Chief of the Air Corps.

The Foreign Minister who succeeded Dr. Argaña is Horacio Chiriani. His policy has tended to resist Argentine fascist advances. Because of its characteristic instability, Paraguay requires careful handling in the period ahead.

Seldom brought to public notice of the outside world and screened behind tight censorship, Paraguay is a nation of fighters wielding influence beyond their numbers. A traveler who came down through Mexico, Central America, and South America into Paraguay remarked after he had been in the country a while: "At last here is a race of men!" Anyone who moves among the Paraguayans will be struck by similar thoughts, even if not in that extreme form. Paraguay has easily the most homogeneous population in South America. The fusing of its particular racial elements has produced a breed of warriors. There are only from 1,100,000 to 1,400,000 people in the whole country, according to differing estimates. Even so, larger neighbors tremble at the thought of ever again having to face them in war. Bolivia within a decade reeled back in the Chaco War before Paraguayan troops who were secretly armed in part by Argentina. Paraguayans do not forget that once their country fought single-handed for six years against the combined armies of Argentina, Brazil, and Uruguay. Doughty Paraguayans under their ambitious dictator, Francisco López, at length were defeated. They lost half of their former population. Before that war of 1864 to 1870 Paraguay had more people than Argentina. Paraguay extended into what is now Argentina's Misiones Territory and parts of Corrientes Province.

It is surprising for outsiders who may have tossed off Paraguay, when they thought of it at all, as an inconsequential speck somewhere in the interior of South America, to learn how proud these people are of their history. In this regard Paraguay is a smaller Argentina. Not only so, but Asunción looks with some condescension down the river toward Argentina's ultramodern capital, Buenos Aires. Was not Buenos Aires finally founded from Asunción after the first try to establish a settlement beside the Rio de la Plata had been wiped out by Indians? Didn't Paraguay have the first railway in South America? Also the first telegraph, first telephone, first revolution against Spain, first elected colonial governor, and the oldest continuous city in South America? In terms of immediate Paraguayan motivations, it is not important whether all of these and other firsts, seriously claimed, would stand up under impartial historical analysis. The main point is that they are believed. They shape Paraguayan attitudes.

Sometimes a personal experience drives home national viewpoints better than hours of reading or conversation. Especially when the instructor is the boot of a Paraguayan Police Captain placed quickly against the pit of one's stomach on extremely scanty provocation, and then pushed, hard. This course of instruction came to me unsought one bright summer day in the sultriness of Asunción. Magnificent cumulus clouds were bleached white overhead by a fierce sun. Entering the cool shade of the colonnade outside what I thought was the passport office, I started into the building. A guard spoke to me. These people have a way of mixing their ancient tongue, Guaraní, with Spanish. Possibly that explains why I had to say, "*No comprendo.*"

The guard spoke again.

Then, without more ado, he knocked my Panama hat from my head.

He told me to pick it up.

By then I gathered that every civilian is forbidden to enter any governmental building without removing his hat. So, in my best Spanish, I began to explain that I had not understood, that I was a stranger, and this handling seemed a bit rough toward a citizen of a friendly American country. I also told the guard he would have to pick up my hat. When he refused and made threatening moves, his Captain came up, wearing sidearms. To the Captain I explained again, not yielding in my demand for respectful treatment. With mutterings, the Captain conceded one point by scooping up the hat and shoving it into my hand. Then he applied the stomach-boot treatment to send me on my way. Going to the passport office next door, I took care of the business in hand and then told the man at the window what had happened. It ended with the Captain's superior officer calling him in and dressing him down in my presence.

An Italian diplomat once had a similar, but milder, hat episode. The guards at the Foreign Office, with bared bayonets, compelled him to doff his headpiece. Turning on his heel, he left without presenting his credentials and never came back.

These incidents are significant only as showing the belligerence that lies close beneath the surface of many Paraguayan skins. Some of it is due to economic instability in a country that could enter a claim to being one of the poorest in the world. Much of it comes from fiery independence of the Guaraní Indians. Although they intermarried with the Spanish *conquistadores*, they prefer their own language and culture. At table on a Paraguay River steamer a modern, well-dressed woman and her companions spoke Guaraní with only occasional concessions to Spanish. When I remarked on this she said with animated dignity:

"Guaraní is my language. You speak English, do you not?"
Along the river I found myself puzzled at first by tones of
this active Indian tongue. I would think I was hearing Spanish,
and then the sounds slipped off like water rippling over a smooth
boulder into the softer accents of Guaraní. It is a language of
double vowels and musical effects.

By nature warriors, the Guaraní are of higher cultural achieve-
ments than many of their South American Indian contemporaries, and gifted besides with a sense of humor. Alert, wiry, and
tough, they make excellent soldiers. Sometimes when Paraguay's
military rulers want to impress their neighbors and stiffen a
bargaining position in diplomatic negotiations, they stage a troop
review and invite their softer colleagues. Expressions on the
guests' faces form a study in human reactions as lines of hardened
Paraguayans march past the reviewing stand. With adequate
weapons they could rank high among infantry anywhere. The
mixture of Guaraní and Spanish strains in colonial times has not
been overlaid or weakened by later intrusions to any important
extent. The result is a hybrid of two fighting races. This fusion
during nearly five centuries has jostled down into a distinct racial
type, different from anything seen elsewhere in South America.
Alien colonies of Germans and others have intermarried to some
extent. For the most part they are active in business on the upper
economic levels, and do not change the national mass complexion.

Asunción houses some 300,000 people. The country has a
small Jewish population, mostly in Asunción. With anti-Semitism
flaring in Argentina and Bolivia, and a fascist reaction under
way in Paraguay, this appears to be another minority problem
in the making. The semiofficial newspaper *El Paraguayo* in a
series of articles against "Jewish infiltration" declared that the
Paraguayan Constitution in its guarantee of religious freedom
does not apply to "races such as the Jewish, whose ideologies are
openly opposed to our national feelings."

A measure of political instability in Paraguay is given by
twenty-six revolutions during the past thirty-nine years. Few
Presidents have finished their terms. General Morinigo has sat on
top of a volcano after more than four years of power. Chief

opposition comes from the Liberal Party which for many years dominated national affairs. Now its leaders are either in jail or in exile. Political persecution has descended on its members by the hundreds in wholesale arrests. Labor made moves toward alignment with the Liberals, and took the consequences. Reprisals have gone as far as assassination and torture.

The most extreme comment made to me about how this poorly endowed country gets along is that it "lives by blackmail." A more moderate statement is that Paraguay is compelled by its geographical position and lack of outstanding resources to use its reputation as a fighter for diplomatic and trade purposes. Asunción's foreign policy accordingly tends to favor one large neighbor above the other in turn, and to exact trade benefits in the process. During a recent swing toward Argentina a Treaty of Commerce was decreed December 1, 1943. Concessions made to Paraguay help this dependent country to maintain itself.

Some progress has been made with Good-Neighbor money from the United States toward helping Paraguay find a solid and wholesome path. Sanitary centers have been built. Some people wonder how these institutions will be staffed and maintained after Washington stops sending this kind of credit south.

Running straight and smooth out of Asunción is a new highway originally intended to link Paraguay with Brazil. The road ended halfway to its goal. North American diplomats who wanted to draw Paraguay away from an absorptive Argentina have been disappointed. So far, the net results of $5,000,000 in Good-Neighbor spending by the United States on this road have been:

1. To tie Paraguay closer to Argentina.

2. To speed some internal Paraguayan commerce.

3. To provide a luxurious jaunt for Paraguay's élite to resort towns, when they can get gasoline for their cars.

Oxcarts with their cutting wheels are supposed to keep off. Sometimes they leave their rutted dirt tracks for a bit of easier going on the hard surface. The route was intended to drive through rough country to banks of the swift and deep Paraná River opposite Brazil's Iguassú region, made spectacular by

Iguassú Waterfalls. To reach Brazil at this point, Paraguayans may fly to the town of Foz do Iguassú. Overland they have one slow route. They may go from Asunción by rail, or the new highway, as far as Villarica in Paraguay. The train carries through to Encarnación on the Paraná. A ferry bridge crosses to Posadas in Argentina. Iguassú is then reached by steamers flying the flags of Argentina or Brazil. Some Paraguayans make the trip upriver from Encarnación in small boats flying their own national ensign. It is a long way around, and it either touches or passes through Argentina.

Wherever Paraguay turns, this interior country finds itself dependent on neighbors for the breath of export transportation. The Paraguay River, after coursing languidly through the center of the country of its name from north to south, ends in the Rio de la Plata at Buenos Aires. Upstream, the Paraguay reaches a Brazilian railhead at Pôrto Esperança. The railway can carry Paraguayan produce eastward into Brazil. Eventually, when this same railway is completed across a new bridge to join Bolivia's rail network, Paraguay will have a western outlet independent of Argentina. The Paraná River parallels the Paraguay as well as the distant Atlantic Coast. More than two thirds of Paraguay's river frontage along the Paraná faces Argentina. The scant northern third looks across at Brazil. For many years Paraguay has been able to send limited amounts of produce up the Paraná to Brazil. But this river is creased by strong and difficult currents. It also is broken by the massive falls of Guairá. Passengers or freight must be taken around the Seven Cataracts by rail from Pôrto Mendes to Pôrto Guairá. There, in normal times, the journey is continued northward in large and luxurious Brazilian steamers to Pôrto Tibiriça and the railhead of Presidente Epitacio. This ties quickly into Brazil's heaviest concentration of railways as it radiates fanwise from São Paulo and Rio de Janeiro.

The aim of former President Estigarribia and of his Good-Neighbor colleagues in Washington was to short-circuit at least one of Argentina's power lines into Paraguay, and balance it with a new Brazilian connection. Fortified by credits of $3,000,-000, President Estigarribia and a corps of United States engineers went to work. The blueprints called for a wide new highway from Asunción through the small town of Coronel Oviedo and on to the Paraguayan port of Tacurupucú on the Paraná. This is across the river and a bit upstream from Brazil's small port at Foz do Iguassú.

How baffling are Paraguay's handicaps whenever it tries to find an outlet apart from Argentina is seen in the remoteness of Foz do Iguassú itself. My first acquaintance with this speck in the jungle came by plane early in 1942. We flew from Curitiba in Brazil's State of Paraná. Hour after hour the magnificent carpet of Paraná pines, interlaced like green snow crystals when seen from the air, alternated with other uncut giants of the forest. Rain squalls spotted the vast horizon and at times obscured our route. When at last we picked up the Iguassú River and followed it down to the falls, a travel-weary lad amused the tourists. Some of us who were seeing the falls for the first time noticed that a young North American in the front seat had fallen asleep. We woke him so he wouldn't miss the sight. Yawning and bored, he informed us he had seen the falls forty times, and rolled back on his left ear. He turned out to be a State Department courier. Many times later I ran across him at widely scattered points in South America as he flew with diplomatic mails.

Our landing that day was exciting and showed how far even air transport has to go in these remote regions. The small airport at Foz do Iguassú was hidden in driving black curtains of rain. With only a half hour of gasoline left, we circled the jungle. Our pilot went down over the landing strip near the tourist hotel on the Argentine side. Grazing horses ran across our path. It was a tight squeeze for our big plane. Fortunately, we didn't have to try it. The dark clouds moved on and we settled to the dripping field in Brazil.

Among the few tourists then at Foz do Iguassú in the small new hotel on a height overlooking the river were a party who had driven from São Paulo, more than 700 miles away. Their road followed the Iguassú River after passing south through the town of Ponta Grossa. Anyone who has ridden on roads in this land of red mud and sudden downpours would hesitate before undertaking 700 miles of it. But Brazil is constantly improving the surface. In time the trip will be easy. A railway also is projected across to Foz do Iguassú. That evidently belongs to the future.

This particular part of the South American interior is economically one of the most promising. Eastern Paraguay, the Misiones Territory of Argentina, and Brazil's States of Paraná and Santa Catarina have pockets of rich soil, magnificent hardwood forests, not too much rain, stores of iron, magnesium, and other minerals, as well as two gigantic sources of potential hydroelectric power. Possibly these attractions, and a semitropical climate, explain why thousands of pioneers from Germany have been settling here for many years. Paraguay is stamped with their impress. The country's business has been dominated by German names. South Brazil and Argentine Misiones also have strong German colonies. These German concentrations, as well as tensions in South America due to Brazil's emergence as a dominant and growing military power, are reasons for establishment by Brazil in this area of two new border territories. The Territory of Ponta Porã blankets the northern border of Paraguay between the Paraguay and Paraná Rivers. The Territory of Iguassú closes in on the remainder of this fuselike line that extends from the Paraná eastward into Brazil's own German colonies.

Builders of the Asunción-Iguassú road started out hopefully toward their distant objective. President Estigarribia pursued a policy of close co-operation with the United States. He completed the basic credits soon after taking office on August 15, 1939. A hero of the Chaco War with Bolivia, he had been elected President while serving as Paraguayan Minister in Washington. A year after he returned to Asunción his term was cut short by an airplane accident on September 6, 1940. Work on the road was carried forward by his successor, President Morinigo, but a variety of circumstances gradually pinched off the original project and reversed its effects. Exactly who decided to give up the tie to Brazil is not made known. North American engineers are said to have found the going hard and expensive in the last part of the proposed route. The first $3,000,000 had been spent, and another $3,000,000 was authorized. Instead of using this money to complete the road, Paraguay and its collaborators from Washington yielded to the opposition. Politicians of Villarica, the largest city between Asunción and Encarnación, had objected all along to the route because it passed several miles to the north. They prevailed, in the crumbling of President Estigarribia's dream. The paving was cut short at Coronel Oviedo and swung south into Villarica. By September, 1942, work had been completed on the curtailed road to its present terminus at Villarica. Later I made the motor trip. As we turned from the eastward-reaching route it became obvious that Argentina, alone among foreign powers, had gained from this expenditure of United States millions. The fact is driven home by the main use of the second $3,000,000. Feeder roads command $2,000,000. These are drawing the Paraguayan countryside and its produce into the Asunción-Villarica highway, which funnels Paraguay into Argentina at both ends. The regular train service from Villarica speeds to Buenos Aires in two days. Fine river transport on Argentine ships makes the run from Asunción in four days to the Argentine capital.

The other $1,000,000 of Good-Neighbor money is being devoted to development of Paraguayan industries.

To clinch the transport advantage with initiative from its own side, Argentina is rushing to completion a motor highway that will tap Paraguay again at Clorinda, just across the river from Asunción. Meanwhile, Brazil glimmers in the distance as seen from Paraguay's capital. Argentine influence in diplomacy is again active with the willing compliance of some young Paraguayan Army officers who like the fascist leadership being supplied by Buenos Aires. What a contrast with my visit to Asunción early in 1942, when pictures of President Vargas of Brazil adorned every public plaza in memory of his state visit to President Morinigo! Then, too, United States diplomacy rode high in the mellow afterglow of the Rio de Janeiro consultations where Paraguay had decided to break diplomatic relations with the Axis.

As if to symbolize the residuum of fascist and anti-United States feeling in parts of Paraguay, an interesting range of hills is in view from the new highway. There, in the *Colonia Independencia,* live some 12,000 Germans, mostly Nazis. They came, 4000 families of them, from Germany, Austria, German East Africa, and Tanganyika after the war of 1914-1918. Although their hillside vineyards prosper, they long to return home. Hitler promised them they would be back in Africa by Christmas of 1941. While I was in Paraguay a trial was being held in Villarica of a German from the colony who was accused of killing the leader of the Free Austria Club.

So, even in these remote parts, the world struggle goes on between fascism and democracy, oppressive violence and human rights. The battle is far from won by forces of right thinking in Paraguay, cockpit of the southern continent.

The Catavi Massacre

It is nearly Christmas in Catavi—Christmas on the calendar but not in the hearts of Bolivia's Indian tin miners. Locked inside barbed wire at the mill town of the world's largest tin mine, they have no food. Outside the enclosure stand armed guards. Women plead for permission to go in search of something for their children to eat.

It is cold on the Andean heights—cold in midsummer. Yet the frost at night could not bite as does the bitterness in the hearts of the miners of Catavi. They had been told that men were fighting, far away, a war to free the world from a cruel and oppressive tyrant named Hitler. They had been ordered to dig tin ore harder and faster than ever before so that those men might have weapons to win the war. They had dug harder than ever. Then they found the war for freedom chaining them to their task. They were forbidden to lay down their tools. That in itself did not stir their sleeping wrath, their constant awareness of being treated as beasts of burden by descendants of white aliens who, centuries before, had invaded and destroyed their once advanced mountain empires.

Smoke burst into flame when injustices accumulated through

a series of labor disputes. The Indians found themselves denied
even the simplest rights for which the "people's war" supposedly
was being fought. At length they struck, well knowing the consequences. Through the days of tension and legal strife they
realize it is nearly Christmas. They long for release in their
gyrating dances of abandon with gaudy headpieces and fiesta costumes, music as piercing as Andean winds, processions and rituals
in semipagan observance of a Christian holy day they do not
fully understand. Yet they know . . . dimly . . . that Christmas
stands for something good . . . for a Savior and Redeemer. They
know there is something wrong with this Christmas in Catavi.

All they ask is permission to send buyers through the fence to
buy food at near-by Llallagua, where some Yugoslavs maintain
independent stores. Repeatedly they are refused. Repeatedly they
ask until their stolid patience breaks under hunger and primitive
anger. Even the knowledge of how brutally they will be suppressed can no longer prevent them from making a mass protest.
Eight thousand of them gather in the plain known as *La Pampa*,
inside the Catavi fence. Some long-lost fire of independence
spreads among them. They form columns and start toward the
company offices. Colonel Cuenca, commanding the Third Military Region, has given his orders. He works closely with the office
of Percy E. Holme, General Manager of Patiño Mines & Enterprises, Inc. Behind the military and the company stands the Government of President Enrique Peñaranda. Behind President
Peñaranda stands the general support of the United States Department of State through its policy of approval for his pro-
Allied diplomacy.

The guns are waiting—rifles—machine guns—a trench mortar.
What the hungry miners intend if they reach the company offices
is not known. Their leaders say they only want to get the attention of some official who might relent from the strike-breaking
weapon of starvation. Spokesmen for the mine operators charge
that the miners carry bombs made of dynamite in tin cans to
blow up the offices and raid closed *pulperías*, or company stores.
Miners have done such things before in labor struggles on the
sere *altiplano*, or high central plateau of the Andes. The officers

responsible for the guns do not wait to find out what the Indians intend. It is midmorning. Into the mass of advancing Indians spreads panic as the vicious muzzles speak. Women and children are in the forefront. There is no way out, no means of escape from those guns. The trapped Indians huddle together and trample each other. Firing continues until the last spark of resistance has been extinguished. Sporadic bursts continue through the morning.

So was broken the Catavi strike, broken by massacre. Where hunger failed, the mine operators and a Bolivian Government subservient to them resorted to mass murder. The exact number killed remains locked in the dark archives of Bolivian censorship. Reliable sources set the number at 400, hastily buried. Many hundreds were injured. Unable to hide so large a flame, the Government officially admitted that nineteen had been shot down, and thirty-five or forty injured. The shots fired would have had to be few indeed to hold casualties that low when a reinforced military garrison fired into a milling crowd of 8000 excited Indians.

Behind this tragedy at Catavi on December 21, 1942, moved far larger issues. Not only the shootings, but the smokescreens of propaganda put forth in the name of the people's war against fascism, make Catavi a somber mirror held up to misdeeds committed by professing champions of human freedom. Political censorship so distorted public reports of events before and after Catavi that nothing short of a political explosion in Bolivia brought some of the facts into the open. An unbiased story is only gradually being pieced together. The official version circulated at the time, and still repeated with an air of wounded innocence by spokesmen for the Patiño mines, is that Nazi agitators had infiltrated among the workers. The agitators' obvious aim was said to be to disrupt tin production, as Bolivia had been a main source of the vital metal for the United Nations since Japan seized Malaya and the Netherlands East Indies. Disputing this apparently plausible explanation, men close to Catavi say that Nazi agitators, if active at all, were a side issue. Any response such agitators awakened among the tin miners was due to deeper social conflicts. Seething for centuries, Bolivia's fiery human flux boiled up to a crater of explosion under the conservative Peñaranda regime. Ever since the Catavi massacre I have been trying to assemble the facts. I have sifted accounts issued by the Government, the mine operators, labor unions, well-informed technicians in Bolivia, and various investigations of private or semiofficial nature. The account of that day's happenings as I have given it is based on points that appear undeniable. From sources able to give a reliable report, these are additional facts, omitted by official versions:

Just plain bad management by the operators and the half-drunk stubbornness of the Army officer in charge set off the final fuse. Someone whose name must be kept out of print put it this way:

"The trouble could have been prevented if there had been any way for workers and management to talk it over."

Nearly three years ago, the element of bad management brought on a preliminary crisis. Then Luis Nogales, a Bolivian in charge of the mines during the absence of the mine superintendent who had gone to the United States, was blamed for not lowering prices in the *pulperías*. Price reductions had been ordered to equalize a drop in contract wages. The workers swarmed and nearly reached Señor Nogales before he escaped. The basic cause of labor disturbances leading to the Catavi massacre was a raising of *pulpería* prices without letting the workers know that a rise in wages formed part of the plan. As feelings mounted, the *pulperías* closed. Food stocks in workers' huts were soon exhausted. The labor story, backed by impartial observers, is that to the end the workers tried to reach the management with a reasonable request to have food sent in or to let buyers cross the fence to Llallagua.

The strike-breaking forces were buttressed by another distortion of this war for human freedom. As Bolivia was collaborating in the war, the Bolivian Government took the line that any strike must be viewed as essentially treasonable. Among all the deliberate falsifications of which political censorship is guilty, not only in South America but in Washington, these Bolivian obscurities must tower when the accounts are finally tallied. That it was done in the name of a war to free the world from fascist oppression only adds steel to the determination that such things shall be made known and set straight. No sound judgment of events in Bolivia is possible without weighing these obscured social facts in the scales with equally valid arguments that Bolivia has been under external fascist influence.

The silenced liberals of South America would say that the way to defeat fascism is to dig up its unpopular and tyrannical tap roots. Bolivia's intelligent labor leaders rightly contend that this is most effectively done by a genuine people's policy, not by shooting Indians to get tin to defeat Hitler and the Japanese.

Bolivia's Reformed (?) Fascists

The story of Bolivia since the Catavi massacre of tin miners has ranged in dramatic sequence over the crags and crevasses of nearly every great issue before the American peoples.

In the pre-Christmas atmosphere of Catavi were unloosed social forces that run all through the relationships of oppressed masses and their exploiters.

In the brutal suppression of striking Indians who had been driven to mob action by mistakes of management that could have been avoided, the Peñaranda Government typified social reaction.

By attributing the Catavi disorders to Nazi agitators, the Patiño mine interests and the Government sought to hide the main cause. They also gave a flagrant example of how the war has sometimes been used in South America as an excuse to withhold human rights being fought for abroad.

By revolting against former President Peñaranda on December 20, 1943, eve of Catavi's first anniversary, the Revolutionary Junta under Major Gualberto Villarroel took a prominent part in the reaction away from what may be called the Rio de Janiero brand of hemisphere solidarity. At Rio de Janeiro early in 1942, emphasis necessarily had been concentrated by Foreign Ministers on opposition to external dangers of European fascism, rather than on uprooting then the seedbeds of native fascism inside countries of the Americas. Swiftly Washington and all of the other American capitals, except Buenos Aires in Argentina, labeled the Bolivian revolution as fascist, pro-Nazi, and anti-American.

The resulting nonrecognition of the Bolivian Revolutionary Junta, on the ground that it was not sincerely behind the war into which General Peñaranda had led the country, launched an experiment of great meaning for inter-American relations.

Finally, one of the most burning issues—nonintervention in the internal affairs of other American countries—came up for review. Bolivians felt that intervention had been practiced quite definitely; so much so that change after change was forced upon the Revolutionary Junta in an effort to meet outside demands. Washington held that what had been done toward Bolivia fell clearly within the meaning of the Good-Neighbor Policy. Three concrete lines of action were followed: 1. Withholding diplomatic recognition. 2. Stoppage of Lend-Lease aid. 3. Curtailment of mineral buying.

The granting of recognition always is a discretionary act of sovereign governments, although international law lays down certain minimum standards that, in normal times, call for recognition. Bolivia's Junta had met those minimums, including ability to maintain internal order for a reasonable period. It also had discharged from the Government persons who were disliked by the other capitals. While I was in La Paz, elections were called for July 2, 1944. Pro-Axis interests were disciplined. As a result, recognition at last was granted on June 23, 1944.

For Bolivia and the United Nations, diplomatic recognition would not have become a crucial issue unless it had affected production of strategic war materials. Actually, the tin contracts went right on during the period of nonrecognition. Wolfram and other minerals continued to flow down from the Andes into Allied arsenals. Termination of antimony contracts had a sobering effect.

Stoppage of Lend-Lease arms was more serious for Bolivia. The country, although at war, was not expected to send troops abroad, but young Army officers wanted all the weapons they could get, just as did their colleagues in Argentina. At this point enters a well-defined policy laid down at Pan-American Conferences since Lima. It is that the American countries will not knowingly strengthen forces which intend to turn American-made weapons against American liberties. So the crux of the decision about Bolivia was whether or not its new masters could prove they belonged with fighting world freemen, instead of with the openly fascist military who had taken over in Argentina. It was a secondary issue, as seen by official Washington, whether the prolabor attitude of the Junta was sincere, or merely political camouflage. Possibly for the reason that social reforms paid no dividends in terms of approval by Washington or other capitals, the Junta greatly minimized that line. Sooner or later, every Bolivian Government has come to terms with the dominant mining operators.

Here again, Bolivia serves as a mirror in which America can see itself, for the prevailing win-the-war-first philosophy as applied by Washington to the exclusion of equally valid policies, steadily strengthens conservative forces in South America and discourages liberal tendencies. In Bolivia, no one seriously holds that former President Peñaranda attained the stature assigned to him by the State Department in Washington. Like many other South American military men and politicians, he was astute enough to jump in the right direction—toward the United Nations. Once that decision had been made, General Peñaranda admirably served the ends of the war. At least so it appeared for a time. The Bolivian upset is seen by critics of Washington's expediency as a convincing bit of evidence. It is held to prove again that a reliable and enduring democratic ally is not won by strengthening a clever politician who at heart is a dictator, a fascist, or an opportunist.

The very excesses to which General Peñaranda resorted in his zeal to show himself a fighting leader on the democratic side speeded his undoing. When he declared war against Germany on

April 7, 1943, this act patently had more to do with internal
Bolivian politics than with defeating the Nazis. He aroused
democratic opinion inside Bolivia by decreeing war without first
calling Congress, which did not approve his action until the
following December. Elections were drawing near. The Constitution, later thrown overboard in the revolution, set the ballot-
ing for May, 1944. Supporting General Peñaranda were four
parties that bore liberal names but had strongly Rightist content.
They were the Liberals, the Republican Socialists, the Genuine
Republicans and the Unified Socialists. General Peñaranda was
not running for re-election, but the four parties had joined
forces to choose one candidate who would carry forward his
policies.

In foreign affairs, those policies were cut to fit the pattern of
the United Nations.

In domestic affairs, the Peñaranda Government maintained the
outward forms of democracy, although even these were steadily
whittled down in the name of the war.

In social motivation, the Government became identified with
the large tin operators and their viewpoint. This is not to say that
such an alignment is all black or all white. But to Bolivian advocates of social reform it can be a call to arms. The standard
political hue and cry for any Leftist group trying to push its way
into control in Bolivia is liberation of the downtrodden Indians
from the mine magnates. Such an opposition against General
Peñaranda appeared inevitable sooner or later. The Catavi massacre testified to the widespread growth of social unrest, and supplied a dramatic campaign slogan. Out of labor conflict, as
much or more than out of fascist maneuverings, came the diplomatic crisis that for months deprived the present Revolutionary
Junta of recognition by all of the American nations except
Argentina. Labor conflict provided soil and seed for pro-Nazi
agitators.

The social revolution that helped overthrow General Peñaranda took form within labor organizations and two principal
political groups. They are the Left Revolutionary Party or PIR,
and the National Revolutionary Movement, or MNR. Inside the

MNR were strong pro-Nazi and fascist elements. They collaborated easily with the *Estrellas Blancas*, or White Stars, a lodge of young Army officers to the rank of lieutenant colonel. Their name comes from the white star emblem worn by officers connected with the General Staff. The PIR emphasized social issues. It took an active part in congressional debates against General Peñaranda for his alleged responsibility toward the Catavi massacre. In the armed revolt, driving power was supplied by the MNR and the young Army officers. The PIR was quickly shoved aside and later persecuted. Its leader, José Antonio Arze, was imprisoned and later escaped, wounded, to exile in New York.

Dr. Victor Paz Estenssoro, head of the MNR and an avowed Marxist, became Finance Minister in the Junta. Civilians who went along with the *Estrellas Blancas* were represented in the original Cabinet by Gustavo Chacón, Minister of Economics, and Victor Andrade, Minister of Labor. Two officials to whom the United Nations objected most strenuously on grounds of their pro-Nazi records were Carlos Montenegro, Minister of Agriculture, and Augusto Céspedes, General Secretary of the Junta. Both were removed during early efforts to win recognition from Washington. While rounding up Axis agents, passing decrees for seizure of Axis firms, and otherwise seeking to convince Washington that tinges of fascism had been washed away, the Junta continued its social propaganda.

"Proletarians!" shouted posters on walls of La Paz when I came through in March, 1944, "The Junta has conquered for you a new right—the syndical law. Defend it!"

This is an affirmation of labor's right to organize and bargain collectively. The Junta's social drive diminished as time passed.

Beneath diplomatic maneuvering remains the underlying economic instability of Bolivia. It exposes this remote Andean nation, landlocked in the center of the continent, to extremes of social agitation. Since the instruments of power have long been held by conservative classes, the drift to fascist thinking is recurrent. Under former President Germán Busch, it took the form of direct links with Nazi and Italian forms of fascism. During that period, Nazi organizers had an almost free hand in Santa

Cruz, a rich hinterland province. The President himself was the son of a German settler in that area. Numerous fascist plots were in the air when I first went to La Paz early in 1938.

It is not likely for some time that basic fascism will cease to exert influence among Bolivia's rulers. They may have to subordinate their feelings in order to win advantages in a democratic world. That is the process whereby the Revolutionary Junta finally won diplomatic recognition. It is comparatively easy for any Bolivian Government to display opposition to alien fascist groups and individuals in Bolivia. There is even economic profit in such a course. Several Latin-American Governments have replenished depleted treasuries by the confiscation of funds and properties belonging to Axis nationals. Proof of deeper anti-fascist policies inside Bolivia is less probable.

Tin is the dominant thread of Bolivian economy, tin coursing down from the Andes as shining rivulets into the arsenals of world democracy, tin running through dark canyons of human oppression. Anyone who learns how uncertain is the outlook for Bolivian tin turns instinctively to the people and asks what lies ahead for them. In the high, thin air of Oruro, a large mining town south of La Paz, I thought of my earlier experiences in Bolivia's tropical lowlands. Oruro's synthetic parks, nourished by soil brought from more fertile regions, reminded me again that people are the most important resource in any country. Bolivia's human equation is being grasped a bit more clearly by the outside world as public interest is drawn to this landlocked country that scrapes the upper skies. Oruro offers an admirable vantage point from which to survey Bolivia's outlook. Citizens of Oruro have made of their bleak habitat a paved and gracious home, perched on the sloping edge of a long valley that climbs in broken strides to the crest of barren ocher ridges. Mine tailings slant almost into town. One of the more important operations of Maurice Hochschild & Co., San José Mine, perforates the nearest slopes. As I stood 12,000 feet above sea level and thought what it means to live, year in and year out, on a floor higher than most peaks of the United States, a different Bolivia, of different Bolivians, merged with the picture. On the boulder-strewn *altiplano* it was an effort to visualize Bolivia's tropical hinterland. Yet the future of Bolivia and of its people is generally agreed to lie in the lowlands, unless new discoveries are made of minerals or other resources in the mountains.

The flame fed by known mineral resources already flickers. Patiño's mines in many instances are dropping their tin content at the rate of .1 per cent every six months. The great mine at Catavi is down to 2.69 per cent pure tin in the ore mined, from 6 per cent some years ago. Patiño is operating at least one mine at 1.1 per cent—just about rock bottom for keeping a mine going. San José Mine at Oruro is near the margin. Miners explain that Bolivia, to meet world competition, has had to cream off the best of its ore for years without bringing in enough new veins to keep up high-grade reserves. Time was when the ores ran to 8 per cent, sometimes higher. Fortunately, the war effort of the United Nations has not been seriously affected by Bolivia's growing crisis in minerals. Nor does Bolivia necessarily face bankruptcy in the foreseeable future. Much depends on how the United Nations and Bolivia itself deal with an admittedly grave situation. For years before the war, Bolivia was kept in the world tin market largely through activities of Simón I. Patiño and his tin cartel with headquarters in London. Without the quota system and the artificial maintenance of a price at which the Bolivian mines could make money, this country might have been forced out of production. If not, drastic changes would have been required inside Bolivia to meet world tin competition.

Señor Patiño started his long and fabulous career as a Bolivian laborer and clerk. His riches began when a debtor turned over to him a piece of property in payment. Señor Patiño may be counted on to protect his extensive holdings in Bolivia. Formerly resident in Paris, he lived in New York during early years of the war, and then transferred his residence to Montreal.

Financial juggling may stave off the day when Bolivia must come to grips with itself and shift economic emphasis from mining to something else. Already Bolivians are talking about their agricultural possibilities. Only in the lowlands of Santa Cruz and the Beni, as yet far behind in any effective mobilization of farm resources, does agriculture hold large promise. The *altiplano,* original home of the so-called Irish potato, is mostly a deep layer of glaciated rock and rubble. Indians, bending nearly double, guide short-handled wooden sticks that serve for plows. The motive power is other men and women or, occasionally, a donkey. I saw soils actually in use that are only a few inches deep on top of boulders and pebbles. Bolivians know, for all their brave talk, that it would be a slow, hard pull to build an agricultural economy anywhere near equivalent to the mining economy that for centuries has made Bolivia world-famed. Nor is mining itself at the end of a long and rich rope that stretches back in time to the Viceroyalty of Peru and caravels filled with gold and silver for the Spanish Kings. It is only that the end of the golden and silvern rope has begun to dangle uncomfortably close.

For the United States at war, Bolivian tin remains not only indispensable, but adequate within the narrow limits of enforced wartime economy. The first crush of emergency in those days when Japan had shut off Far Eastern tin has passed. African and other sources are increasingly available, although far below the Far Eastern output. Salvage operations have eased shortages. The balance pointer of American war plants already hovers on the line between "must" and "desirable" for Bolivian tin. Washington and La Paz have entered the period when renewal of tin contracts is increasingly a matter for serious negotiation, instead of being a foregone conclusion. Britain's position must also be weighed in the scales. Before the war, Bolivian tin went exclusively to Britain or Continental Europe for refining. Now the United States has its own tin smelters at Texas City, Texas.

Tin is only the best-known of Bolivia's minerals. In Catavi there are said to be enough tungsten, antimony, and bismuth to supply the world—at least for a time. Bolivian antimony of 61 per cent fine content was bought by the United States until about the time of the revolution in December, 1943. When antimony buying was not renewed, Bolivians took it as part of Washington's pressure to bring the profascist regime in line on foreign policy. Actually, antimony was increasingly being obtained in Mexico. The wartime tin price of 60 cents a pound allowed Bolivia a short margin of profit, due to high production and transportation costs. Copper is being bought by the United States in Chile, Peru, and elsewhere, rather than from Bolivia. Among Bolivian mining men, I was kept aware that they know how narrow and broken is the mountainous path they tread. This economic instability accounts for much of the country's political and social unrest.

Bolivia is a country of which one of its thinkers said in a melancholy moment: "My country has only one future— disintegration."

The large dent made in Bolivia's *Chaco* borders by Paraguay; earlier inroads by Peru and Chile that cut from Bolivia its Pacific coast; the natural economic ties of the tropical Bolivian hinterland with Brazil, Argentina, and Paraguay rather than with the *altiplano*, would seem to support this somber prediction. Certain it is that only statesmanship of a high order can preserve Bolivia. The country's social and economic structure illustrates in exaggerated form the general South American lack of an adequate middle class. Bolivian scenes tell the story.

In Cochabamba, 8400 feet high on eastern Andean slopes, Señor Patiño has three palaces. The quiet attendant at Portales, one of the palaces in this small city of predominantly Indian population, opens the side door which I have reached through elaborate grounds. He ushers me into sumptuous but empty corridors, and leads the way to the Grand Salon. A white marble mantelpiece of ornate and sculptured lines rises to the level of the second-floor balcony. On the opposite wall hangs a Gobelin tapestry, one of three in this palace. French export taxes alone on the artistic value of these masterpieces when they were brought from France amounted to 300,000 francs. The staircase is modeled on that of the Sistine Chapel in Rome. The furniture is covered as though the residents had gone for the summer. Actually the palace has never been occupied. Room after room reflects the genius of some thirty European architects who were brought to this remote city to lavish their talents on residences for the Tin King of the world.

The attendant uncovers piles of elaborate draperies and cushions. Their color and design gleam richly in the silent house. Here is the setting for an Arabian Nights' Tale. Spread those royal fabrics and let the dance begin! Silence echoes, and there are no dancers. Treasures of the Old World have transformed Cochabamba with unused and unseen glories. All that money could buy has been brought from the ends of the earth to furnish a palace for a Bolivian who proudly preserves near by the heavy stones he once moved with his own arms to grind his first tin ores. The palace roof is of solid copper and cost $160,000.

Portales is located on the city's outskirts, and is set in a pleasant parked estate. Cochabamba is a natural homesite for a Bolivian of means. Whoever can break away from the 12,200-foot altitude of La Paz drops down to this pleasant valley for an occasional respite.

The second Patiño residence is downtown. It occupies the second floor over the Patiño Mercantile Bank. On the street floor a large blackboard is marked with spaces for quotations from London, Paris, New York, Madrid, Rome, Tokyo. Upstairs, Señor Patiño's European architects combined business necessities with their ideas of a town house. Presumably business visitors were to be entertained as befitted associates of the man who controlled the world tin market. Expense was evidently no concern of the architects and interior decorators. Oriental and Greek art vie with French and Italian. The Versailles influence is marked. Living accommodations are provided for the entire Patiño family, and guests. Of the five children, three have survived. Antenor Patiño, the second son, has seen the downtown palace, and Luz Mila Patiño, one of the two daughters, came in 1942. Señor Patiño saw the building in construction, but not completed. Furnishings of his palaces include elaborate oddities such as fifteen push buttons beside his bed, and folding tables lined inside with mirrors.

The last Patiño palace is Villa Albina, in the country near Hacienda Pairumoni, his model dairy farm fifteen miles from town. Villa Albina, named for Señora Patiño, is the oldest of the three palaces. Its exterior and grounds are palatial, but in subdued tones. On the rear terrace are the rough stones that started Señor Patiño's vast enterprises.

The cost of all Patiño installations in and around Cochabamba is estimated at $30,000,000 in United States currency. The palaces have lain idle for more than twenty years. It does something inside to anyone who knows Bolivia, to learn that the man who lavished such sums on palaces for himself and his family, has never seen the two elaborate ones, and has reached an age that precludes his ever coming to these altitudes again. He has built a monumental burial place near the country palace. Residents of Cochabamba look on the reminders of Patiño wealth in their midst, and remark with feeling that he never has shown concern to build institutions that would raise the people's standard of living. The model dairy farm is a worthy move in that direction, but an influential resident of Cochabamba said to me: "It is a hobby rather than a public service." This same Bolivian added that Señor Patiño's actions made him "want to go Communist." When I visited the farm, my impression was of carelessness rather than of model conditions. Indian women rolled and lifted heavy milk cans. On the property I saw men in clothing so ragged that patch had been sewed on patch until the original garment disappeared.

In the same country that houses those unused Patiño palaces may be seen Indian men and women straining under loads almost beyond human endurance. In La Paz it is a daily occurrence to see Indian women bent under loads of building tile a foot square and two inches thick stacked in piles that press with relentless weight from their shoulders to their hips and are held in place by straps across their foreheads.

In such a land, fascists may reform outwardly, but basic fascism goes on. It grinds Indians down lower than beasts of burden, instead of lifting them to walk erect as men.

Chile: A Breath of Freedom

From the atmosphere of fascist plottings in Brazil, Argentina, Paraguay, and Bolivia, I emerged in the Chilean city of Punta Arenas near the center of Magellan's Strait and could feel the clean winds of freedom blowing. It was after dark when the car from Gallegos in Argentina deposited me at the Hotel Savoy. For nearly five months I had been hemmed in by armor-plated censorships. I was loaded with stories. My first concern was to know whether in the South America of early 1944 I would at last find an outlet for the free press.

The cable office turned out to be opposite the central plaza where a splendid statue of Magellan faces his Strait between two great oceans. The mariner is grizzled, eager, searching. There was only time for a passing glance as I searched for my own passage through barriers of illegitimate political censorships. To the young cable clerk behind an old-fashioned wire partition I said:

"Are your messages sent through Buenos Aires?"

He answered without hesitation and with Chilean emphasis:

"The farther we keep from Buenos Aires, the better we like it. Our circuits pass directly through Santiago to the United States."

There was my Magellan's Strait, wide open after five months of dead ends in jungles both geographic and political.

"How late tonight will you take press dispatches?"

"We close at ten-thirty."

"*Muchas gracias.*"

I sought out at once the office of the morning newspaper, *La Prensa Austral,* to catch up on late bulletins before starting to file. The editors placed every facility at my disposal in the low-ceil-inged newsroom with its sheet metal stove. To be among whole-hearted democrats again who could speak freely instead of hiding from secret police of fascist regimes, gave me a foretaste of coming home. The abortive revolt led by Colonel Duco had just been quelled in Argentina, and I poured out some of my long-suppressed information. Ten-thirty passed, and the night cable operator showed me a side door. He took copy until well after midnight.

Here were democrats in South America, men of Latin extraction who, according to the teaching of some law schools, lack the Anglo-Saxon capacities for popular self-government. I felt that exceptions could be taken to this teaching as I talked with the Chileans. They differed little from the other liberals I had met in Brazil, Argentina, Paraguay, and Bolivia. Such men exist throughout South America. The tragedy is that they so often are silenced inside their own countries, and find scanty understanding or support outside. United States Ambassadors, and even former Secretary of State Cordell Hull, often appear to have lost sight of South America's forgotten liberals. Such an attitude on the Secretary's part could not have been intentional, in view of his broad democratic sympathies and untiring labor for Pan-American friendship. When I talked with the Secretary after my last trip to South America, he was so intent on military aspects of winning the war that he expressed impatience with criticisms of his policies then current in the press. I came away from the interview with the unhappy impression that he supported governments which co-operated in the war to such an extent that any opposition to them was resented. While I am not permitted to quote him under the circumstances, he was aroused and used language that made me feel he viewed South Americans who opposed even one of the dictators collaborating in the war as politically ambitious people trying to get into office, and trouble-makers.

A diplomat of the United States who has had ample opportunity to see Vargas in action told me at a moment when Brazil was seething with political unrest as I had learned during my trip through the interior, that the political situation could be summarized as follows: "President Vargas never was stronger. Everyone is satisfied except a few wealthy malcontents. He has labor with him. The political opposition has no *povo* (people). All of the people who count, in cities, are for him. Of course, he is a dictator."

The same diplomat referred to the work of Allen Haden, one of the few news correspondents who has dared to write some of the darker facts about Brazil, in low terms. Mr. Haden is a talented, discerning correspondent. During the 1942 consultations of Foreign Ministers at Rio de Janeiro, as a staff correspondent of the *Chicago Daily News,* he saw through Argentinian and Chilean policy when many of his colleagues were bemused by over-optimistic propaganda. Because he later wrote fearlessly about Brazil, DIP made an attempt to prevent him from ever again entering that country while the Vargas regime lasts. The Brazilian Foreign Office saw how shortsighted such a step would be, and he was allowed to re-enter, briefly.

When I asked this critical diplomat what he thought about the shooting of students in São Paulo, apparently he attached no deeper significance to it than that it was an unfortunate police mistake, and was evidently content to leave it that way. Signers of the Minas Gerais manifesto seemingly fell within his definition of "malcontents."

As long as such attitudes emanate from highest diplomatic quarters of the United States, it is not surprising that South America's genuine advocates of the democratic way feel deserted, tossed to the fascist wolves, cut off without a kind word. Because of such attitudes, Washington has obscured the actual course of events, in some instances, almost as effectively as have the political censorships of South American fascist regimes.

Such thoughts were with me as vivid personal experiences while I drew deep breaths of freedom in Chile. I knew it would be a short respite, for my trail led back across the Andes into Argentina, and then north through Bolivia and Brazil.

Chile, I discovered, was in the position of being under fascist pressure without having yielded more than a portion of its integrity. There are fascists in Chile, as in the United States and around the world, but this writer would not at present use the term fascist as applying to the primary motivations of the Chilean Government. How persuasive and pervasive Argentine influence is in that part of the world may be seen in Chile's act of promptly recognizing General Farrell when he took the seat of President Ramírez in February of 1944. Chile ever since has been defending the move. Presumably, Bolivia and Paraguay would have recognized General Farrell anyway, but their path was smoothed by Chile. The inside story of Chile's desertion—so it was viewed in Washington and in many other American capitals —shows how important is the personal element in South America's explosive situation. The Chilean Ambassador in Buenos Aires, Conrado Rios Gallardo, appears to have maneuvered the Argentine recognition. He is known to have been harboring an old grudge against the United States. Under the dictatorial Ibañez regime in Chile, he had served as Foreign Minister at the time of the Tacna-Arica dispute with Peru. He disliked the report by General Pershing that Chile had sent 20,000 people to vote in the plebiscite. This same Ambassador stood out flatly, early in 1943, against Chile's break with the Axis, but was overruled. When seen about town in Buenos Aires soon after Chile had accepted his recommendation to go on with General Farrell as though no change of government had occurred in Argentina, Señor Rios Gallardo was visibly enjoying his momentary success.

Yet in Santiago, the Chilean Foreign Office found itself plunged into hot water. The articulate liberals of Chile let it be known in no uncertain terms that they disapproved. The Confederation of Workers stated publicly that the "premature recognition of the Farrell regime is a means of favoring the advance of antidemocratic, retrogressive, and brutal forces in the American Continent."

That there exist genuine democratic thinkers in South America who make their weight felt where they still are free to speak is disclosed in what follows of the Chilean workers' statement. Chile's act, they said, had "aided the Axis in its attack against the peoples of the United Nations, and impeded a rapid and just democratic solution of the Argentine crisis." There, out of the mouths of Chilean liberals, is a sad commentary on what happens when freemen sleep and let their democratic liberties go by default. Not only in Argentina, but in the United States, Brazil, and the world, millions now kept in the dark have yet to show whether they want freedom enough to resist and defeat the most subtle forms of enslavement.

In South American diplomacy, Chile has aligned itself at times with Brazil as a counterweight to excessive Argentine influence. Brazil has sought to maintain cordial relations with Chile, aiming to prevent that country from being drawn into an Argentine bloc, as well as to establish a foothold for its own influence on the other side of Argentina. As one of South America's three leading powers, Chile figures prominently in any calculations of power politics.

Coming south through Patagonia I saw Argentine military activity greatly augmented on the threshold of Magellan's Strait. The city of Gallegos is Argentina's closest military center, since all of the strategic waterway falls within Chilean territory. Argentine troops trained in the German tradition and wearing uniforms decidedly influenced by Prussian tailors were much in evidence. Young conscripts with whom I traveled in the southbound bus were likable lads, resembling their fellow Americans of high school age in Tucson or San Diego. Gallegos has one of the training camps where the present military dictatorship is rushing to build an Army at least able to hold its own in an arms race with Brazil. Brazil speeds ahead under the propulsion of a foreign policy that has opened the purse and the arsenal of the United States to the Vargas regime. Relations between Argentina and the United States worsened during this period, adding to Brazil's headstart in diplomacy as well as in armaments.

It is characteristic of Argentine thoroughness that the whole nation feels the call to arms. South of Gallegos, Argentina has a sizable part of Tierra del Fuego, the large island that dominates a labyrinth of smaller islands, glaciers, and channels as the continent draws in to the detached rocky promontory of Cape Horn. Argentina did not show as much initiative as Chile in early setttlement of this zone. Chile maintained a fort on the Strait. In a series of accords from 1855 to 1903, Chile's claims were recognized to the extent of excluding Argentina from land frontage on the Strait itself. Their frontier south to Latitude 52 was traced by the division of waters along the Andes. Transit through the Strait was declared open to all nations in the treaty of 1881 under mediation by the United States, and fortifications were forbidden.

Chileans profess to be undisturbed by Argentina's martial moves on the Strait's northern threshold. They pride themselves on a military tradition that appeals to them as more substantial than the present tactics of Argentina's barracks-room politicians. Although outnumbered nearly three to one, Chile is peopled by a race of fighters. After all, wasn't their most famous President an O'Higgins? With their blue eyes and their Irish or Scottish background crackling through their superimposed Latinity, many Chileans are as little "South American" in the usual mold as are the formidable, skirted Scotch Highlanders.

Between them, Argentina and Chile divide the whole southern end of South America. The only other power within close range is Great Britain in the Falkland Islands. Argentina to this day does not recognize British occupation in 1833 of those strategic bits of land 300 miles east of the Atlantic entrance to the Strait. Argentine maps and books persist in calling the islands *Las Malvinas*, the Spanish name. Undoubtedly one of the prizes which German-trained Argentine Army officers hoped to gain, when they thought Britain was going down before the Nazis, was this island outpost. Berlin could hardly have overlooked such a persuasive promise in its bids for Argentine neutrality. All such Nazi world-reshuffling has ceased to have practical meaning for some time now, yet Argentina's military caste appears to be reluctant in giving up its dream.

Knowing that fascists of Buenos Aires have indulged in talk of expansion, Chile is alert but confident. Territorially the only part of Chile where Argentina's ambitious military might strike is in the neighborhood of the Strait. Chile would not be alone in defending that international waterway. The United States and Great Britain would come to Chile's rescue at once if any menace arose to free transit around South America. Magellan's passage is still the only protected water route between the Atlantic and Pacific, should the Panama Canal ever be temporarily out of commission.

While Chile has held aloof from Argentina's projected South American bloc, the need continues for understanding and skilled diplomacy toward Santiago by other democratic capitals. Brazilian influence has its wholesome side in Chile as against aggressive Argentine diplomacy, but Brazilian influence is also fascist in many subtle ways. I met in Rio de Janeiro an official of the Chilean Government who had been sent there to study methods of DASP, the department whereby Dr. Vargas centralizes governmental administration in his own hands. Emulation of a fascist system is not an encouraging sign to find in Chile, but that country of fiery independence is still a breath of freedom, a welcome respite.

Uruguay: Democratic Bulwark

Anyone who glances across Montevideo harbor to the outer river, where the shattered mud-bound hulk of the Nazi *Graf von Spee* is rusting away, can see that South America's most democratic country isn't going to be engulfed by aggressive fascists. It is a rare day when the protective shape of an Allied warship does not move across the waters between Uruguay and Argentina. From three to four major units of United Nations fleets would probably be within easy calling distance at all times, should anyone try to make trouble for Uruguay. These are not military secrets. They are public knowledge in the essential strategy of a world-wide peoples' war against fascism.

For Uruguay towers above all its Latin-American contemporaries in democratic stature. This small country, wedged between differing fascist regimes in Brazil and Argentina, is known and admired among world democrats as the center of highest promise in South America. Conversely, Uruguay is too bright a light for the comfort of South American fascists. It is through the open window of Uruguay's free press that fascist plottings have been exposed in Argentina, Paraguay, and other countries in the southern half of South America. If this light could be extinguished, press darkness would settle over everything except the thin strip of Chile across the Andes. Bolivia under its modified revolutionary program may return to more freedom of the press, but fascist influences have become assertive during a period of political terrorism, executions, and assassination early in 1945.

As long as Uruguay remains stalwart and erect on the Atlantic coast, and Chile can be kept from falling under fascist influences on the Pacific, South America has small but vital buttresses for its long upward path of struggle toward popular rights. A traveler in South America these days emerges from the surcharged atmospheres of Brazil, Paraguay, and Argentina into the freedom of Uruguay and Chile as he might come to the surface for deep gulps of air after immersion in a swamp tingling with electric eels. Uruguayans and Chileans know and cherish their heritage as some of the freest peoples in a continent of dark oppressions and darker political hypocrisies.

One of the most refreshing experiences of travel through South America during the past seven years has been to see the triumph of Uruguay's liberals after a temporary interlude of the Terra dictatorship. Under former President Gabriel Terra, his ready propaganda artists in white-and-gold Army uniforms rocked on their heels and assured me in 1938 that Uruguay and Argentina were almost indistinguishable, amounting, in effect, to one country.

"We have the same traditions, the same culture, the same aspirations," they said. At the time there was no particular wrench needed in adjusting this propaganda to the facts. Uruguay for the moment was actually less democratic in its government than Argentina. Deep down, the Uruguayan people wanted real democracy. So do the Argentine people to this day. Yet the two peoples are not as much like peas in a pod as the Terra propagandists said. This fact became unmistakable as the world crisis developed.

At the darkest hour for world democracy, when France had gone down and the United States still slumbered in the thinning edges of an unrealistic neutral dream, Uruguayans spoke out courageously. They had restored their own country to internal democracy. Even to strangers like myself they would talk freely on the streets of Montevideo about high politics. They had cheered as the *Graf von Spee* went down to defeat off their own shores before guns of the British Navy. Tars of the fleet later sat in sidewalk cafés as heroes in a home port. When Uruguayans routed the Nazi fifth column in their midst, they did not retain fascist forms of government themselves, as the Vargas regime has done in Brazil. Uruguay cleaned house on fascism of the domestic as well as the imported varieties. The press is free, Congress functions, and the United Nations have no more loyal supporter, within the narrow range of Uruguayan powers and resources.

The country of which such fine things can be said is not even as large as the neighboring Brazilian State of Rio Grande do Sul. It is about the size of South Dakota. There are only some 2,150,000 Uruguayans, compared with Argentina's 13,700,000, and Brazil's 44,000,000. Every argument of caution that was advanced by Argentina's shapers of foreign policy to explain their "prudent neutrality" might have been used with more justification by Uruguay. Instead, Uruguay's Foreign Minister Alberto Guani, now Vice-President, scorned subterfuge. He and his democratic teammates have declared and maintained independence from Argentine pretensions to dominate Uruguayan affairs.

No doubt Dr. Guani saw beyond the immediate footwork of Argentina in early 1942 to the way that was being cleared for a fascist march. Now that the Argentine Army has seized the Government and exposed plans for drilling fascism into the nation, with external aggression as a possible goal, Uruguay is under increasing pressure. Buenos Aires finds willing Quislings even in a country such as this. There are some profascists in the Uruguayan Army, just as there are in other armies of Latin America. Certain political forces also find it to their advantage to draw on Argentine support, including funds. As for the Uruguayan people and their leaders, they are as stanchly democratic as any other in the Americas. Their very tolerance toward opposition is democratic. While Uruguay is willing to grant equal political rights to Communists, fascists, or other opponents of its national traditions, this nation can be quick and decisive in making the law felt by those who overstep. The former Nazi fifth column overstepped so far that it brought down on its head a truly national reaction.

Uruguay is one of the buffer states between South America's two giants. The other intermediate countries where diplomacies of Argentina and Brazil frequently clash, are Paraguay and Bolivia. Chile and Peru are more remote, and more powerful. The aim of Argentine fascists and their Uruguayan henchmen is to bring about situations inside the country that cannot be dealt with by Allied warships offshore. This is an almost forlorn hope in Uruguay, because the fascists are far outnumbered. Also, the Government of President Amézaga is alert and forewarned. He enjoys not only the assurance of military aid in case of assaults against Uruguayan freedom, but fullest assistance from the United States. Under present conditions, these safeguards do not need to be formalized in treaties. Existing Pan-American rules of general application for defense of the hemisphere are ample to protect Uruguay, or any other small democracy that might be menaced. The alien Nazi fifth column no longer figures as a practical danger in Uruguay.

Argentina is working through various native channels. An obvious one is the nationalist movement in Uruguay, headed by Dr. Luis Alberto Herrera. Prominent in its directorate is Senator Victor Haedo.

A target of repeated attack by the fascists is the building of naval and air bases with United States aid. Uruguay's position at the mouth of the Rio de la Plata divides the military control of that strategic waterway with Argentina. The shorelines of the two countries roll back from the estuary on nearly equal, but opposite, promontories. For years the Argentine has risen to protest, with vigor, whenever Uruguay appeared to be letting United States or Brazilian armed forces gain a foothold across the river. While naval vessels of the South Atlantic Patrol put in at Uruguayan ports, during my visit there was no sizable traffic by Allied military planes, out of deference to Argentina. Work, however, goes steadily ahead on commercial and even military air bases that could come in handy in case of untoward developments. Twenty-four miles from Montevideo is a new Pan American-Grace Airways base of four magnificent runways, built with United States money.

Even so, Uruguay's future depends far more on the growth of democracy in South America, especially in Argentina and Brazil, than on warships or warplanes from up north. Those weapons could drive back a bully. They cannot build South American peace. That requires North American statesmanship of consistent democratic effect among the large as well as small nations of South America.

GENUINE GOOD-NEIGHBORLINESS

"Resolute Self-Respect"

APPLICATION OF THE Good-Neighbor Policy has fallen short of its possibilities because sound principles have at times been abandoned in favor of delusions that inter-American friendships could be bought for a price, although that price undermined the policy's foundations. When President Roosevelt in his First Inaugural Address launched the Good-Neighbor Policy as a phrase and a going concern, he based it on mutual self-respect.

"In the field of world policy," Mr. Roosevelt declared, "I would dedicate this nation to the policy of the good neighbor— the neighbor who resolutely respects himself and, because he does so, respects the rights of others—the neighbor who respects his obligations, respects the sanctity of his agreements in and with a world of neighbors."

If the Good-Neighbor Policy had been applied consistently in accordance with this original definition, South America could have been spared much of the ordeal through which it is passing. More important, the United States would stand on firmer ground in its task of helping to rebuild a world shattered by fascism. Washington's betrayal of the Good-Neighbor Policy began with partial self-betrayal. The State Department adopted as fixed policies toward Latin America such evident inconsistencies that the mere statement of them makes them seem incredible. Yet they are still solid fact. Their impact has not been lost on the logical mentalities of South American peoples and their astute leaders.

While nearly 12,000,000 young North Americans were fighting to free the world from fascism in its German, Italian, and Japanese phases, the State Department not only winked at fascism in South America, but strengthened it. Instead of adopting a clear-cut attitude of opposition to fascism in all its forms,

Washington has pursued a course of expediency. This may have been inescapable in some instances, due to urgent military necessities of the war against the Axis. Expediency, however, has gotten out of hand, with unfortunate consequences. The most dangerous single departure from a consistent democratic diplomacy has come in dealings with Brazil and Argentina. Those two nations are the powerhouses of South America. On the synchronizing of their high-tension voltages depends the peace of that continent. They will largely decide whether democracy or fascism is to prevail among their smaller neighbors.

When the Good-Neighbor Policy was enunciated, signs of fascism already had become visible in the Vargas dictatorship of Brazil.

Argentina at that time had a going system of representative government, when allowances are made for South American irregularities. The Argentine press stood high among national mediums of public expression. *La Prensa* and *La Nación* added luster to the most glorious traditions of editorial independence and integrity. They stood for democracy openly and vigorously. They attacked every slightest tendency of the Argentine Government to slip into undemocratic or fascist methods. Their big guns were unlimbered against electoral frauds and corruption in high places. Without fear they gathered news from the world and printed it in pages of breadth and depth that inadvertently put to shame many of their contemporaries even in the United States. Their interests were world-wide, and their journalistic skills on a par with the best. Latest mechanical equipment made their plants marvels of the profession. I have seen the best equipment in the United States, and it does not exceed *La Prensa's,* where four-color supplements were printed twice a week.

To Buenos Aires in 1936 came the Inter-American Conference for the Maintenance of Peace. It carried forward the work of good-neighborliness begun at Montevideo in 1933 by Secretary Hull himself. President Roosevelt visited Buenos Aires and received an ovation from the democratic Argentine people.

Then Dr. Vargas had six years of dictatorial power behind

him. He was about to sweep away the betrayed Brazilian Congress and launch his fascist *Estado Novo.*

United States foreign policy in those days hewed more closely to the line of resolute self-respect than was to be the case later. As the world crisis developed between fascism and democracy, both Brazil and Argentina avoided taking decided stands on either side. They entered a period of diplomatic fence-walking that was to characterize most of the Latin-American nations until Japan struck directly against all of their liberties at Pearl Harbor. The most conspicuous fact in South America during that period was the growing fascism of the Vargas regime. Step by step the Brazilian dictator eliminated his opponents, individual and collective. The more absolute became his power, the more he sought to hide the fascist nature of his rule by a studied propaganda of sweetness and light. When the nation had been taught by violence and guile that opposition of any kind would not be tolerated, he used various devices in an effort to sugar the bitter pill of lost civil liberties. Just as the Japanese set up puppet governments in troublesome parts of China, so he set up puppet governments in São Paulo and other centers of potential danger to his regime. Always the smile and soft hand were extended to a nation in chains.

The Vargas strategy inside Brazil did not escape Argentina's thinkers. They saw through it. So did other leaders in Latin America, both fascist and democratic. It is amazing to report, but true, that many diplomats of the United States for seven years have joined with the paid propagandists of Dr. Vargas in trying to convince me and other impartial observers that the Vargas regime is not fascist, but at base democratic. Possibly they mean a base kind of democracy, degraded beyond recognition.

Washington's winking at Vargas fascism did no large-scale harm in South America as long as no tangible weight was injected by it into power politics of the southern continent. South Americans of the ruling classes are pragmatists in politics, not idealists. They spin legal niceties and abstractions on paper, but do not allow moral considerations to interfere with the actual seat of their semifeudal privileges. Argentines who knew what was going on in Brazil were not unduly alarmed while Brazil remained inferior to, or roughly on a par with, Argentina's own armed power and industrial potential. If they thought at all about Washington's naïve swallowing of Vargas propaganda as to his democratic intentions, they attributed it to inferior political acumen of the idealistic *gringos*. It was not until the Good Neighbor indirectly entered the game of South American power politics that Buenos Aires became alarmed. Argentina saw hundreds of millions of dollars being spent to build air bases within easy striking distance of Buenos Aires. Washington extended favors to fascist Brazil by the basketful, and pursued a studied diplomacy of building up Dr. Vargas as a South American bulwark of "democracy" against "fascist" Argentina.

It can be argued, and is, that the force of events after Pearl Harbor drove the State Department as in a hurricane. So it was, but the damage in South America had been done long before Pearl Harbor. Also, Washington's faulty diplomacy in South America goes on unchanged in essentials, but intensified in harmful effects, three years after dictators' collaboration had to be bought—if ever it had to be—at the expense of the self-respect of the United States of North America.

You Can't Buy Friendship

Paraguay offers a sobering illustration of an old maxim that applies to current results of the Good-Neighbor Policy at many points in Latin America: "You can't buy friendship." Even before the large new hospitals, paved roads, and other Good-Neighbor bounty had been completed with United States money, Paraguay fluctuated in its cordiality toward the United States.

Nor is Paraguay alone among Latin-American countries in this regard. It gave a convincing preview of possible reversion to deep-seated attitudes that had been overlaid, but not fundamentally changed, by recent United States spending. A Brazilian businessman put it frankly when he said in the United States that after the war Brazil will buy from Germany—of course—or anywhere else that prices are attractive. Quoting North America to itself, he said, "business is business."

North Americans of realistic bent know this. They also know that for some time now their principal business toward the other American countries has been Good-Neighboring. Anything affecting this relationship is vital to them and to all of the American peoples. Prominent public controversy over application of the Good-Neighbor Policy has surged in the United States. Republican Senator Hugh Butler of Nebraska returned home from a tour to Latin America during the summer of 1943 with sensational charges of "boondoggling," "graft," "wastefulness," and "inefficiency" he said he had found in Good-Neighbor spending. He had skimmed through all of the countries. High officials at Washington rose in self-defense.

The Junior Senator from Nebraska compiled figures purporting to show that a total of $5,733,953,534 had been expended, earmarked, or extended as credit to the other twenty American countries during 1942, 1943, and 1944. He said the actual total might go much higher. Senator Kenneth McKellar, Democrat from Tennessee, denied the figures and their accompanying attack on New Deal policies in Latin America. He found just 95 per cent of error in Senator Butler's figures on the basis of his own official summaries. Against the critical Butler total which had been publicized in round numbers as $6,000,000,000, Senator McKellar cited a net total of $1,483,373,000 for the years 1941 through 1943. He estimated another $1,000,000,000 for 1944.

The re-Butler to this was that the Senator from Tennessee had covered 1941 to 1943, whereas the original charges had been based on 1942 through 1944. When the estimated outlay for the later year is added to Senator McKellar's figure, he admits $2,483,373,000 for a period longer by one year than Mr. Butler's nearly $6,000,000,000.

The account of this controversy as detailed in the *Congressional Record* makes fantastic reading for an impartial observer.

Not only the grotesque discrepancy in figures, but the petulant tone which both sides allow to mar their arguments, is a sad commentary on the level of official conduct in such a sensitive field of foreign relations. Where actual facts stand amid the welter of charge and countercharge may not be fully known until the history of this fast-moving period is finally written. Anyone who possesses current firsthand knowledge can easily perceive strange inaccuracies in some of Senator Butler's figures, even though he has gone through the process of having them certified. It is harder to assess the Government's tally, but in several departments the figures given are surprisingly low. If it is claimed that anything can be proved by statistics, the reverse is also plausible in such a case of jumbled and confused arithmetic.

Yet beyond the political computations move human values. Americans throughout the hemisphere need to know all they can learn about how their money is being spent, and the effects of this spending. Senator McKellar asserts that the United States spent only $324,185,000 in Latin America from 1941 through 1943 on all accounts except the purchase of strategic war materials and ships. When broken down into some of its component parts, this figure may be correct, but it taxes credulity.

Naval Lend-Lease and other co-operation with fleets of Latin America is totaled at a cost of $25,206,000. Another $13,000,000 went for current expenses at the base of Guantánamo in Cuba, an almost exclusively North American installation. When the Latin-American sum outside Guantánamo is divided over the three-year period, it comes to $8,402,000 a year for current U. S. naval expenses ashore, and all naval Lend-Lease material sent to Latin America. This is a bargain, if the whole charge has been entered.

The United States Army expenditures on a chain of magnificent bases and other activities also seem low. Secretary of War Henry L. Stimson gives $476,980,000 as covering construction of airfields, personal services, and military matériel for the fiscal years 1942, 1943 and 1944. This covers everything south of the Rio Grande instead of only the independent Latin-American countries. When heavy outlays in the Panama Canal

Zone and in other entirely United States bases are deducted, a remarkable example of economy seems to have been achieved. Secretary Stimson held the door open to additions in the form of spending by field commanders not then reported to Washington.

Purchases of strategic materials to carry on the war are summarized by Senator McKellar at $1,102,637,000 spent by the United States. He makes the point that this outlay on wild rubber, tin, tantalite, and other indispensable sinews of United Nations armies cannot fairly be charged against the Good-Neighbor Policy. On the contrary, it is implied that the ability of the United States to obtain this much material is due in some measure to the Good-Neighbor Policy itself.

So Senator McKellar arrives at what he calls "the relatively modest war figure of $324,185,000" for all Good-Neighbor activities of the three years 1941-43, including those of the State Department. He then whittles this sum down by deducting items which directly benefit the war effort, such as capital investment in airports and military facilities, expenditures on sanitation, and repayments expected from Lend-Lease advances. The result of this figure-whittling is the extremely moderate sum of $178,000,000 which Senator McKellar is willing to admit as comparable with the $5,733,953,534 compiled and publicized by Senator Butler.

While the Senator from Nebraska would agree to an analytical breakdown of his billions, the impact he originally made on public opinion was that the Good-Neighbor Policy had cost $6,000,000,000 in the three latest fiscal years. He also stated forcefully that the program was loaded with scandalous corruption.

Of the expenditures conceded by Senator McKellar as justifiably chargeable to the Good-Neighbor Policy, the Co-ordinator of Inter-American Affairs takes $29,169,000. Spread over three years as it is, this comes to $9,723,000 a year. Anyone who has watched the stream of good-will missions both ways and seen the staff initially organized by Nelson A. Rockefeller at work would have to admit that $810,250 a month represents a large measure of economy. It also is a small investment in good will with

twenty countries. Provided, of course, that the net result turns
out to be good will.

Warren Lee Pierson, as head of the Export-Import Bank, was
the man chiefly concerned with the controversial issue of loans to
Latin America. Shades of defaulted bonds from the giddy
'twenties restrain reckless lending. Latin Americans, who suffered
more from the ensuing collapse than North Americans, prefer
sounder finance. During the three years listed by Senator Mc-
Kellar, the Export-Import Bank reports cash loans of $120,-
028,000. Other agencies advanced $536,000, making a total
of $120,564,000. Mr. Pierson has steadily given assurances that
his lending policy in Latin America would be based on loans
capable of promoting friendship. As he sees it, this means loans
which can be repaid. Bad loans make bad friends, he holds. Cash
loan repayments of $57,820,000 accordingly are entered in the
three-year accounting.

Elsewhere in his reply to Senator McKellar's questions Mr.
Pierson discloses that since 1934 the bank has authorized lines of
credit totaling $778,987,767. But not all of this has been taken
by the authorized borrowers. In all, $201,567,308 was canceled
or has expired. Actual loans effected are given by Mr. Pierson as
$212,182,962, of which more than half, or $107,284,391, has
been repaid. There's music in these words by Mr. Pierson: "No
loans to any Latin-American country or political subdivision or
agency thereof are in default."

Those are the peaks of statistical defense on which the Roosevelt Administration ranged its Latin-American line in the
election year of 1944.

Senator Butler, apparently nothing daunted by the weight of
official evidence against his original detailed blast, returned to the
attack with his figures certified by James A. Councilor & Co.,
Certified Public Accountants. This firm carefully specified that
its confirmation of Senator Butler's figures did not extend beyond examination of his source material. Reliability of the
material itself they naturally could not confirm.

My own trail through South America brought me across
Senator Butler's at various points. Some people who had given

him information expressed displeasure over the way he used it. Some charged he had shaped it to suit his own purposes. There are points at which my own factual sources are sufficient to uncover surprisingly loose and partisan juggling of figures and facts by Senator Butler in those instances. This does not extend beyond well-defined topics, but because of them I would have to see indisputable proof before accepting his totals.

For example, he repeats a figure for wild-rubber production that makes spectacular propaganda, but crumbles under a well-sharpened pencil point. Anyone who mentions $500 a pound as the cost of rubber needs only to multiply this by 2200 pounds to get $1,100,000 per long ton, the measure used for raw rubber. At that rate, some eighty tons of rubber would have been produced by the Rubber Reserve Company and the Rubber Development Corporation (RDC), since they began operations in Latin America. The least amount of rubber rightly creditable to activities of RDC totals thousands of long tons. Senator Butler tried to prove a deficit of rubber production in return for $78,000,000 spent! RDC is open to valid criticism, but not by such careless tactics.

Elsewhere in these pages I report at length on the wild-rubber program and other concrete examples of Good-Neighbor spending in wartime and before the war. These include the Rio Doce iron project, the Asunción-Iguassú road that ended halfway to its goal—so reversing the purposes of its Good-Neighbor spenders, and field activities of the Office of the Co-ordinator of Inter-American Affairs. In terms of practical results, a heavy percentage can be discounted as inescapable wartime expenditure, with the usual haste and waste of emergency measures. This was particularly the case with wild rubber in early stages of the program.

Apart from the war, it is a tenable proposition that long-range benefits can accrue to South America only from North American spending that has natural rather than artificial effects. To stimulate South America by building projects beyond its capacity to maintain does not result in permanent friendship. The Good-Neighbor spending that has been most effective is often the least spectacular. Friendly individuals have come to know and understand each other better through numerous interchanges of recent years. Some good has resulted from officially sponsored tours of writers, scholars, exchange students, and a wide variety of individuals. These tours have been expensive, and could not be maintained indefinitely. I have seen both sides of the tour picture, as a member of one party and as a newsman covering the visits of others. Not the lavish entertainment and overdone rounds of sight-seeing, but the opportunity to mingle with other people in more natural ways has paid the actual dividends.

In the field of propaganda, United States methods have been singularly inept. I was in South America when an advertising campaign began in newspapers there. The aim was to give money to South American editors in a way that would preserve their self-respect. The advertisements then began urging South Americans to travel to the United States! Chileans and Bolivians whose *pesos* would have to be saved for a lifetime to finance such a trip, were made to feel more poverty-stricken than ever. The campaign ended abruptly. *En Guarda,* a magazine issued by the Co-ordinator's Office in Washington with Spanish and Portuguese editions in color on high-gloss paper, has been spectacular from a North American standpoint, but obtuse and poorly conceived for Latin America because of overemphasis placed on the war. It has exalted the armed might of the United States to a degree that could not fail to revive South American fears of the Colossus of the North. Struggling South American editors have known what *En Guarda* must cost to produce. The same money, wisely distributed to a few genuinely democratic papers in South America, could have built more enduring friendship.

On the long range, genuine Good-Neighborliness takes form in everyday ways rather than the dazzle and glitter of recent years. A poor neighbor next door is not heartened by a ball given in his honor so much as by a helping hand to find steady work. A rich and proud nation such as Mexico, Argentina or Brazil, does not want to be flooded with propaganda from a more powerful neighbor who tactlessly writes about little else except his own planes, tanks, and battleships. They would prefer, even in wartime, a more balanced diet of give and take, with emphasis on the human values that build lasting understanding among peoples.

Latin Americans prize culture more than what they call the materialism of North America. They are learning to appreciate some of the spiritual values they had not discerned before in Anglo-Saxon culture. This awakening is reciprocal as Latin-American music, poetry, and literature find their place among us. Such values are not for sale. They can be advanced, and have been advanced by some of the more wisely expended Good-Neighbor billions. Yet the returns in currency of enduring friendship represent a small percentage of the amount invested. As the artificial spending stops—and it must—peoples of the Americas have to consider how they can build, with sounder money, the year-in and year-out foundations of mutual understanding and community well-being.

Signposts of Policy

Good-Neighboring, to succeed, must be maintained from both sides of the street and across even the back fences. In the crucial period of world readjustment now opening, all of the American Governments and peoples need to revaluate their mutual relations. Each will shape the outcome by making right decisions on how inter-American friendship may best be strengthened.

National responsibility rises in proportion to power, and so the United States of North America cannot escape making the most influential decisions, not only in the Western Hemisphere, but in the world.

Agreement is general that the Good-Neighbor Policy as originally enunciated is fundamentally sound. Since its essentials were in operation under the Republican Administration of President Hoover before President Roosevelt gave it dramatic impetus and a name, the policy has become national rather than partisan in the United States. Resolute self-respect, tolerance,

a friendly desire to understand your neighbor and help him along
—these are imperishable signposts for every nation.

In practice, Washington has succeeded as a Good Neighbor
when the State Department held closely to the sound line of
constructive principles, and has failed by resort to power politics.
The inescapable conclusion is that the first necessity for peace
and progress in the Western Hemisphere is for Washington to
reinstate the original Good-Neighbor Policy and advance from
that firm position. This calls for drastic revision of prevailing
attitudes, at the top, in the State Department. Those attitudes at
present are not coherent, and are changing under Secretary of
State Edward R. Stettinius, Jr., but for a long while were fixed
along the following lines:

1. A limited definition of fascism as external aggression. While
accurate as far as it goes, this incomplete approach to the underlying world struggle causes inconsistent actions. Under this definition, Washington falls an easy prey to an astute Brazilian
diplomacy that fights fascism on European battlefields but uses
the power gained by this policy to solidify fascism inside Brazil.
The same shallow definition caused Washington to fulminate
against Argentina while that country was being driven deeper
into fascism by the State Department's support of a notoriously
fascist Brazilian regime. The net result was to strengthen fascism
in Argentina. Washington's early blunders aroused nationalistic
instincts of the democratic Argentine people so that they did not
resist a fascist dictatorship as they should have done. Similar bad
effects result from contradictions of policy that run all through
Washington's dealings with Latin America. The cure is for the
State Department to lay down a clear line of consistent democratic diplomacy. Since the issue of freemen versus fascism is
acute enough to send millions of young North Americans into
battle, it should be acute enough to shake the State Department
into adoption of a clear-cut attitude of resistance to all forms of
fascism. To base a foreign policy on resistance merely to the
external aggressions practiced by fascist regimes is to invite the
kind of disaster that descended on the world when the democracies from 1931 to 1938 refused to open their eyes to what was

going on inside Germany, Italy, and Japan. In its handling of fascist regimes in Bolivia and Argentina the State Department has been more perceptive of late.

2. Washington extends armaments, credits, and honors to any South American regime which helps to win the war against fascism abroad, regardless of how fascist that regime may be at home. Brazil is the most conspicuous example. During a brief period, Paraguay fell in the same category. So did Bolivia under the reactionary rule of former President Peñaranda. Washington has gone beyond even the bargaining position of a foreign policy based on sheer expediency. A procession of dictators has been brought to Washington and paid honors that could not be understood by Latin America's liberals who had been driven into hiding or exile by those same dictators. The United States has degraded itself and discouraged the genuine democrats of Latin America by such tactics.

3. There is no sustained program in the State Department for strengthening democratic forces among the southern neighbors. While Latin America itself would not rest until it had bound the United States by formal Pan-American commitments of 1933 and 1936 not to intervene in the internal or external affairs of any Latin-American country, that fact does not entirely cover the case. It is hard to draw a line between intervention and non-intervention in relations of powers differing as greatly as do the United States and Bolivia, to take one example. By not acting at all on certain issues, the United States can overthrow Bolivian Governments. Such was the case when a Revolutionary Junta came into power by revolting against former President Peñaranda on December 20, 1943. The Junta was forced to make drastic internal changes before it won United States recognition. In the case of Argentina, effects of nonrecognition have not been as rapid. Instead, the inconsistency of Washington's actions toward Brazil and Argentina on the issue of fascism at first rallied public opinion behind the military dictatorship and tied the hands of Argentine liberals. The effect of Washington's diplomacy has been to place unassailable military weapons, including warplanes, in the hands of Dr. Vargas and other dictators. Popular revolu-

tion against oppressive regimes is thus rendered nearly impossible, due to actions of the United States Government. This is intervention on the wrong side. It must stop. In its place must be installed a genuine and consistent democratic diplomacy that will hearten Latin-American liberals and withhold from fascist or semifascist dictators any outside aid in imposing themselves on defenseless peoples. That can be done through actions motivated by resolute self-respect. It does not require violation of the Montevideo and Buenos Aires pledges not to intervene in domestic politics of the Latin-American neighbors.

4. The State Department is still weakening its diplomacy toward Argentina by its Brazilian policy. There can be no solution of the Argentine problem on the basis of power politics directed from Washington. That path would lead inevitably to war between Argentina and Brazil—provided Brazil's fascist regime did not betray the United States and play its own power politics with Argentina's fascists. Before any progress can be expected in constructive results from United States diplomacy toward Argentina, that highly intelligent country must see that Washington has ceased to strengthen the fascist Vargas regime. A powerful and principled United States diplomacy, not a powerful fascist Brazil, holds promise of South American security and peace. Proof of this view is found in support by Argentine liberals for Washington's action against the fascist regime in Buenos Aires, while Brazilian liberals dislike the United States for supporting Vargas. Similar reactions throughout Latin America provide the most convincing evidence that the State Department has wandered far from the original objectives and inspiration of the Good-Neighbor Policy. The time to return is now.

On the Latin-American side of Good-Neighbor paths, much constructive work also remains to be done. The present fascist upsurge, unless checked from within the countries where it appears, would hold back their progress for another indeterminate period. Right-thinking forces in Latin America should not shirk from their part in the world-wide struggle to lift fascist yokes from human necks. Native fascists in the ruling classes will fight to the end by open and secret means to retain their power. A new revolution of independence has begun, this time not to win freedom from a distant European Empire, but from fascist dictatorships in the Americas.

A prime necessity is for Latin Americans to meet the United States halfway, especially in fields where Latin America can benefit by modifying its traditional customs. The artificiality of social attitudes that place appearance ahead of substance is unwholesome. North American frankness in the press may shock sensitive Latin Americans, but truth-telling is better for them in the long run than an unrealistic politeness. Latin America is retarded by personal and social faults that can be overcome only from within. Refuge is taken in poetry from the actualities of an admittedly harsh environment. On the train from Buenos Aires to La Paz a Bolivian in the compartment next to mine recited poetry all day long for four days. Meanwhile his country outside the windows, boulder-strewn and poverty-stricken, appeared headed toward national bankruptcy unless strenuous countermeasures are taken. South America's thinkers tend to spin mental abstractions instead of coming to grips with practical problems of their everyday world. They have much to learn in elementary sanitation of mind and body. They are learning, just as North Americans are coming to appreciate the aesthetic values of their neighbors' music, dancing, and poetry.

In short, a sincere effort must continue on both sides to understand the other neighbor's point of view. Doing so, the Americas can shape their future into mutual helpfulness, provided they never lose sight of the spiritual and moral values that have given them whatever they share of greatness. They then will find tangible means for building America as a bulwark of freedom, a refuge for the oppressed, a citadel impregnable to forces of fascism from without or within.

"Constellation of America"

Foreign Minister Ezequiel Padilla of Mexico reached the hearts of Brazil's democratic people as no other official did during the consultations of Rio de Janeiro in the lengthening shadow of Pearl Harbor's black smoke. Mexico's Dr. Padilla is a man of the people who has known hunger and climbed the long, hard stairs of self-education. Scholarly erudition has not deprived him of the common touch. Essentially he is a poet-statesman. His speech in private and in public rises naturally to a Lincolnian simplicity of phrase that combines penetration and power with sheer beauty.

At Rio de Janeiro on January 28, 1942, the Third Consultative Meeting of American Foreign Ministers came to its closing plenary session. The course of negotiations had been stormy in this first inter-American meeting after war at last engulfed the Americas. Undersecretary of State Sumner Welles labored without success to form a united American front against the Nazi-Fascist-Japanese Axis. Argentina and Chile refused to sign a resolution bluntly agreeing to sever diplomatic relations with Axis powers. The other nineteen delegations seated at Rio de Janeiro had the choice of going ahead without Argentina and Chile, or of weakening their own forthright position to meet the dissenters' formula. Mexico, Uruguay, Costa Rica, and other nations which had taken their stand with the democracies against the Axis, advocated vigorous action. Mr. Welles clung to the hope that his original objective of a united and strong statement could be achieved.

The crisis came on the night of January 21-22. Foreign Minister Juan Antonio Rossetti of Chile and Foreign Minister Enrique Ruiz-Guiñazú of Argentina were the storm centers. Chile had taken the initiative in calling the Foreign Ministers together, and so its defection was puzzling. Argentina's ultra-conservative Castillo regime had no intention of breaking diplomatic relations with the Axis powers. Pressure was exerted by

Buenos Aires on Chile and the other Latin-American nations in an effort to keep them from going along with Mr. Welles.

The Undersecretary met frequently with correspondents of the United States press. On the afternoon of January 21 he called us together in a special news conference and told us with satisfaction that the Argentine and Chilean delegations had accepted a strong declaration in favor of breaking with the Axis. So dark had been the outlook one day previously that he visibly showed relief.

During the early evening the National Brazilian Academy of Letters held a session where Louis Dantes Bellegarde of Haiti delivered an oration in his polished French. Foreign Minister Ruiz-Guiñazú was there. After the meeting, as he stood on the curb waiting for his car, I presented myself and sounded him on the encouraging turn of events. He was icy, aloof, abrupt, and terminated our brief conversation by pretending not to hear questions. That night over the long-distance telephone from Buenos Aires, Dr. Castillo repudiated the text to which his delegation in Rio had agreed. It is possible that the affair was arranged by Argentina's diplomatic stage managers to embarrass the United States. If so, even Mr. Welles appears to have been taken in by the ruse. He found himself, with us, on the end of a long and shaky limb soon after he gave us unqualified assurances that the conference had solved its central problem.

How far the consultations had fallen short of hemispheric unity became apparent the next morning. Feeling ran high as Argentina's betrayal of the meeting became known in the city. Rio's people reacted visibly. From the start of the sessions, when they had massed at the seaplane base to watch Mr. Welles step from his camouflaged Stratoliner, they followed the course of negotiations with keen and informed interest. They knew who the delegates were. To none did they respond with more spontaneous affection than greeted Dr. Padilla whenever he appeared.

All day Thursday, January 22, Dr. Padilla and the other advocates of a forthright democratic stand labored to repair the damage done by Dr. Castillo in his long-distance telephone orders to Dr. Ruiz-Guiñazú. No solution had been devised by Friday afternoon. It became evident that Argentina's position was immovable, and that the reasons were larger than any single Argentine official. The conservative wave in that country, already rising to tidal proportions, rose higher during the Rio consultations. The more diplomatic prominence Brazil attained, the more Argentina asserted itself in reaction.

Day by day, United States backing of the Vargas regime appeared more unmistakably as a spotlighted event on the world stage. Whatever conciliatory tendencies might have existed in Argentina were overwhelmed by the surge of nationalistic resentment. So the fascist tinge of government deepened in Argentina.

By late afternoon of that Friday a compromise, but not a solution, had passed through the red-hot rollers of negotiation. Neither Argentina nor Chile was willing to offend Nazi Germany, but the motives of each country were somewhat different. I discovered in Chile after the conference that Foreign Minister Rossetti had accurately reflected Chilean public opinion, although his belligerent personal attitude in Rio partially obscured this fact. Chileans were afraid of what might be done to their vulnerable coastal economy by a few submarines. Not many shells would be required to wreck power plants, oil tanks, harbor installations, and shipping, on which the country is almost entirely dependent. Because of the Andes, Chile's economy is compressed into a narrow strip along the sea. At that time the United States Navy was still reeling from Pearl Harbor losses, and Chile felt in danger from Japanese naval power. Argentina also dreaded reprisals by U-boats against its merchant marine. In addition, the Castillo regime responded to pro-Nazis in the Argentine armed forces, to anti-British and anti-United States elements, and a related complex of influences.

As Argentina and Chile drew back from the advanced position of the other American nations, attention focused on Brazil. Would the pressures exerted by Argentina and Chile prevent Brazil from breaking with the Axis? Also, would soft-spoken Foreign Minister Oswaldo Aranha be willing to take a strong stand against the actions of his two largest South American neighbors? With characteristic personal and national moderation, Dr. Aranha placed unity ahead of an uncompromising statement. Mexico, Colombia, Venezuela, and many of the smaller nations were prepared to hew to the line of their own convictions, even at the expense of traditional Pan-American unanimity. Mr. Welles indicated that he would have preferred the sacrifice of this limiting tradition, rather than of his minimum program for a break of diplomatic relations with the Axis. As I analyzed the reactions of delegations during those critical hours of decision, it seemed that the balance was tipped by Brazil toward tolerance of Argentina and Chile. Dr. Aranha personally made every effort to fill and smooth the gaping crevasses that had opened under his feet as chairman of the consultations. In his press conferences he showed no disposition to read Argentina and Chile out of the party. This point of view prevailed. The resulting declaration eliminated a clear-cut commitment and made possible the cherished unanimity. Along the way in this linguistic juggling, a Spanish phrase which declared that the American nations *no puedan* (cannot) maintain diplomatic relations with the Axis, was changed to *puedan no* (may not). The final draft omitted even such tenuous obligations and merely recommended that relations be broken. Within the four paragraphs of this document may be read the inner conflict, the ideals, and some of the dominant methods of Pan-American relations.

Reaffirmation is a revealing word in the text. The American Governments, including those of Argentina and Chile, had unanimously adopted at Havana in 1940 a declaration that any act of aggression by a non-American nation against one of them would "be considered as an act of aggression against" all of them. This commitment occurred as number XV among the final acts. Such a clear affirmation would appear automatically to have bound Argentina and Chile at least to break diplomatic relations with Japan, Germany and Italy after Pearl Harbor and the ensuing declarations of war. Havana's resolution was so interpreted by Costa Rica, first American nation to declare war against Japan. Acting a few hours before the United States Congress, diminutive Costa Rica—with more schoolteachers than soldiers—said to the Axis: "You can't hit my big brother." Argentina's defection at Rio caused the other delegations to *reaffirm* the words of Havana.

Pan-American resolutions are loaded with this device. It is an open confession that worthy statements have been ignored or violated. Rio repeated this procedure, and then summed up in Paragraph III its lowest common denominator of unanimous agreement in these weak words: "The American Republics, in accordance with the procedures established by their own laws and in conformity with the position and circumstances obtaining in each country in the existing continental conflict, recommend the breaking of their diplomatic relations with Japan, Germany, and Italy, since the first-mentioned State attacked and the other two declared war on an American country."

That was the text before members of the First Committee when they assembled around the long rectangular table of carved Brazilian hardwood in a room of Itamarity Palace overlooking the swan pond with its rows of royal palms. It was a semipublic session, meaning that any qualified person who could crowd into the small room would be admitted. Writers and photographers were jammed in with secretaries and a few representatives of the general public. Surcharged feelings crackled in the air as Foreign Minister Aranha took his seat informally at the center of the table's side that faced the door. Air-cooling units had been installed—a welcome modern touch in the midsummer heat of the old palace.

Foreign Minister Ruiz-Guiñazú soon was given the floor and launched into a legalistic discourse that spun a long tissue of meaningless words. On he went, and on. He stood across the table from Dr. Aranha, and to the right. To the chairman's left sat Uruguay's Foreign Minister, Dr. Alberto Guani. A great democratic statesman, he can be puckish on occasion. Diplomatic amenities do not stand in his way when he is confronted with actions he considers unworthy of respect. Seated diagonally across the table from Dr. Ruiz-Guiñazú, he was seen to be aroused.

With side glances toward his equally aroused colleagues he picked up a newspaper and began reading. The bold headline he held so it could be seen by the Argentine consisted in a blistering indictment by a Brazilian editor of Argentina's action in trying to torpedo the conference. Such Guani frankness, while of a kind native to the United States Congress and the British House of Commons, seldom breaks the smooth tenor of Pan-American speech-sessions. The delegates heard Dr. Ruiz-Guiñazú through to his last legal nicety, and applauded perfunctorily.

When Dr. Guani's turn came to speak, he faced toward the Argentine and said simply: "We Uruguayans came to Rio de Janeiro to break relations with the Nazi-Fascist-Japanese Axis. I shall telegraph my Government tonight recommending that we break." He sat down amid salvos of applause.

It was a situation to summon the Mexican Foreign Minister to the floor with controlled emotion that showed in the movements of his strong artistic hands. Tall and commanding, he rose to speak with his whole being visibly in revolt against the evasive tactics of Argentina. Addressing his remarks at times directly to Dr. Ruiz-Guiñazú with pointed emphasis, he said that in times of peace "diplomatic courtesies and protection flourish like orchids in the hothouse of world civilization,—but faced by the problems of war we must speak another tongue. . . . It could not be otherwise, for the homelands of the peoples, their heritage of freedom and spiritual values, are in jeopardy. . . . This is no time to defend material wealth—the hour of sacrifice is upon us."

So was prepared the final session, five days later, in Tiradentes Palace, former home of the Brazilian Chamber of Deputies and now used for offices by fascist press manipulators of the Vargas dictatorship. It is customary at final plenary sessions of Pan-American meetings for everything to be cut and dried. This was different. Brazil had not yet publicly announced whether it would break with the Axis. The territorial dispute between Peru and Ecuador had not been settled. Dr. Aranha built the meeting to its climax by shaking his leonine gray hair as he dramatically ranged Brazil beside the forces of world democracy in protest against Axis aggression. Then, with public fanfares that did not accurately record the depth of hostile feeling still remaining in Ecuador and Peru, Rio rounded out a tempestuous wartime session by hailing the settlement of the border dispute between those two countries.

Nothing remained to be done—or so the diplomats thought. The spotlight rested where it should, on the chairman. He was about to declare the meeting adjourned when something occurred that never before had jarred a Pan-American speech-fest out of its complacency. From the right rear corner of the hall came a rising tide of voices. The gallery was speaking. The people of Rio would be heard. They wanted the Mexican Foreign Minister to speak. With their Portuguese pronunciation they chanted:

"Meh-shee-ko! Meh-shee-ko! Meh-shee-ko!"

Dr. Aranha hesitated. He obviously wanted to shut off this unscheduled event. There was no stopping it.

"Meh-shee-ko! Meh-shee-ko! Meh-shee-ko!"

The chairman yielded. Dr. Padilla rose from his seat on the right aisle. In the ornate theatrical box that filled the corner behind and above him as he came forward sat Sebastião Cardinal Leme da Silveira Cintra, Archbishop of Rio de Janeiro, in scarlet robes. The floor was filled with delegates and distinguished guests under the lofty dome. Silence filled the hall as Dr. Padilla neared the lower rostrum. He bowed to Dr. Aranha on the level above, and to the rows of dignitaries on sloping tiers of seats behind the chairman. What Dr. Padilla said that afternoon has been taken down and translated. The Carnegie Endowment for International Peace considered his three speeches at Rio so important that they were singled out and published. The words on paper give only a faint impression of the contribution he made to genuine good-neighborliness in the Americas. I was standing within a few feet of the rostrum as he began to speak extemporaneously.

"We are all of us anxious to hear words of faith and hope at a time like this, when the continents are torn asunder in tragic strife, and the warlords are intent on destroying the weaker peoples. . . ."

Ranged before Dr. Padilla a few rows back from the first curving line of delegates sat Dr. Ruiz-Guiñazú and the other

Argentines. Across the aisle sat the Chileans, visibly uncomfortable. Both delegations had remained seated when Dr. Aranha announced Brazil's break with the Axis and all the other delegates stood up cheering. The atmosphere in the dissenters' neighborhood was frigid. To them Dr. Padilla addressed himself. He said that it had been in his heart a long time to speak to them . . . that he spoke as to brothers. Then he drew from his storehouse of poetic imagery words of such beauty and depth that his audience rose with him.

"Just as, in early evening, not all stars of a constellation appear, but the deepening darkness finds each shining in its place, so the Constellation of America will come out clear and strong, all twenty-one stars, brave and united across the night."

One year later Chile's star came from behind the clouds. Still another year and Argentina's star gleamed fitfully in the Constellation of America before being again hidden temporarily by the same vapors of fascist power politics that dim other stars in the western firmament. Above the black mists, it still is true that the constellation of human freedom grows in beauty, for the light of democracy can never be extinguished. Its strength is above the sun, beyond all stars, safe in the divine source of man's brotherhood.

PORTRAIT OF A CONTINENT

Prologue: Mirages

IT IS DOWNRIGHT dangerous for people to harbor illusions about South America of the kind that easily shimmer through golden hazes of the unknown. Millions of young men and women look to South America as a new horizon, a fresh start away from older or war-depleted continents, a beckoning frontier awaiting sturdy pioneers.

Just in case anyone is planning to sell the family homestead and set forth in search of those fabled riches, it would pay him to read the pages that follow before going too far. I have seen most of the territory he might enter. There also runs through me a broad streak of pioneering. The ring of an ax in my hands is more agreeable than the chatter of typewriter keys. I grew up with the tang of sagebrush and the call of distant peaks. In those days there still was enough of the early West in California to give some faint savor of pioneer times. It was natural for me, when I started going to South America seven years ago, to make trips to the interior instead of spending all my time in cities.

South America's frontiers attracted me. Whose imagination has not been quickened by the Amazon and Andes, Cape Horn and Magellan's Strait? In practical terms of economic relief for a world that struggles with recurrent unemployment and over-crowding in Europe, Asia, and even parts of North America and Africa, I wanted to know what South America has to offer.

I have found out enough to enable me to draw some reasonably definitive conclusions. In the following word-portrait I present a balanced view of South America as I have seen it. Promising resources highlight the canvas. Formidable obstacles are not omitted. In other parts of this book are portrayed human elements both favorable and unfavorable to anyone seeking a new home or field for investments. Full weight is given to the shadows

143

of restrictive governmental edicts and other forces responsible for delaying South America's progress. *In Search of Frontiers* follows the portrait with more detailed examination of pioneer possibilities.

South America often has come before the world in spectacular ways. Rivers of gold flowed from the Viceroyalty of Peru to speed Charles V toward mastery of Europe in his day. Sugar poured from Brazil. Chile long had a near-monopoly of nitrates. Amazonia pioneered in rubber when bicycles, and then horseless carriages, were the latest novelties. So it has gone, except that each of these spectacular South American resources in time lost its commanding position on international markets. Others, such as petroleum, meat, cereals, coffee and tropical products have fared well, but not as monopolies.

Much of the land that lures from afar as virgin country awaiting only the axes and plows of adventurous pioneers, actually has been abandoned. This view of South America is well known to the United States Department of Agriculture, the Rubber Development Corporation, field workers of the Office of the Co-ordinator of Inter-American Affairs, and other agencies which in recent years have sought those fabled riches. This view also is well known to South Americans who day after day wrestle with the actualities of a difficult continent. South Americans are proud and polite. They seldom call attention to their handicaps. Occasionally they remind North Americans that the United States, in its geographical make-up, does not have to contend with obstacles equal to the Amazon and the Andes.

It should appeal to anyone's reason that the acquisitive human race would not have allowed fortunes to lie around loose for 450 years in South America. The plain fact is that easily accessible wealth was creamed off long ago. First it was carried away as gold and silver in Spanish galleons blown toward far Seville. Highly capitalized modern firms took up the search. Industrial minerals therefore are largely a staked preserve. Many mines of the Andes have been exhausted. Others are fading, including Bolivia's once bountiful tin veins. The black gold of petroleum

Cordillera Paine Beyond the *Salto Chico* of Rio Paine
Towers rising in sculptured simplicity amid lakes and glaciers near the Strait of Magellan in Chile.

Photo Studio, Punta Arenas **Lago Argentino Through Ice Walls of Moreno Glacier**
One of several large lakes south of the region usually reached by tourists, Lago Argentino
fed by ice fields hundreds of miles long.

F

Otavalo

nquil and remote
the Andes of
uador, Otavalo
rs the fruitage of
rural Indian econ-
y into Market
y. At dawn this
n square begins
fill. Before noon
traders and their
ilies, in holiday
od, disperse into
town or start the
g dusty miles
meward. Skilled
avers, the Otava-
is preserve an-
nt designs of re-
ement and com-
e them with a
e appreciation for
olor harmonies

Right, André Roosevelt

Spinning, left, in porch of
an adobe home. The child's
early maturity is typical in
the Andes. Good cheer,
wit, and humor prevail
among Otavalo's land-own-
ing Indians. Brilliant
scarves hold papoose for
his long, swaying rides.

G

Grand Upper Hallway in Patiño Palace at Cochabamba
One of three sumptuous residences in a remote Andean city, Portales, has never been seen by
its Tin-King owner, a Bolivian who lives abroad.

Bolivian Tin Miners at a Soccer Game, San José Mine, Oruro
Sports, especially *futbol*—as soccer is known in South America—have gained rapidly in pop-
ularity. Maurice Hochschild maintains this field.

H

**Bolivian
Scenes
of
Luxury
and
Poverty**

Above, ragged peons on
the Patiño Model Dairy
Farm near Cochabamba.
One of the three Patiño
Palaces is on the farm.

Right, a *Balsa* boat on
Lake Titicaca. These
raft made of reeds
lashed solidly together
ly between Bolivia and
Peru at an altitude of
2,500 feet. There is
also steamship service,
said to be the highest of
its kind in the world.

1

Sculptured Mantelpiece in Grand Salon Opposite the Gobelin
Europe's best furniture styles and accessories, including brocaded drapes and cushions in many
colors remain covered. They are flawlessly preserved.

J

High Noon in the Plaza at Arequipa, Peru

An ancient Inca metropolis, Arequipa lies in the mid-zone of moderately high valleys—7,000 to 9,000 feet elevation—in the central Andes. The *Altiplano* beyond is from 12,000 to 15,000 feet.

Paseo de la Republica in Lima, Peruvian Capital

In contrast with Arequipa, Lima lies nearly at sea level on dusty flats. Behind the city rise foothills of the Andes with massive abruptness. Lima is in an irrigated oasis.

K

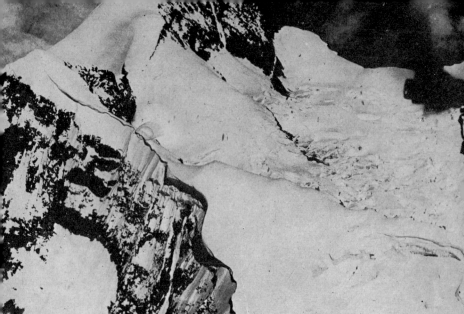

Right, Courtesy
Pan American Airways

Santa Marta Mountains
Attaining nearly 20,-000 feet, the Santa Martas in northern Colombia overlook the Caribbean as the forerunners of similar peaks farther south. Although near the Equator, they are snowcrowned all year.

Kaieteur Waterfalls
In British Guiana on wild borderlands near Venezuela, Kaieteur is characteristic of tropical falls, many of which are several times the height of Niagara. The Indians are *Selva* types, markedly distinct from pre-Spanish tribes of the Andes.

L

Venezuela: Caracas and Mile-High Angel Falls
Top, National Pantheon, a monument to Bolívar. Boys, center, draw water on outskirts of the
city. The hovel is typical of housing in poorest districts.

A Channel of the Amazon River in its Jungle Setting
Inset: a semi-civilized forest Indian near a missionary settlement on the Perené River, a Peruvian tributary of the world's largest river system. The feathers show he is son of a chief.

High-water Marks of Culture in Amazonia
Top, Belém, ninety miles from the Amazon's mouth, is port of entry and export for most of the basin. Lower, the *Teatro Nacional* in Manáos.

Reception Committee and Soil Erosion on the Beni River

Wade Stiles

Shipping Casualty in Log-choked Chapare, Bolivia

Down to the River at Riberalta, Frontier Outpost of Beni

P

Wild Rubber
The Second Boom
in
Amazonian History

Top: rafts and 'snakes' of rubber balls being delivered at Guayaramerín, Bolivia.
Insets: rubber tapper on Ford plantation at Belterra, left, and in Bolivian jungle, right. The
hand-pushed rail car passes rapids at Cachuela Esperanza on the Beni.

Jangadas, Sailing Rafts of Brazil's Northeastern Coast

Recife, 'City on the Reef,' Capital of Pernambuco State
Its harbor sheltered behind the Great Barrier Reef, Brazil's metropolis of the strategic bulge faces Africa.

R

São Salvador de Bahia in Brazil's 'Mediterranean' Zone

Bahia, City of Two Levels United by an Elevator Tower
Situated on a large ocean bay, Brazil's former Colonial Capital crowns its hills with modern
and old Portuguese architecture.

Migration on the São Francisco River, Brazil

Colonization in São Francisco Valley
This crude home must be abandoned during part of the flood season.

Brazil's Mosaic Sidewalks
Hand-set, these colorful walks are still ing built.

Gavea Peak on the Ocean Side of Rio de Janeiro

Modern Rio
...ctional architecture makes best use of
light and air.

**Changing Outlines of
Avenida Rio Branco**
Brazil's capital centers its activity along
this thoroughfare, a blend of tradition and
experimentation.

Three Periods of Design in Facades of Ouro Preto, Brazil

Goiânia, New Capital of Goiaz State on Brazil's Plateau

Cauê Peak Brazil's Iron Mountain

The trucks are hauling this ore, one of the richest exposed hematite deposits, down a road cut through 69 per cent iron. The whole peak will eventually be blasted apart and poured into Brazil's expanding industries, or exported. *See Rio Doce Iron Project in index.*

Transport Handicaps Being Overcome

A new concrete bridge, not quite complete, is used by a bus on the way from the Iron Mountain to Santa Barbara with its rail connection to Brazil's industrial areas. Ore from Cauê Peak is hauled another way, down the Rio Doce Valley by road and rail to the port of Vitória.

Corumbá, Mato Grosso, on its Paraguay River Palisade.

Volta Redonda Steel Mill—Start of Brazilian Steel Age

São Paulo Rubber Industries—Left, Goodyear; Right, *Orion*

and Waterpower

Practicos poling the *Octavio Carreiro* off the rocks of rapids in the São Francisco River. Lower, the small hydroelectric plant below Paulo Afonso Waterfalls, Brazil. A hand-drawn cable car is crossing the gorge.

Y

Iguassú Waterfalls
Inset tree, a Paraná Pine

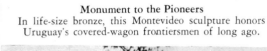

Monument to the Pioneers
In life-size bronze, this Montevideo sculpture honors Uruguay's covered-wagon frontiersmen of long ago.

El Gaucho
uestrian study of
traditional nom-
who filled the
mpa region with
stalgic folklore by
customs and ex-
its when frontiers
re still unfenced.

Paraguayan
Lime Kiln
ne of the country's
w nonagricultural
industries.

Z-1

Uspallata Pass, Main Andean Crossing from Argentina to Chile

Chile's Coastal Passages Between Puerto Montt and Magellan Strait

A Mongoloid Type Among Chilean Mussel Divers in the Passages

Chiloé Island, Chile, with its Quilt of Potato Patches

The Strait of Magellan
The explorer's statue in Punta Arenas faces the passage to the Orient, at the southernmost point of the South American continent. The beached ship was the first steamship to transit the Strait.

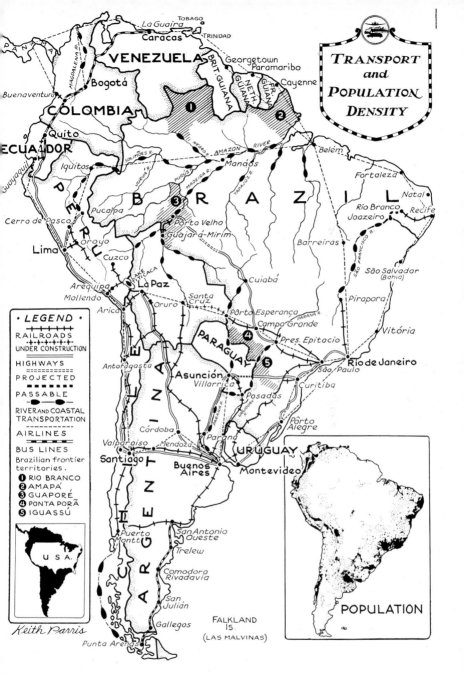

TOBAGO
La Guaira
Caracas TRINIDAD
VENEZUELA Georgetown
Paramaribo
Buenaventura Bogotá Cayenne
COLOMBIA ❶
Quito
ECUADOR
Guayaquil Iquitos Manaós
Pucalpa BRAZIL Belém
Cerro de Pasco ❸ Fortaleza
Oroyo Porto Velho Natal
Lima Guajará-Mirim Rio Branco Recife
Cuzco Joazeiro
Arequipa Barreiras
Mollendo La Paz
Arica Oruro Santa São Salvador
Cruz (Bahia)
Cuiabá
Pôrto Esperança Pirapora
Campo Grande
PARAGUAY ❹ Vitória
Antofagasta ❺ Pres. Epitacio
Asunción Rio de Janeiro
Villarrica São Paulo
Córdoba Posadas Curitiba
Valparaíso Mendoza Pôrto
Santiago Paraná Alegre
Buenos URUGUAY
Aires Montevideo

TRANSPORT
and
POPULATION
DENSITY

· LEGEND ·
RAILROADS
+-+-+-+-+-+
UNDER CONSTRUCTION
HIGHWAYS
========
PROJECTED
■-■-■-■-■
PASSABLE
●━━●━━●
RIVER and COASTAL
TRANSPORTATION
AIRLINES
●━━━●
BUS LINES
●━━━●
Brazilian frontier
territories .
❶ RIO BRANCO
❷ AMAPÁ
❸ GUAPORÉ
❹ PONTA PORÁ
❺ IGUASSÚ

U.S.A.

Keith Parris

Puerto
Montt
San Antonio
Oueste
Trelew
Comodoro
Rivadavia
San
Julián
Gallegos
Punta Arenas

FALKLAND
IS.
(LAS MALVINAS)

POPULATION

Z-5

RESOURCES
AND
HANDICAPS

Desert

Caracas
VENEZUELA
BR. GUIANA
Georgetown
SURINAM (NETH.)
Paramaribo
Cayenne
FR. GUIANA
Bogotá
COLOMBIA
Quito
ECUADOR
Equator
Belém
Maranhão
Poor Soils
Excessive Rains
Floods
Leached Soils
Recurrent Drought
Natal
Recif
PERU
Lima
BRAZIL
Bahia
SN
Poor Soils
La Paz
BOLIVIA
Poor Soils
Mountains
Desert
PARAGUAY
São Paulo
Santos
Rio de Janeiro
Asunción
CHILE
ARGENTINA
URUGUAY
Valparaíso
Santiago
Buenos Aires
Montevideo
Concepción
Poor Soils
Cold Rains
Falkland Islands (Br)
R. Lenz

KEY

	Maize		Nitrates
	Cotton		Fruits
	Sugar		Wool
	Tin		Rubber
	Cattle		Gold
	Coffee		Silver
	Wheat		Diamonds
	Oil		Copper
	Manganese		Cacao
	Iron		Quartz

is still abundant, but past the pioneer stage as oil flows through pipelines.

On a smaller scale of exploitation during many centuries, South America's own hard-pressed peoples have been at work. They reduced, and sometimes ruined, their own natural wealth in the struggle to wrest a bare subsistence from this difficult continent.

The South American bounty that remains is sometimes tremendous in its potential value. Brazil has 22 per cent of the world's iron ore reserves. Much of it is high grade. So far not enough industrial fuel has been found to match the iron. Oil and coal are located, but neither in sufficient quantity nor quality. These may be discovered in Brazil, but until they are, we do well to face present facts.

On the whole, South America's resources are spotty. They are hedged about by handicaps that must be seen to be grasped by North Americans or Europeans. Not least among handicaps are the human ones. These frequently hinder advancement even more than do the misplaced mountains, the poor soils, and the jungles with their almost unbridgeable rivers and misleading luxuriance. These conclusions have been thrust upon me by South America itself. I originally set off southward with the usual assortment of mirages. One by one, the beckoning frontiers exposed their bleakness or stark poverty behind that golden haze. Instead of virgin territory, I often found lands that had been examined at intervals by hardy and intelligent pioneers during hundreds of years. Some of the explorers left enduring settlements. Others, if they survived, gave up the quest as unprofitable.

There are opportunities in South America, but seldom if ever will they be found in the romanticized form made popular by uninformed enthusiasms. Actually it would be difficult to design a continent with more massive natural handicaps.

Andes: Unyielding Barrier

Tides of human advancement, as waves of the sea, wash against the Andes only to recede and surge again. Wherever men beach their craft along the entire northern and western shores of South America, they face a wall of steep ridges leading up to glacier-riven peaks. Sometimes a narrow coastal strip provides a base of operations for efforts to surmount the wall. Never does the wall itself lower forbidding heights enough to provide easy or profitable passage toward the interior.

Sheer magnitudes of extension and height explain why the Andes dominate South America's scene. To measure these mountains and square around them the frame of our canvas in its world setting, we need a compass with arms equal to the earth's radius. When the compass has been extended to embrace the Andes, significant comparisons with other continents are possible. One compass point, pivoted at Gibraltar, projects the other point beyond the North Pole to Bering Straits. An arc swung southward from that Alaskan point takes in Russia and most of Siberia. The line bisects China, passes Ceylon, Madagascar, and Africa's Cape of Good Hope—with open ocean to spare as wide as Texas. The same compass, set in the Atlantic Ocean a thousand miles offshore from New York, would dip its other point in the Pacific a thousand miles beyond San Francisco.

Such is the length of the Andes. With related ranges they total 5500 miles from the Peninsula of Paria on South America's northeastern shoulder to Cape Horn. Their breadth varies from a few miles, near the extremities, to 400 miles in Colombia and Bolivia. Their height is exceeded only by the Himalayas. Yet in total volume the Andes dwarf Asia's most impressive mountain chain. The Peruvian Andes alone nearly equal the Himalayas' total base area. All of Europe's Alps, including the summit of Mont Blanc, would disappear under the floor of the *altiplano*.

The remarkable continuity of South America's mountain wall is its distinguishing feature. In such an extension of mountains it is reasonable to expect some gateways, some valleys all the way through, some natural aids to the engineer. Not one pass is opened at levels or locations that would speed economical and large-scale traffic. The only low passes are so far south that the lands they serve on either side of the Cordillera require no more than a track for herds of sheep. An occasional adventurous tourist matches the springs of his car against the bad roads. At their extreme northeastern extension the mountains are little more than ripples of rock compared with the soaring mass of the main Andes. Yet those ripples would be considered high mountains almost anywhere else. Starting in Venezuela and combing the eroded gorges all the way south, explorers during hundreds of years have located no break to release the narrow Pacific Coast into the broad hinterland.

Only one fragile pair of rails so far provides a way for laboring locomotives to shove and snort their way clear across. This is the line between Santiago, Chile, and Mendoza, Argentina. To ride by rail or automobile across that pass, Uspallata by name, is to realize how slight a dent men have made in the Great Wall of South America.

It is a tortuous hundred miles. By air or by land, the massive pyramid of Mt. Aconcagua, 23,081 feet high, is seen as a reminder that the Andes here attain their highest, even while breaking serrated crests to permit a rugged and costly passage. From earliest times this cleft has served barefoot migrants, then beasts of burden, Spanish *conquistadores*, and finally, modern transport.

In a commercial plane on the main transcontinental run, Uspallata is crossed in an hour. The ship climbs twenty minutes, sometimes spiraling with a condor's easy grace of wing, then levels off across the hump at from 16,000 to 20,000 feet, depending on the weather. Twenty minutes at top altitude, and another twenty sloping down to Mendoza on the Argentine side, or Santiago when the flight is to Chile—such is the compression of time made possible by Andean scions of Kitty Hawk.

On a clear day, this flight can be one of the most majestic and satisfying known to aviation. Opposite Aconcagua the plane seems barely to move in full view of ridges that thrust upward and north and south until the upper world glistens with crystalline whiteness in a sky of wind-swept blue. It is awe-inspiring to realize that the procession of mighty peaks in view to farthest horizons is only a small sample of the Andes. Then the canyon narrows. Black precipices rise, snow-seamed, dead ahead. They slide past so close that one wing tip seems about to scrape.

Barren rock prevails all the way across, for this pass is in an arid zone. The sun gleams on a kaleidoscope of colors from buff to slate gray and reddish hues. Lago del Inca, emerald green between rock-strewn slopes that wedge it in a deep declivity at an elevation of 9000 feet, is the only sheet of water passed. Thin white torrents foam toward the small rivers of this canyon maze.

The air passage is so easy that the Great Wall seems hardly to exist except as a scenic attraction. On land the wall rears its bulk, creased by a tenuous line, but unconquered. An experienced and fast driver can cross in twelve to fourteen hours with time for border formalities and transit of the international tunnel. In an Argentine car, I left Santiago at 4 o'clock one morning. We stopped briefly at Los Andes. This is the usual overnight stop for train passengers, who leave Santiago one day, and arrive at Mendoza late the following afternoon.

That is, when the train runs. So exposed is the roadbed to freshets and landslides that whole sections have been swept away at times. For several years a large gap had to be crossed by automobile. Chileans charged that Argentina deliberately delayed repair work for political and economic reasons. Shortly after my last crossing, rail service was resumed.

Riding in a car packed with Chilean and Argentine passengers, I saw what this wall means to South America in terms of obstruction. The road is gravel. It cuts through the treeless pass in view of an arroyo marked with signs of frequent floods, although the steady volume of water is small. This characteristic of the Andes is puzzling at first. They are so high, so expansive, it seems those snow-covered roofs should pour down all the water needed by thirsty lowlands. It is not so. Only where tropical rains deluge the Andes, along the upper rim of the Amazon Basin, do great rivers form. In the entire length of their coastal side, and on the southern half of their eastern slopes, the Andes produce only two significant rivers—the Magdalena in Colombia and the Guayas in Ecuador. For the rest, there are only small streams that carry no shipping, or soon become unnavigable as they rise in rapids. Evidently the explanations for scanty water from the Andes are many. Upper airs at such altitudes deposit less snow than might be expected. Moist air is heavy and seldom is driven to the heights. At 20,000 to 23,000 feet, snows turn to ice and only slowly yield their relief to parched valleys. The very expanse of the Andes and their general lack of moisture-gripping forests cause tremendous losses through evaporation except on lower slopes of the wet tropics.

Such thoughts journey with us—the Chileans, the Argentines, and the lone North American—as we thread through desolate ravines where only an occasional oasis of green appears at some wayside village. As we climb, even the oases disappear. Ordinary conceptions of size fail to take in the scene. There are gorges too immense to comprehend during the jolting moments while they are in view. The next-to-last barrier raised by the Andes across this lowest pass of the central massif is a rock slide that cascades from above as an amorphous staircase. Tackling that slide resembles rushing at a steep glacier turned to rock. There is a feeling of underlying instability, as though the slide may give way at any moment. The road builders have piled surface stones to form switchbacks of acute angles and sudden upward surges.

In the rapidly thinning air, we level off at the western entrance of the international tunnel. Uspallata Pass above us crosses at 12,795 feet elevation. The tunnel bores through solid rock in a costly effort to make this lofty pass economically feasible by reducing its height. The crude tunnel is two miles long. Its highest elevation is 10,486 feet. A single set of rails and the rough roadbed for automobiles leave an impression of how slight is the grip held by men on transport across this barrier. Yet Uspallata represents the pinnacle of Andean conquest on land after centuries of effort.

The only other railways that reach the central Cordillera,

without crossing it all the way, are compelled to climb even higher. There are five. One is from sea level at Antofagasta in the coastal desert of northern Chile. Another begins at Arica to the north of Antofagasta and makes connections on the *altiplano* after crossing passes of 15,000 feet elevation. These lines have access to Cochabamba, 8400 feet high on eastern slopes of the Bolivian Andes. A third railway runs from the Peruvian port of Mollendo to Lake Titicaca and Cuzco. The fourth rises from Lima, Peruvian capital, to the copper-smelting town of Oroyo. This is the highest standard-gauge railway in the world, touching 15,806 feet. The last Andean rail crossing connects Guayaquil, Ecuador's principal seaport, with Quito, the capital. Otherwise there are only short and isolated lines.

To grasp what Andean railways have to contend with both in construction and operation, North Americans have only to imagine that the Andes have been lifted bodily and placed cross-wise on the United States. At each end the lower ranges would extend seaward. Across the entire North American continent, an obstruction would suddenly have been raised so high that even the loftiest peaks of Colorado and California would serve only as underpinning for the upper plateaus. A mountain climber on the highest pinnacle of the Rockies would find himself looking out across level ground. That would be the floor on which people plow and run railways and breathe the rarefied air, from Denver to Chicago.

Then the mountains begin, and go up—up—up—to more than four and a half miles above the sea.

In the presence of the Andes, all mountains of the United States shrink in magnitude, but expand in utility. The Rockies, Sierra Nevada, Alleghenies, White Mountains, and lesser ranges are so placed that they can be by-passed or crossed with comparative ease. The Andes are not similarly convenient. Suppose every railway from the northern United States to the South had to cross passes of from 12,000 to 15,000 feet!

South America's *altiplano* is a world apart, largely because modern transport has hardly begun to open its doors. Peoples native to its atmosphere are of necessity rugged. Here only the strong survive. Chests expand to draw more oxygen from thin air. Toil shapes massive torsos. Legs are muscular and sturdy from daily treks of unbelievable distance across the rough terrain. Foreheads brace against straps that run over the shoulders to hold loads seemingly beyond human capacity. Cheeks of bronze show rich color under the nippings of frost. Faces often are refined, not flat-nosed or coarse. The South American mountain Indian is far more advanced in physique and culture than the river Indian. In the Andes have flourished empires of the Incas and earlier peoples long lost to human knowledge except in their mute temples. Skill in masonry was not matched by chiseled hieroglyphs. Writing, if it appeared among those early peoples, did not reach a form permanent enough to tell us their story. More can be read about the past in the bearing of some Andean Indians. At a few points may still be seen individuals and communities retaining qualities worthy of a once independent mountain race.

At Otavalo, north from Quito in Ecuador, night fades toward market day. Along every road in predawn dimness move lines of men, women, children, and animals. Color makes itself felt even before its hues can be distinguished. Brighter tones first appear—brilliant crimsons in wool fabrics tossed with careless grace over the upturned brims of heavy white felt hats, other scarves that remind me of luminous yellows used by Andrea del Sarto, pale blues, cerise, turquoise, emerald. As the crisp air becomes a golden transparency beneath skies of blue native only to the upper atmosphere, costumes disclose an advanced community taste. Navy blue predominates, with pure white used to give accents. The vivid tints are used with moderation, not gaudily.

A magenta headpiece combines beauty with utility. Arrived at the open market square, the Otavalan Indian woman removes the fabric and it turns out to be nothing more than a square carryall. In go a few handfuls of wool bought to keep the slender spindle whirling as she walks home the dusty miles. Six eggs follow . . . vegetables . . . pinches of dye selected with mature care from the score of pots in front of the dye merchant and done up in bits of old paper . . . a square of fabric . . . some new necklaces . . . potatoes and dried beans—to mention only a few of her purchases.

An Otavalan of lordly mien strides through the market. His head is erect. Braided black hair runs straight down his back in a queue from under the brim of that characteristic upturned white felt. It is a stiff headpiece three-sixteenths of an inch thick. The crown is fitted close to the head inside the brim's broad circle. Not a trace of the downtrodden Indian shows in this figure. With quiet self-confidence but not assertiveness, he moves as one conscious of a dignified heritage. His wife follows a step or two behind. Both are immaculately clean, even though their bare feet are dusty from the road. White woolens are kept white by scrubbing in the lake. These Indians bathe, many of them every day. They use various soapy substances, including a reed that makes suds.

Lines of design in costumes show refinement and discrimination achieved with utmost simplicity. As in India, feminine elegance is expressed by overlapping two plain fabrics, or forming circular spirals around the figure without benefit of stereotyped patterns. Color is consciously combined with prevailing good taste. So the plaza of moving humanity glints with the subdued richness of a stained glass window.

Dimming this native South American glory of color and intrinsic art are squalor and drunkenness, filth and poverty, in the same market. I have been describing the élite of all the Andean peoples who had their own cultures here before the Spaniards shattered them.

In and around Otavalo are Indian landowners whose wealth is calculated at 30,000 *sucres*. In its setting this sum, equivalent to $2100, is a sizable fortune. One of the few non-Indian residents of Otavalo complained to me that the Indians own nearly everything in the countryside! The best of these Otavalan Indians could walk down Fifth Avenue in New York, bare feet and all, without loss of dignity. They would fit into any cosmopolitan setting as easily as a lady from Chungking with her split silk skirt and high plain collar, or a Burmese prince in London.

Among the Otavalans flashes a lively wit and sense of humor. In the cool evening after market has closed, they foregather in homes of friends, or sit in the open plaza to watch their own brand of fireworks. Skyrockets are made of cornhusks tied around the end of a stick. Explosions are set off after powder has been pounded into a rock mortar.

Music here retains a rhythmic pattern all its own even when sifted through modern band instruments. Every player is an individualist bound by no written score. Many evoke native tones of the Andes from flat rows of bamboo pipes held in their hands. Lips move along the open upper ends of this crude but effective instrument. Pitch depends entirely on the depth and diameter of each bamboo note. There are no reeds or mechanical adjustments. This is music of high winds fluting against mountain crags. The piercing melody is caught on a handful of crude pipes and poured, throbbing, through a village street. Somewhere, sometime, a few brasses made their way into this band. Woodwinds known to the outside world also swell the strange harmonies. A definite melodic cycle unfolds with cold fire and crescendo, with melancholy and release, always fused in an underlying rhythm that sways both the musicians and the feet of dancing Indians who mass around them.

These are basic intonations of the Andes, as characteristic as the *Samba* in Brazil or the dance known as *La Cueca* in Chile. For these people, music and dancing are one inseparable artistic outlet. Local variations occur from Ecuador southward through the highlands of Peru and Bolivia, but the same motivations drive individual dancers in their gyrations. There is a whirling, hopping step under it all, woven in and out with paths chosen at random by other dancers. Heads and shoulders bend low and then rise with waving arms to give an effect of human whirlpools, flowing together in ever-changing contours. Vivid coloring of everyday clothes or the special costumes worn on days of fiesta blend rare dyes in the scene. Colors are mixed with the untutored skill of nature, as wildflowers that never clash, however brilliant their pigments.

Otavalo, for me, excels among Indian communities in the New

World. The closest approximation comes in Guatemala. Not even the Indians of upper Peru and its famed Cuzco attain the quality of the Otavalans, in my judgment. Bolivia's colors are brilliant but brash in comparison with the clarity and modulated richness of Otavalo's.

Although the Andes are heavily populated in relation to the Amazon and many other parts of South America, these mountains have none of the livable qualities found supremely in the Swiss Alps. Men move in an austere, overpowering setting at altitudes far above those to which most of mankind is accustomed. One of the most characteristic sights of the *altiplano* is a lone Indian bent under a heavy load and hurrying across the boulder-strewn plateau where herds of llamas and alpacas graze. These animals thrive on the thin fodder. Snow-covered peaks or cones of volcanoes adorn the horizon.

Violent contrasts occur along the entire mountain chain. Opposite Trinidad, jungled forerunners of the Andes rise from typical river lowlands. A range is crossed. The land becomes suddenly arid. It might be Utah or southern Palestine. Folds of ocher earth lead back to the sea, where islands lump like fantastic dinosaurs molded of clay in some past age and set down on a sea of polished emeralds to bake vermilion in the sun.

This misplaced desert and others farther south are explained by winds, the Andes themselves, ocean currents, and a fierce tropical sun. Latitude has nothing to do with it. Jungle and desert alternate on the same parallels. Upward-jutting Andean ridges thrust their baffle plates two, three, or even more than four miles straight up across the path of winds moving in from sea level. Masses of air are hurled literally thousands of feet. So it is that a moisture-laden stratum of atmosphere rolls up one side of a ridge and drenches the jungle, then bounces from the top and does not strike earth again for miles, or possibly drops in the sea. Flying into Bogotá, Colombia's capital, I have been caught in an updraft that lifted the plane a thousand feet in a few seconds. Our seats in the trembling fuselage become individual elevators driven upward as by rocket propulsion.

Coastal deserts occur along the Caribbean, then give way to

jungle. Wet tropics prevail southward through the wild Chocó
region of Colombia, opposite Panama, to Guayaquil, chief seaport
of Ecuador. Not many miles beyond Guayaquil the coastal Andes
change almost as by the turn of a switch. Scores of foaming
torrents have been visible at the same time in deep jungled
canyons. The plane heads across a bay. The next land seen is
desert so nearly absolute that gray dust blows as though water
never has touched it. Here begins the moonlike desolation that
rises slowly from the Pacific and then abruptly vaults in piles
of rock resembling clinkers and broken furnace brick. I recall
with what incredulity I inwardly received a comment by Dr.
Víctor Andrés Belaúnde, eminent Peruvian scholar and publicist,
when he said to me in 1931 during an Inter-American Institute
at Gainesville, Florida:

"My country is a land of rock and sand."

He shouldn't be wrong, and yet—could that be all of Peru?

Dr. Belaúnde spoke as a cultivated Peruvian to whom Lima
with its broad avenues set in an irrigated oasis, and other parts of
the easily accessible coast, constitute the country in all essentials.
A later generation is breaking through into the interior, crossing
the Andes, and discovering a new empire in the tropical hinterland—decidedly not rock and sand. Yet in terms of the entire
Peruvian coast except a bit in the extreme north, and the whole
massive bulk of the Peruvian Andes west of their forested
Amazonian slopes, Dr. Belaúnde's remark is strictly accurate. He
overstated his case for effect. Possibly Dr. Belaúnde had found
that North American illusions about South America's fertility
would not budge under moderate statements. This is still a
puzzling preference of many intelligent people who seem to cling
to childhood notions about South America even against eye-
witness reports by qualified observers.

Lima proves that wherever water awakens this Peruvian dust,
it springs with verdure. Anyone looking for ways to relieve the
parched plains and slopes along 2500 miles of Peruvian and
Chilean ocean frontage turns instinctively to the snow-topped
Andes. In the midst of coastal aridity I scan distant snows and
wonder whether irrigation may not be possible on a far larger

scale than anything yet seen. The answer is no, beyond relatively small gains. The Andes, in one of those strange contradictions that abound here, do not provide enough water for the coast, even if all of it were impounded and ditched. The side of the Cordillera that most needs irrigation has small and uncertain streams, yet on the other side torrents pour down into already drenched jungle. So the Andes in this central sector constitute a double deficit that weighs heavily. They throttle passage eastward to the watered hinterland. They cut off wet winds blowing from the east that might share some of their moisture with the coast.

As though these weren't enough handicaps, the ocean reaches out from Antarctica and snatches away most of the rain that normally should sweep inland from the humid expanse of the South Pacific. It is heartbreaking, when you know the desperate need for water ashore, to stand on the deck of a ship and see rain pouring down as cold gray pellets into the sea.

Our ship has sailed from Panama. There the weather was hot and moist. Ship's officers were in tropical whites. Heat prevailed to the sea passage between Ecuador and the Galápagos Islands, named for their large turtles. During the night we have steamed into a different climate. Low fog all but hides the blaze of the equatorial sun. We are squarely on the Equator, yet this might be the North Atlantic except for the strangely felt presence, above the fog, of that burning sun. Its heat collides forcibly with waves of cold air that move above icy ocean currents.

Again South America, even at sea, proves itself a continent of violent extremes. The Humboldt Current, laden with frigidity from ice cliffs of Antarctica, here swings away from shore after changing the climate of half the South American Pacific Coast. So an ocean current causes Peruvian and Chilean deserts where there should be lush vegetation. Enough rain falls into the sea to make a garden of this wasteland. Coastal plains and those lower clinker peaks could be clothed with green up to the timber line. Agriculture could thrive. Waterpower could course down from upper ridges to increase industrial possibilities.

Instead, the entire land from Peru's oil fields at Talara south nearly to Santiago de Chile lies stripped to the naked rock. Volcanic ash that carries fresh fertility from depths of earth and could support many crops, fills sterile gullies. In flight I have seen the dove-gray sprinklings of ash blown into patterns of fern fossils on rusty red stone.

Only at rare intervals a stream manages to survive from some glacier that turns toward the Pacific at distant altitudes of 16,000 to 20,000 feet. Lima's oasis is kept vernal by the Rio Rimac, a boulder-strewn torrent of such small volume that it would rank as little more than a brook among rivers coursing by thousands down eastern slopes of the Andes into the Amazon Basin.

This coast is a zone of melancholy superlatives. Washed by the world's largest ocean, it is within 100 to 200 miles of the world's largest river system in a drenched jungle. Yet here is one of the most desolate coasts on earth.

Warm winds freighted with relief from the Pacific are dehydrated as they blow through cold air above the Humboldt Current. Their moisture is removed as effectively as though labyrinths of blotters rose in their path. When they emerge on the other side and reach land, they bring no regular showers, not even the "small rain upon the tender herb." Once in a great while the mist or fog that prevails for several months becomes heavy enough to be called a sprinkle. More rarely, a brief rain actually falls. Then the mountainsides burst into transient bloom. Hidden in this ankle-deep dust are many latent possibilities, as Lima proves with its brilliant flowers and luscious strawberries. Yet young Peruvians who have been reared in Lima tell me they never saw rain as we know it until they went into central and southern Chile.

The other apparent avenue of relief for this parched land is blocked by the Andes. Winds blow in the right direction, since Amazonian rains are borne inland from the northeast. Already moist from the Atlantic, they gather new vapor as they pass over 2000 to 3000 miles of saturated river lowlands and tropical rain forest. They arrive at eastern foothills of the Andes so laden that on slight provocation they condense in cloudbursts. All along the eastern slopes are forests and rivers, until this paradoxical continent reverses the picture farther south. Yet opposite the entire 2500 miles of desert coast, wet tropics prevail from Peru's jungled interior to the "Garden of Argentina" in Tucumán Province.

It seems incredible that any wall could restrain such wind-blown luxuriance from washing over the other side, at least enough to feed a few great rivers, and break this no man's land here or there.

It is incredible, but the Andes are like that. There is no pass, even for the winds. Searching, they drop their vaporous ballast and roll ever higher. The higher they blow the drier they become until, as they tumble over crags and crests and plateaus to fall at length on the Pacific side, nothing remains to awaken the coast from its torpid sleep beneath undulating blankets of radiated heat, or oppressive fog. Such conditions prevail along half of South America's Pacific shore.

Because of the Andes, there are geographically three distinct parts of the countries from Venezuela to Chile. They are the coast, mountains, and hinterland.

On the Caribbean, Venezuela's coast alternates between jungle and desert. The mountain-rimmed valley of Caracas at 3000 feet is typical of livable uplands that continue through Colombia and Ecuador but disappear in the central *altiplano*. Venezuela's interior along dwindling ranges steps down to the Orinoco Valley. There grasslands, or *llanos,* combine with tropical rivers and jungle, some desert, and spectacular mountains in the border-lands toward British Guiana. This is the region of remote escarpments where the aviator Jimmy Angel discovered a waterfall that is not yet officially accepted at his altimeter reading of a mile high.

Colombia largely escapes deserts on its coastal plain and lower Andes. Both are heavily forested beyond the marshy valley of the Magdalena River. Bogotá, Colombia's capital, is set in a broad and fertile plateau 8660 feet high. The Andes here are almost unbelievably jumbled, yet Colombia is favored with pleasant highlands. Valleys and climate are more reminiscent of North American plateaus than are many other parts of the Andes. Colombia's hinterland drops away from the mountains through grasslands and occasional forests to the Orinoco-Amazon wilderness.

In Ecuador a short train trip dramatically illustrates the effect of the Andes where they interpose their climate-juggling bulk across a zone of the wet tropics. This is the start of the overland trip to Otavalo and its colorful Indian market. It is also the setting for Ben Hecht's play, *To Quito and Back*. Guayaquil is the coastal terminus, set inland on the estuary of the Guayas River. Along an esplanade of unexpected grandeur, Guayaquil is replete with statuary, a clock tower, river wall, paved streets, landing platforms, and parked walks where seats are shaded by trees. In the river float islands of vegetation that has broken loose from jungle banks. Hyacinths predominate. Their lavender and white blossoms bob along above silt-laden currents. The launch shoves off. It chugs upstream to the opposite bank where a train waits. A first-class ticket for a numbered seat does not mean a shoehorn wouldn't be of use in squeezing yourself on board through passengers and towering luggage. This is typical Andean train travel, so few are the railways.

The train clangs forward through marshlands. Palmetto huts are built on stilts six or more feet high to be above flood level. Earth has been filled under some of the huts to form islands in the swamps. Pigs lie in the shade. Banana plantations and cacao provide the principal occupations of the lowland dwellers. These people are drab in clothing and subdued in bearing compared with the more independent highlanders. Along the line at way stations, venders offer bananas—fine large juicy ones—for the equivalent of 1½ cents the dozen in United States coin!

Even by train the transition from wet tropics to semiarid tropics is remarkably swift. Soon the laboring locomotive starts to climb along a small river. From languid waters the stream rises to foam in quickening rapids. Stilts under houses shorten to the vanishing point. Banana plantations become steep, and finally give way to cactus. Dust blows. Yet through the same windows only a short while before, I had seen distant flocks of white egrets settling over marshes.

Difficulties of railway construction in the Andes are driven home by a set of switchbacks known as the Devil's Nose. A precipice bars the way. Engineers have vaulted it by running their tracks forward on a shelf that has been cut in the face of the cliff. The train runs ahead on this shelf and then backs on a switch until it can resume forward motion on a higher level. Our conductor shouts at a sleepy Indian who almost doesn't throw the hand switch in time as we near the edge of the abyss!

Trees that have crowded the lower slopes give way to barren ranges and valleys. Eucalyptus groves are being planted to provide windbreaks and firewood. They are seen all along the upper Andes, as well as increasingly in Brazil. Not native to South America, these imported forests from Australia thrive. They are changing the contours of South American landscapes and introducing uniformity where great diversity once reigned. As a fast-growing and hardy producer of wood, the eucalyptus pays, but it is taking away the continent's individuality. It is unfortunate that some native tree could not be found to do the same work without making this part of the world look like Southern California or Australia.

As soon as the mid-zone of rocky canyons has been left behind, a different world appears. This is the realm of Indians who live on the tops of rounded mountains where soil is deep and fertile, at altitudes most people would find oppressive. The patchwork fields are reached by deeply rutted footpaths. Already the human color of the highlands is boldly stroked across the landscape as Indians tread those paths.

Gone is the drab coast. Gone is the rain-soaked forest. Within a few hours by slow train we have sampled one of the most significant and characteristic features of the Andes all along their northern extension from parts of Venezuela through Colombia and Ecuador into the northernmost tip of Peru. We have left sea level in the wet tropics and climbed over a pass 11,842 feet high. The route has been lined with volcanoes. Often their slopes rise from the bleak *páramos,* or lofty moors, to curve upward along the line of old lava flows in a weird half-light. They plunge from sight in a heavy cloud ceiling. Once in a while the fortunate traveler has a day of full sunlight on the glistening cones of Chimborazo, Tungurahua, or Altar. From Ecuador's heights it is only a short distance eastward to low wet tropics of the interior, but transport is almost nonexistent.

All of coastal Peru except the northernmost tip is desert. Thin lines of green mark watercourses that cut briefly across the desolation. Only beyond the Cordillera does Peru luxuriate in a watered realm that is gradually being tapped by transport, and settled.

As the Andes march south through Bolivia, they are mirrored in Lake Titicaca. *Balsa* boats of reed, as well as the steamship line between Peru and Bolivia, ply its surface, 12,500 feet above the sea. Here the Andes buttress their central massif between the white pyramids of Illimani and Illampú. La Paz, Bolivia's capital, is cupped in a deep valley at the foot of Illimani. The upper rim of the valley is eroded to form rows of minarets. Highest capital in the world, La Paz at 12,200 feet elevation exceeds even Lhasa in Tibet.

Gradually, as the Amazon Basin is left behind, eastern slopes of the Andes thin in vegetation. Opposite the *Gran Chaco* and *pampa* in central lowlands of the continent, Andean ridges become as scorched as they are on the Pacific exposure. At this point the Chilean and Argentine border along the Andean divide bisects an arid zone that continues far south. On the Chilean side, coastal deserts merge north of Santiago in the fertile and watered central valley. Argentina's arid plains, hemmed in by the Andes from rains that fall liberally in Chile, sweep southward into Patagonia. There are occasional deserts. The treeless expanse only yields to forests in the lake district that begins some 500 miles south of Santiago.

Chile's normal rains from the South Pacific blow inland across the central valley without being condensed offshore by cold ocean currents. Those strike farther north. Between the Andes and the Coastal Range Chile centers its national life. To describe this land is to run the gamut of scenery. Crossing from Argentina by the main pass to Santiago, a traveler enters almost at the mid-point of Chile's shoestring territory. Here the land resembles Southern California. Even the same light haze, translucent with cloudless sunshine, tinges the hills with purple that pales at each successive range to the opalescence of far horizons.

Arriving at their seashore, Chileans step from fast interurban trains in Viña del Mar. The atmosphere is a composite of California beaches. There are long crescents of sand. Surf runs high. It breaks on rocky promontories.

The central valley, like the San Joaquin Valley in California, washes against great mountains on the inland side, and is separated from the Pacific by low coastal ranges. Unlike the San Joaquin, this Chilean valley has no deserts. Those are all in the northern half of Chile. Instead, the valley deepens in verdure as it goes south. Rows of poplars, planted to break the wind over well-tended fields, give place to huge stumps in cleared pastures, and then to uncut forest.

In Chile's southland there is always the breath of ice just under the edge of the air. It is felt even when the sun beats down with shafts of warmth, raising wisps of steam from bosky meadows to float among gigantic trees. Along forest paths stand trunks resembling small Sequoias and Redwoods. Yet twelve to fifteen feet is not an unusual diameter. The orange-red bark rounds away upward to disappear in erect branches and a tufted top of vivid green. Chileans know and love this part of their country. First of the Chilean lakes south from Santiago is Lago Villarica, reflecting in its waters the stately cone of a volcano bearing the same name. This volcano and Lanín form the most famous pair of peaks in Chile. Snow-clad all year, Villarica and Lanín adorn the landscape and are used as motifs for many illustrations. Resembling Fujiyama and Vesuvius, they represent Chile's spectacular southland.

Through the Chilean countryside here grow wild blackberries in profusion. Women and boys gather them in baskets and buckets. I, too, have emerged from the thickets looking like the small boy who has been in the pantry. Wild roses, wild blackberries, and wild Fuchsias often are found growing in one colorful and delicious bouquet of Chilean nature. Leaving the main north-south rail line at Loncoche, I turn inland toward the Cordillera. The climb at times is sufficient to send creakings of effort through the train. The rail terminus in the town of Villarica is reached at the western end of the lake. Busses then bound along for an hour to Pucón at the eastern end. Pucón combines the atmosphere of a western cattle town with that of a lakeside resort, the whole in a setting that is all Chilean. The main street, wide and dusty, runs from a small bay of the lake directly toward the Andes. The road beyond winds across into Argentina over one of the few passes suitable for motor transport. Clapboard houses gray with dust resemble those of many a cattle town in the United States. The adobe houses usually associated with Latin America do not occur in this part of Chile. Timber is abundant.

Oxcarts creak past, their drivers standing against loads of ripened grain, and controlling the animals with prods of a long bamboo pole. The lake's shores are rocky, and the forest remains uncut as a reminder of how magnificent this country was before fire ran through its redolent evergreens. The hotel fronts a curving beach in the grand manner. The atmosphere is as far removed from the cattle town outside as though a bit of the Riviera had dropped down across the Andes. Sporty vacationers ply rod and reel, ride horseback, or sail. A small excursion steamer docks across a peninsula near the hotel. Long before the hour of departure the crew toots the whistle to attract passengers, and toots again. The cruise resembles those on the Lake of Geneva, except that some of the snow-clad mountains in view here are smoking volcanoes. Villarica towers behind the hotel as the boat rounds the peninsula. A wisp of white fumes trails from the distant crater. At the eastern end of the lake the steamer anchors while those who want an extra excursion take rowboats into the *rinconada*. *Rincón* means corner in Spanish. In winding channels of the *rinconada* there are many nooks of unsuspected charm. Clear water reveals waving vegetation beneath the surface. Banks are overhung with shrubs that have a diminutive, storybook quality. At one point a slender waterfall springs from the heights above, its whisper blending into the quietude of the *rinconada*. This beautiful spot has lately been ravaged by fire, the scourge of Chile's southern regions.

The countryside in this part of Chile is so distinctive that anyone who has seen it once could be dropped by parachute at night and soon know where he is. An unmistakable feature is the custom of making fences from the logs of trees. These barriers might be called walls rather than fences, for each log is cut and set upright in the ground tight against the next log. As the diameter runs up to a foot and a half at times, or even more on occasions, whole droves of cattle would have a hard time pushing the fences over. Another feature that stamps the region as close to pioneer days is the prevalence of bare tree trunks still standing. Long ago they were stripped by fire of their leaves and smaller branches. The process of clearing the land goes on. Flame is the ax that first cuts into dense forests. Where the stumps have been removed, fields roll pleasantly. Elsewhere the skeletons of trees provide a seared foreground that runs up the slopes of Andean foothills. Beyond, the peaks compensate with untouched magnificence.

Chile's fertile valley is well-watered, and the loveliest river of them all is justly named the Rio Bueno. A chain of lakes, increasing in size, drops this stream by stages from the crest of the Andes. The last of these is Lago Ranco, mirroring islands and fed by many clear currents that converge at the outlet to form the Bueno. Something there is in the character of this river that sets it apart. The main rail line follows the Bueno for a few miles. That brief acquaintance is enough to explain why Chileans call it the Good River. If ever water smiled and exuded good cheer, this is it. The Bueno rolls over and over as it goes, much as a seal disports itself for the sheer joy of rhythmic motion. Where the railway crosses, Rio Bueno is coasting toward the sea through level meadows. Yet the whole surface pirouettes in eddies that bubble up from clear depths. However placidly the Bueno appears to flow when seen from a short distance, this is no sluggish stream. Born in rushing rivulets that rise where the Chilean-Argentine Andes cup the most secluded of world-famed lakes, the Bueno carries its clarity and vitality into the lowlands.

Each river in this region of Chile, and there are many, is distinctive. One of the tributaries of the Bueno is the Negro, or Black River. Whether the dark color is due to the soil, or shadows of the deep banks that overhang its course, this moody stream contrasts sharply with the open friendliness of Rio Bueno.

All of the watercourses lead down from the Cordillera to the Pacific. Benjamín Subercaseaux in his richly human book on Chilean geography complains that the rivers escape through the coastal range too soon, instead of running lengthwise along the central valley. Had they done so, this part of Chile might have been made as rich as the Valley of the Nile with sedimentary fertility now swept into the sea.

Even so, Chile's valley extending southward from Santiago for nearly 500 miles is the heart of the country. The sandy wastes of the north yield to pleasant fields. In a climate resembling that of Southern California thrive fruits, olives, grapes, cattle, and wheat. Central Chile provides a welcome relief from the fierce glare of the northern deserts and moody clouds that darken the southern region for much of the year. The pioneer land below Puerto Montt overpowers with its untamed beauty on those rare days when clear sun reveals its gigantic trees in uncut forests, its ice fields hundreds of miles long, its fjords, icebergs, lakes of milky glacial blue, and violent rivers. By contrast with the subantarctic south and the baked sterility of the north, Rio Bueno represents the Chile of mellow harvests. As I caught swift glimpses of distant snow-covered volcanoes across the ripened wheat, and took interest in the diversity of streams sent hastening down from the Andes, I met and left too soon the Bueno, a distillation of snow and sky, rollicking toward the sea.

In Southern Chile, as in Maine, the aroma of wood smoke floats pleasantly on the rural air. Both are about the same distance from the Equator, in opposite hemispheres. Chile, too, has a rockbound coast. At Valdivia, an indentation leads inland to the city by way of a bay and river channel. Shipping is concentrated at the port of Corral, just inside the shoulder that nudges aside the heaviest swells of the South Pacific. Between Valdivia and Corral runs a wood-burning packet line—German-Chilean, as it would be in this part of the country. These river and lake boats are one of the most pleasant features in a land of many delights for those who enjoy nature on the near edge of pioneer days. The full story of wood-burning boats in Southern Chile and Argentinian Patagonia would fill an alluring volume. Some of these boats have been transported overland in pieces. They were reassembled on the shores of lakes frigid with glacial water that reflects walls of ice or the grandeur of peaks on surfaces of milky blue.

Each day in season on the large lake of Llanquihue at Puerto Varas, the wood-burner that carries tourists and residents into the heart of the Lake District may be heard tooting merrily for its departure in early morning, or scurrying homeward at sunset with a whistling that seems reinvigorated after a day on such waters. Always there is the spicy aroma of wood as it is pulled from the hold in sticks about three feet long and heaved into the sizzling furnace. There are no Keep Out signs to prevent an intimate view of the fireman at work. He also is engineer, majordomo of the cargo, and an amiable conversationalist. After a few minutes aboard one of these Chilean boats, the passengers feel like shipmates. If it is chilly on deck—and it usually is—the small cabin with its wide windows offers a welcome retreat every so often. Inside the cabin formality melts. Yet of all the excursion and pleasure boats known to this writer, none has been more courteous.

On the Valdivia-Corral run, we were advised some time ahead of sailing by the usual series of whistles. Mellow waves of sound permeated the quiet town. The *Bremen* was tied up in the river. On the opposite bank, the sign of a large German firm was in full view. As passengers arrived, the German element predominated. Young men who could have been Hitler Youth merely by stepping into a uniform, *Frauen* busily gossiping in German as they shepherded their *Kinder* down the short gangplank, blonde *Mädchen* without a trace of Spanish about them, older German men of the citizenry which controls most of the business in and around Valdivia—so they came. There were Chileans of non-Germanic descent, too, in a distinct minority. As the boat slips downstream past wooded hills and cultivated fields, many of the groups on deck speak animated German. Spanish is heard in even more animated tones where several young Chileans engage, as they like to do, in good-humored debates and philosophical discussions that range far afield. Chile is a country of great intellectual curiosity. Its bookstores are filled with titles on an amazing array of topics. Inexpensive editions speed the process of popular reading.

Several times the boat stops alongside wooden quays. A *madre* in black shawl tries to unload a sack of flour while holding her *niño,* and ready hands come to her aid. The air begins to smell of the sea, and then Corral is reached. Chile has an iron smelter here. Its black stacks fill a ravine to the left of the town as we come in. German business signs are spread to view on the dockside. I soon hear of a German resort hotel around the promontory seaward. German-Chilean merchant ships lie at anchor. As I land, another of them bears in from the sea. It is not to be concluded that all of these German-Chileans are Nazis, although the proportion of those who instinctively respond to the call of their distant *Vaterland* must be high. They and their forebears colonized this part of Chile. In early evening I left Corral. The *Bremen* slipped away from the dock at the German hotel, and churned upstream pungent with its own invisible perfume of burning wood.

No impression of southern Chile is more vividly with me than the basement in Valdivia where a few courageous Chileans were publishing a weekly newspaper, *El Popular,* while the Nazis were bestriding a temporarily conquered Europe. Four German-Chilean papers dominated the southern press. Edgardo Mewes, youthful Chilean democrat, faced a German boycott when he raised his voice against the Nazis. He had to import newsprint and ink from Santiago, nearly 500 miles to the north. Shut out of suitable buildings by Germans who own most of Valdivia, he carried on from a basement, helping readjust the news balance at one of the focal points as Chile struggled to find itself in relation to the war.

Over these southern parts of Chile and Argentina, where magnificent lakes and forests grace both sides of the Andes, broods an indefinable sense of transition between the Temperate Zone and the subantarctic. The dusty carelessness of easygoing vegetation gives place to grasses virile and supple, waiting in hushed animation to withstand polar winds. South from Chile's port of Punta Arenas in Magellan's Strait the Andes reach out toward Weddell Sea and Little America.

Although the mountains are far lower than in the northern ranges, they still shoot great peaks skyward. San Valentín soars 13,300 feet near Lago Buenos Aires in a region of lakes farther south than those usually reached by tourists. Mt. Darwin looks down on Beagle Channel from 7640 feet where a tapering promontory formed of mountainous islands points to the last wind-swept and sea-swept cliffs of Cape Horn.

Set as the rarest jeweled mosaic of mountain scenery I have ever seen along the length of the Andes, is Cordillera Paine. Chile's port of Punta Arenas near the center of Magellan's Strait was my point of contact for reaching Paine. The Cordillera is named for its English discoverer. Chileans pronounce it "Piénee." I had come down through Argentine Patagonia overland. In advance I had no assurance of being able to reach Paine. It is on a private sheep ranch, or *estancia*. Sometimes months are required to make arrangements with the owners for a visit. At first no doors opened. I did not have weeks, or even days, to wait during that trip.

By a fortunate chain of events the path to Paine cleared. Several bus lines operate between Punta Arenas and Puerto Natales, the city nearest Paine. I had tried to book a seat on the best day for me, without success. At the last minute a few helpful words were said on my behalf by friends of the bus line operator. As we talked, I learned that he was a brother of Rodolfo Santucci C., General Manager of *Estancia del Rio Paine*, then in Punta Arenas on one of his infrequent business trips. The next day he was leaving for Paine by car with his family. A seat was found for me in another car that accompanied the bus.

Early that morning we were methodically packed in for the long run to Puerto Natales.

At first there was no sign of mountains. Punta Arenas on a clear day catches views of a few distant peaks, but is itself in low and rolling open land. About halfway to Puerto Natales the remnants of superb forests hint the natural glory that luxuriated here before fire and axes laid it low. There are pleasant resort hotels of modest type, where Chileans who have come from Santiago by rail and boat ride, hike, and just vacation. As we neared Puerto Natales the first snowy ranges came into view along a deep fjord. The city lies on the near shore, commanding a view of steep mountains and glaciers.

Puerto Natales is a city built almost entirely of sheet metal exteriors to turn the wind, and so has the color of weathered tin. From Puerto Natales I rode on a small truck of the *estancia* to *La Peninsula*, first outpost of Paine's domains. The Santuccis arrived later that night. We were to sail the following morning on the *estancia's* small steam launch. It had been sent across the Lago del Toro, or Lake of the Bull, for the long run through bays and windy straits to Paine. The launch comes only on special occasions. There is no other way to reach the *estancia* except by horseback.

It turned out to be a choppy voyage after we slipped away from the sheltered pier. As the launch rounded the last headland, Paine's glory began to unfold. The panorama expanded until it filled the horizon on our starboard bow. Rising 8760 feet from nearly sea level, Paine sends a river of the same name through Lago del Toro to fjords and passages that terminate the Andes where they sink beneath icy seas.

Weeks in the saddle would not be too much in the varied environs of this natural masterpiece. The towers of Paine rise in sculptured simplicity above glaciers, lakes, and rivers that tumble in opalescent spray. Ivory-colored stone of the massif has been eroded in deep canyons. Glaciers still cling and carve there aloft. Capping the towers, as they narrow at the top with grace equal to the statuesque lines of a Sequoia trunk, are black crowns.

The stratum of which they alone remain once sloped in such a way that now the strokes of this basaltic brush adorn Paine as Greek architects vivified their luminous temples with black marble accents.

One of the *estancia* riders injected the human element into such magnificence of scenery when he waved a hand and said as we jogged along the trail: "Long ago I have tired of all this."

Sheep started up before us. Otherwise the sound of our horses gave the only sign of habitation. Out on some of the lower mountain pastures another day I was struck by the herding methods. Two men and their dogs were rounding up sheep from distances so far apart that the men's shouts came through as whispers. Since two men could cover that area, it was obvious this wind-swept land could not support new thousands unless and until drastic changes of basic economy occur.

After I had ridden out from *Estancia del Rio Paine* and sailed from Punta Arenas for the six-day voyage through the western half of Magellan's Strait, I entered Chile's coastal passages. There an even less-inhabited region appeared. We rounded the southernmost point of the continental mainland and soon were drenched in a cold, misty rain. For three days the sun hardly broke through. Islands we passed shone vivid green through the murk. This zone begins north of Cordillera Paine and extends to the Peninsula of Taitao. Waterfalls and cascades too numerous to name trace their foaming white threads down to narrow gray passages. These island-mountains are solid rock with hardly a layer of soil anywhere on them. They are lumpy, as though mud had been shoved before cosmic bulldozers and then petrified. The lush green is illusory in terms of fertility. Valleys of apparent promise are beds of moss a foot or more thick on top of solid rock. It is depressing scenery at that point, but mountain-lovers could spend months exploring other parts of the southernmost Andes.

Lago Argentino, where crevassed walls of ice send icebergs crashing into turquoise water to float at length in mirrored majesty . . . Lago San Martín . . . Lago Viedma . . . glaciers hundreds of miles long and others inching down from heights of thousands of feet into Norwegianlike fjords—such are scenic compensations of South America's unyielding barrier at its spectacular termination.

Amazonia: Earth in Solution

To understand the aberrations and lack of balance in South American politics and economics, anyone seeking a unified portrait of the continent must discern how heavy is the deficit of Amazonia, in addition to the barrier of the Andes. The two— Andes and Amazonia—cannot be separated. Unquestionably the Amazon River would shrink by a third, possibly half, its present size, if the Andes were erased in an arc 2500 miles long. This arc, like a pair of anchor arms, swings across the central shank of the river.

How different South America would be if the Andes, instead of rising abruptly from the Pacific, had thrust up somewhere near the center of the continent and been supplied with a few viable passes! Then there could have been two broad coastal plains with a more equable distribution of rivers. As it is, the Andes choke half of the Pacific Coast with dry sand while scooping rains from eastern clouds to drown the Amazonian lowlands.

Again South America is found geographically without restraint. Where this continent is mountainous, so many of them are piled in one line that tides of human advancement break against them. Where South America has rivers, it pours out enough to fill inland waterways of every nation in the world. Then, instead of distributing the waters advantageously, the perverse continent plays such pranks that potentially magnificent inland waterways are wrongly placed or lined with hazards.

Grasping, even in part, what the Amazon means requires far more than flying over its mouths near Belém in Brazil. We must do that, and then range across the inner valley, climb the Andes at several points along the headwaters, sail on river steamers and ride or portage around rapids where the low plateaus of the southern periphery form an almost imperceptible continental divide on the east-west axis. It helps to spend nights alone in the jungle, as I have done, or push through trails that leave hardly a mark in the green immensity and would disappear if left uncut a few weeks. We need to meet rubber tappers on their solitary rounds in the wilderness, and visit the few cities such as Manáos or Santarém. Doing all this, and more, we shall have sampled the world's largest single frontier, the last to be brought even to fringes of human habitation.

Over nearly all of the Amazon Basin, population density averages less than one person to two square miles. Even this would not be so except for the concentrations found in the few cities. South America's Great Basin, in much of its expanse, is as devoid of people as some empty green planet floating through space.

Most of us, when first flying across this expanse of navigable rivers, magnificent tropical forests, open savannas, and apparently inexhaustible fertility, are likely to wax enthusiastic over prospects of Amazonia. This is neither a surprising nor a new emotional reaction. The only trouble with it is disregard for reason, experience, and centuries of hard fact. Long before North Americans indulged in romantic dreams about Amazonia, Europeans had their fling. Eminent personages in London and Paris allowed their imaginations to run. Lyrical descriptions of Amazonian fertility were written by self-styled authorities who never had been there, or had glimpsed only the edges.

Deception stalks through this land. The very luxuriance of vegetation is a green camouflage for some of the world's most poverty-stricken soils. Few laymen, few ardent young pioneers, could be expected to see through this paradox of the wet tropics. I certainly, being no farmer or soil chemist, was as innocent of the agricultural facts as anyone even after I had flown thousands of miles over the Brazilian jungle on my first trip in 1938, and penetrated overland from Lima to the Peruvian hinterland at three widely separated points early the following year. Gradually I learned what lies behind Amazonia's green façade. After my last trip I put to Robert L. Pendleton, Principal Soil Tech-

nologist of the Office of Foreign Agricultural Relations in the
Department of Agriculture at Washington, this question:

"If an acre of the best Iowa soil should be moved bodily to the
center of the Amazon Basin and used as a truck garden, how
long would it last?"

Mr. Pendleton has spent twenty-six years in the field of tropical agriculture, mostly in the Far East. He has studied similar
conditions in the Americas.

"The Iowa soil, if exposed to the rain with no cover other
than light row crops," he told me, "would be greatly depleted
in a year. It would almost certainly be leached beyond profitable
use in two years."

Since Amazonian rain could do that to some of the world's
best soil, what has it done to the valley's own soil? Standing in
the prow compartment of a Catalina flying boat over the deepest
reaches of the valley between the upper Negro and Japurá Rivers
at the height of the rainy season, I met this soil-destroyer in its
cloudy lair. The small windows curved around me. Within arm's
reach out front the flying boat's nose thrust through vapors into
open patches. Below, the country of head-hunters lay drenched
and apparently empty of habitation. Across the level circle in
view on the horizon many rainstorms were in progress at the
same time. I could count scores. There must have been a hundred or more. The black columns of rain trailed from cloud-
packs which at times were fired with white flame where the sun
touched their tops.

We flew for a time with a double rainbow—two complete
circles—vivid and beckoning before us in concentric beauty.

Then we would hit one of those columns of rain.

It was as though the ship had plunged into a wall of water.

For a moment I saw nothing through the windows. At 180
miles an hour the wind could not blow the panes clear. Gradually, outlines came through, waving and liquid.

The plane's nose quivered like a rabbit's. I couldn't see the
wing tips.

Captain Frank L. Sage of the Rubber Development Corporation Flying Service shouted down from the pilot's seat to ask how I liked it.

Other times, on the ground, I had seen the same kind of rain pounding, pulverizing, and washing away the chemicals on which agriculture thrives in Iowa, on the steppes of Russia, or other Temperate Zone lands including the Argentine *pampa*.

No amount of money can change the rains of Amazonia or remove the western barrier of the Andes that shuts much of it away from profitable exploitation.

Like the Andes, the Amazons are overpowering by their sheer size. I say the Amazons, because no single river channel bears to the sea such a freight of silt-laden water. Chroniclers use the plural, oftentimes in memory of the mythical race of Amazonian warrior women rather than the river's multiple courses. Conceptions of size abandon me in the presence of this natural phenomenon. Time and space gyrate as gears that don't quite mesh. I find myself beginning to understand why Amazonia in nearly half a millennium of European and American settlement has hardly been nibbled along the edges of its river banks. Flying over the lower Amazon, I feel that the earth itself has become liquid, and moves. Nearly all of the northern half of the continent pours its waters into this single labyrinth of channels.

On the Amazon's main tributaries—the Rio Negro, Solimões, Madeira, and Ucayali, to name only a few—human habitation has advanced far enough to establish two substantial cities. They are Manáos, on the Rio Negro near its confluence with the Solimões, and Iquitos in Peru, more than 2300 miles from the sea. A few other towns, such as Santarém near the Ford rubber plantation on the Tapajóz, approximate civilization. For the rest, there are clearings big enough to give breath to a hut or two in the deep forest. A dugout canoe drawn up on the bank; an occasional sailboat or a steamer on the larger rivers; agricultural clearings so small that they are little more than flecks in the green immensity—that is the typical human penetration into Amazonia. When the plane heads across deeper reaches into country inhabited only by aboriginal tribes, a whole day's flight may disclose only a few of their clearings.

This land of the Amazons is flat, with hardly any outcroppings. Dense forest rolls to the horizon in every direction. Rivers of unbelievable meanderings and swamps or open savannas are characteristic over most of the valley. In the wet season, from November to April or May, the sun's searchlight glints on water through the matted roof of the forest. During hours of flight, no dry land appears. Then a hut clings on a fragment of sodden earth a few feet above the flood. Such conditions prevail for months over wide areas along the rivers. Yet it is only near the rivers that people can find adequate transportation. There they must live.

On fringes of the basin are higher lands. These slope upward to the Andes on the west, and to the low plateaus of Bolivia's hinterland, as well as to Brazil's Mato Grosso and Goiaz on the south and east.

The Amazon Basin accounts for nearly half of South America, and so is roughly equal to the United States. One other large river, the Orinoco, drains southern Venezuela and Colombia and the low continental divide that runs from the Andes to the Guianas. This divide, marked by some spectacular peaks and lofty plateaus near the Guianas, curves irregularly in the interval between 2 and 5 degrees North Latitude. A fact of singular interest is the joining of the Amazon and Orinoco systems over a river that literally runs both ways. This versatile stream is the Casiquiare. It unites the Rio Negro, a major tributary of the Amazon, with the main Orinoco. For a distance of 100 miles the Casiquiare is in effect a long slender lake, or canal, draining at each end into a different river network. Other tributaries of the two valleys come even closer, but do not quite break through low barriers between them. That shows how slight is the uplift of land along the first transverse divide south of the Caribbean coastal mountains. On its southeast watershed the Orinoco draws rivers such as the Caroní from a jumbled wilderness. The Sierra de Rinocote, where Angel Falls turns into vapor on its long plunge from the clouds, and Roraima, 8620 feet high, are summits in broken country that starts south of the Orinoco delta near the British island of Trinidad and sweeps southeast through the

Guianas. Numerous large and spectacular waterfalls line the escarpments where this isolated realm breaks off into British Guiana.

Aloft and on land there are humor and amenities that ease the tensions of these times. Take, for example, the electrifying peanuts of Trinidad. Take them with care, unless you are one who lives dangerously, even recklessly. For their sponsor and commercial entrepreneur on Charlotte Street, Port of Spain, hangs out this sign:

VANTERPOOL'S PACKAGES
OF FRESH ROASTED PEANUTS
WILL TONIFY, ENERGIZE, & ELECTRIFY YOU.
SOLD HERE.

Such peanuts could not be passed by. Entering the corner store I learned that all of this could be had for the modest sum of tuppence. Emerging into the white glare of the street I sought a shady spot before opening the paper sack. After all, they might explode in this sun! Well, they didn't explode, and somehow I didn't detect any special tonifying, energizing, or electrifying effect. But they were good peanuts, small as peas and round, and well roasted. The sign alone was worth more than tuppence.

That portion of Charlotte Street is as cosmopolitan as Trinidad itself. The Crazy House Store advertised:

HAVE THE GOODS AT KEEN PRICES.
G. B. SINGH, PROP.

The universal Chinese laundryman near by, Lee Wo, was running an American Steam Laundry.

Two other signs, not amusing but appealing, and not in Trinidad but in Surinam, or Dutch Guiana, deserve recording. On the neatly painted gable of a wooden house in Paramaribo I saw the inscription: Self-Help House. Thinking it might be some kind of society for helping people help themselves, I knocked to inquire. No, the young couple said, it was not a society, but they had helped build the house, and so had named it Self-Help. Many houses in Surinam have their own names, more distinctive than the coldness of numbers.

Not far away, on a semicircular wooden arch that spanned the gate leading to a small church building, not even my unfamiliarity with Dutch could hide the meaning of these words:

Jezus zegt, Komt herwaarts tot Mij!

In the planes, too, there is a wealth of human interest. One of the Clipper Captains struck me as acting with the maximum of easy informality and modesty in the way he dealt with passengers and crew. It came out after we knew each other quite well that he takes secret delight in writing children's stories drawn from his world-roamings as a pilot of Pan American Airways.

I retain an enthusiasm for the flying boat as against the ultramodern land plane. There is an intimacy about the Clippers, and especially the older, smaller Clippers, that makes up to me for the advantages of being whisked somewhere faster, with never an opportunity to stand at the door of the control cockpit and watch four men navigating the blue. One of the enjoyable aspects of my latest trip was the opportunity again to fly in the old S-42 Clippers, possibly some of the same ones that introduced me to ocean flying. The S-43 Baby Clippers are more like private planes than commercial carriers as they nose down the coast, putting in at little bays or river towns scorned by the super-super land planes. Give me a ship of the air that also knows the feel of the sea. Yet the times are set against flying boats. Slower and less economical, they are slated to be displaced. Already, most of the people flying around South America miss coastal stretches where sea, sand, wind and rivers have fashioned beauty that is seldom seen.

I once spent an unforgettable and revealing Christmas in Surinam. All the way from Miami southward in that flight I had seen the floral brilliance of crimson Poinsettias, avenues of them, enough Poinsettias for the world's Christmas. In the British island of Jamaica, in Colombia's main port of Barranquilla on the Caribbean, and in Caracas, Venezuela's capital 3000 feet high in foothills of the Andes, Poinsettias luxuriated among other equally gorgeous displays free to any passer-by. Trinidad added its gifts of flowers. Translucent hibiscus, cerise with a crystalline fragility in the sun, covered bushes twice a man's height. Some of the blossoms were six inches or more across. In form and coloring they resembled orchids, except for a hardiness to withstand the tropical sunlight. Whole trees bloom in this continent of superlatives. Flying over the jungle I saw yellow trees, purple trees, and flaming dashes of crimson.

Yet none of these meant Christmas. Even the Poinsettia appears here in the lush, extravagant tropical tradition, not in the silence of night over Bethlehem, or the purity of white New England steeples aspiring toward the stars in a world crisp with the breath of snow. As I flew southward toward the Equator, Christmas seemed more remote. Not that the outward signs mean so much, but it was hard to realize the day had nearly arrived. We crossed the Orinoco delta and entered Guiana skies. Jungles and chocolate rivers led on to Surinam, and then I began to sit up and take notice, for there in the jungle it was plain to be seen that the Dutch had been long at work. Neat canals bisected the land in great rectangles. White houses began to appear, replacing thatched huts of the countryside. Then beside the tawny Surinam a bright city came into view, a city as Dutch as the tropics permit. Colonial spires and towers that might have been in New Amsterdam beside the Hudson, before the Dutch traded the future New York for this tropical colony, rose among typical wooden gables of Paramaribo. I wondered how the Dutch would observe Christmas in Surinam, among a population not only of Europeans, but of Javanese, British Indians, Negroes, a few Bush Negroes in from the jungle to trade their wares, and various racial mixtures in one of the most polyglot communities of the world.

The day before Christmas I was invited to a plantation across the river at Mariënburg, the colony's most famous sugar establishment with 5000 acres under cultivation. United States Vice-Consul Carl Norden, son of the bombsight inventor, took me across the river on the ferry. We drove to the plantation along the river that leads to the main bauxite mines then providing most of the aluminum for United States defense.

At the door of a breezy dwelling raised high on brick pillars painted white, we were met by our host and hostess, Mr. and Mrs. Herman Luitink. In the yard he showed us his orchids. A resplendent yellow one, its branches aglow with small petals swaying in the breeze, spread a full eight feet across. Orchids were everywhere, outside and inside the house. They have one special type called the Christmas orchid. It is a small blossom of deep lavenders and purples. Backs of the petals are covered with a rich dark tufting in regular patterns.

At table we were served by Javanese women in native garments. Mrs. Luitink showed us a small branch of faded, fragrant evergreen, brought from the Netherlands before the war. That was their symbol of Christmas at home, although they have long lived in the colony where he is Supervisor of Production on this large plantation.

Returning to the city on Christmas Eve, we saw efforts to simulate the evergreens that are not found here. From the Botanical Garden were cut branches of a tree with long, slender needles resembling pine. A Christmas tree was formed from such branches and set up in the lobby of the Palace Hotel. The proprietor, who also operates a motion picture theater downtown, spread sand for snow on the theater's porch, set up a cotton snow man, and hung flakes of cotton on many threads to make a winter scene. The background was black with silver stars.

Thousands of pounds of turkey were imported for the United States troops, in Surinam on invitation of the Dutch to help guard their bauxite mines. At the hotel we had native turkey, a tropical equivalent of pumpkin pie, and cranberry sauce.

Christmas in Surinam came otherwise. Something in the luminous town with its streets of shell and sand made radiant by a full moon, was akin to the true meaning of Christmas. Then as I trod lightly through the quiet glow of Paramaribo, away from the few streets where modern noises intruded, I heard voices, children's voices, raised in irresistibly sweet singing. At the door of a strange, angular building ungraced by a steeple, I saw children peeping in. It was a Christmas night service, specially for children, at the Netherlands Reformed Church. Inside, a Dutch lady in white waved her baton and a large child choir responded, mixed voices, high and melodious. Many of the faces were jet black, others chocolate, some white. In the semilight flickering from candles on the Christmas tree, rows and rows of child faces filled the church on four sides. A raised pulpit of colonial design, reached by spiral stairs and canopied as in Colonial New England, stood high above their heads. When the singing blended into silence, the preacher mounted his pulpit and read from *The Bible* in measured, understanding Dutch, read the story of Christmas to the dusky children of Surinam.

A few days later as I flew south toward Belém, unbroken wilderness spread below the plane most of the time. I searched for signs of human habitation outside the few Guiana towns. Along the coast I saw huts of fishermen and an occasional settlement that might be called a village. The Guianas represent the highest stage of development on northern coastal borders of the Amazon Basin. British, Dutch, and French colonizers are gifted, yet so far even these advanced Europeans have not conquered climate and terrain sufficiently to make a home attractive for anyone except the few who may enjoy the wet tropics at their hottest and most humid.

After the Guianas have been left behind with their sweltering clearings, jungle reigns supreme. The searchlight of the sun glints on water even where I thought there was dry ground under the trees. At times, salt water encroaches inland for miles. At other places the low-lying river systems make their own fresh-water swamps that join those of the sea and wipe out all transport except by dugout canoe over large areas. Anyone who moves must float between the dim shapes of mossy jungle trees and dodge the cables of trailing lianas. Where could a city be built? On stilts? A Venice of the Amazons? Intriguing, but not practical.

Of savage beauty there is an abundance. Green of jungle predominates, that heavily pigmented green which gleams somberly by day and absorbs by night every vestige of illumination from the sky. Rivers in their coloring and their meanderings enliven the flat jungle. There are rivers within rivers, where some clear stream from an occasional sandy elevation above flood level enters a muddy current and keeps its own identity. Enough earth is suspended in most of these rivers to provide a bed for other watercourses. Some rivers have two ends and apparently no outlet. I have seen temperamental channels meander to within a few hundred feet of the sea, and then swing inland to wander for miles before finally tasting salt water. A phenomenon hard to believe, until it has been seen repeatedly where no human hand could possibly have done the work, is the planting of jungle trees in rows along concentric arcs laid down by the sea or by old river channels. The process of land formation can be traced in stages inland from blowing sand dunes to the forest. Evidently the ridges back of wide bays are sufficiently pronounced to shape the jungle. Seeds are blown into the troughs. Whatever the explanation, there are the trees, furrowed and combed as though some gigantic harrow had carded and woven this living tapestry.

A seeker for his first glimpse of the world's largest river should not expect to look from the plane window and say: "There it is; there is the Amazon!" He might be jumping at a ripple on its edges, or some long-abandoned channel filled with water that no longer moves. Even at 12,000 feet in the air, one sees only a limited circle of the Amazon delta at any given moment. Suddenly he may realize that he met the Amazon long ago. As far north as Surinam, some of that muddy tinge in the sea had drifted from the Amazon. I recall a sea voyage when the deck pool was murky with Amazon water—300 miles offshore!

As I first neared the Amazon's delta in flight I wanted to make sure I was reading the living map correctly. When the plane's Captain came aft to see how we were doing, I asked him some questions. Returning to the pilot's cabin, he brought a chart.

"We have to map these islands ourselves," he said, pointing to outlines made in pencil. "They keep changing."

From the air, even a layman can see the watery fingers of the

Amazon molding and shaping the soft silt into new land. So heavy is the deposit each year that channels clog and others break through. Islands rise and are swept away.

Bridges? Where would they find footing? No outcropping of rock has humped up the jungle roof since the last ripples of the Guiana ranges waned in Brazil. Moreover, the Amazon delta is 200 miles across. Farther up the Amazon there are some high banks, but to throw a single bridge across this river at any point within its first 2000 miles from the sea would be a task equal to that of building all of New York City's existing bridges, the two long ones at San Francisco, and a few more for good measure.

The Amazon is one of those natural marvels that must be seen to be believed. Even after seeing it at hundreds of points along the main stream and its headwaters, I try to assemble the pieces into one coherent whole, feeling all the while that I haven't straightened out even the main design. Broad generalizations about the Amazon would be as unsafe as for a casual visitor to this earth to conclude that it is all as he sees it during the first year, even if he were to travel constantly. The central stem of this river labyrinth breaks around the large island of Marajó opposite Belém. Marajó, with the j pronounced in Brazil's Portuguese as in Joe instead of hoe as the Spanish-speaking parts of South America would have it, is as large as Belgium. The Amazon could hold Belgium in its teeth as a dainty morsel, yet how different is Marajó from the land of the Walloons and Flemings! Run as a feudal fief, Marajó spreads to the horizon, its marshes and grasslands apparently empty. Actually there are extensive cattle ranches, settlements, many *jacarés* or crocodiles, and traces of long-lost civilizations. The islands in the delta are summed up by Brazilians of Belém as *Las Ilhas*. There wild rubber is gathered. River boatmen ply their rakish rigs, sailing as on an inland sea.

Literally thousands of channels converge here in knotted convolutions of the river as it unwinds toward freedom of the open sea. No longer confident of distance judgments in such a realm, I clocked the last channel before Belém. It is actually the Pará River, compounded of waters from the main river as well as the most easterly watersheds of the Amazon Basin. By my wristwatch it was five minutes at two miles a minute. Ten miles for a single outlet of this river, ninety miles from its mouth! Nor is this merely a broad flat estuary similar to inlets along the Atlantic seaboard south of New York. This is a river of great depth and powerful currents beneath its lakelike dimensions. One feels the surge of it. This is not water flowing, but earth in primeval suspension, earth being formed before one's eyes.

When New York City is imagined at the mouth of the Amazon instead of the Hudson, a resident of the United States has a basis of comparison for realizing what Brazil has to contend with in Amazonia. As far inland as Chicago, the central maze of waters would then constitute a barrier that splits the country. This barrier would be due to the attempt of nearly the whole United States to disgorge the Mississippi, Colorado, Columbia, and all its other rivers from one mouth at New York, and to do this after tropical rains have swollen floods beyond the imagination even of levee tenders at Cairo or New Orleans. Building levees along the Amazon would be as though children scooped up banks of sand against the sea. Floods are not controlled. They spread over both banks and often range so far they meet other flooded areas. Such conditions prevail during three to six months over large segments of the basin. If the first thousand miles of the central Amazon were serpentined between New York and Chicago instead of Belém and Manáos, the upper river with its flood area would extend nearly to California.

Even in flight it is hard to be sure that all of the Amazon's width is being seen. The picture of a neatly banked river must be discarded at the outset. The Amazon is a connected series of mighty currents, lakes, channels new and old, marshes, a few moderately high banks eagerly seized upon for human settlements or towns, and tributaries by the thousands—many of them great rivers in their own names. So level is most of the central basin that few restraints check temperamental giants of this liquid realm. Spread below is evidence of centuries spent in making and unmaking river courses. A favorite device is the silting in of a curve, so that a new loop is formed to one side or the other. The original river becomes an inlet at that point, and in time may close at both ends to form a lake. As on the coast, I saw again the handiwork of a green tapestry weaver whose needles are shafts of water miles long, and whose thread is spun from whole forests. The land is swirled and cut abruptly. It lays fold on fold and crease on crease as far as eye can see. Only rarely has land near the rivers reached stability. Any year the thrusting wall of mud in flux may burst old barriers and run its shears through the fabric of variegated green.

Ahead lie pleasant meadows—or so it seems. Their color is lighter than that of the jungle. Apparently a plane could land on this billiard-table level without bouncing over a hummock.

Deception, all deception.

The sun has been gleaming on water beneath forest. The reflected ball of fire reaches the edge of the meadow and changes its color as though an iridescent sheen had spread slowly over the surface. The meadow is a swampy pool, covered by floating leaves of various growing grasses and lilies. In secluded bays are scores of Victoria Regia pads, several feet across and crimped upward around the edge in a flange. From plane's height they seem pale green plates of fragile chinaware spread for a picnic.

Tremendous tributaries enter the main river trunk. Junction areas are vast. About where a city like Pittsburgh would rise at a fork of Temperate Zone rivers, no city of any kind could possibly stand beside the Amazon. Only rarely is an Amazonian junction point suited to its natural use as a traffic center. Manáos, on high red bluffs of the Rio Negro a few miles above its confluence with the Solimões where those two form the lower Amazon, occupies one of the favored sites, and is the metropolis of the valley as a consequence. At Manáos the normal rise of the Negro is fifty feet. In view of the fact that the whole river falls only 250 feet in its first 2000 miles, plainly there are wide regions subject to flood. Few banks are high enough, as at Manáos, to absorb the height and weight of currents from ten to twenty miles wide and as much as 500 feet deep in places.

How much land the inner basin offers that is drained well enough to support all-year habitation is not known precisely.

One thing is sure. Most of the habitable country, beyond flood limits, is so far removed from the main arteries of river transport that development becomes more costly than resources justify. Farms, towns, or cities on the high ground would have to maintain roads during the dry season from April or May through October, and see them swept away, or at least sunk beneath five to fifty feet of water during the rains. The year is roughly divided in half by those extremes. Immediately along the rivers are natural levees. There are found most of the huts. Farming depends on a Nile system of annually replenished soils. Yet security against flood is by no means assured, and many settlers count on moving by rowboat each year, returning to repair or rebuild whatever remains of their homes when the waters recede. At least they live during half of the year on the main line of traffic.

Inland from Manáos, the valley broadens. It is relatively narrow at the Atlantic, only 500 miles. This is the sluice gate for a pear-shaped drainage basin 2000 miles deep and nearly as wide. On eastern slopes of the Andes thousands of foaming torrents roar toward the lowlands. Some notion of the volume of water flowing into the Atlantic beyond Belém is given by following along these Andean headwaters, 3000 miles from the delta. Even in the higher levels, so much water comes down at times that floods of thirty feet are usual. Many oil reserves in southeastern Colombia and northeastern Peru would have to be exploited under such flood conditions. Engineers have told me the world will have to need oil more than it now does, to justify crossing the Andes, or cruising the length of the Amazon, and then contending with six months of high water.

The extraordinarily low gradient of the central valley has the advantage of providing a magnificent canal for ocean-going ships all the way to Pucalpa on the Ucayali, and even beyond for bottoms of lower draft. Several tributaries, including the Negro, Madeira, Tapajóz, and Xingú, carry large ships on their lower reaches. The result is a network of inland waterways reaching across the continent to within 300 miles of the Pacific— but that last 300 miles raises its own wall nearly three miles high even in the passes. Nor is this system of natural canals as useful as it appears on a map. Hazards of Amazonian navigation are numerous.

From the prow of a river launch on the Beni River in Bolivia I watched a submerged log grind past. Its root-end pointed downstream and rotated as a gigantic drill. Snags of broken hardwood churned the muddy surface. The massive shank rotated slowly, powerfully, out of sight. It could turn its drill through the bottom of an iron hull and hardly quiver from the impact. Loose alluvial banks of these rivers give way constantly, tumbling trees into the current.

Also, along the southern rim of the inner valley a series of cascades breaks shipping connections. The drop is almost imperceptible from the air, but by land near Pôrto Velho on the Madeira I saw huge red rocks in the dry season, ground and rounded. Returning at the height of the wet season I saw rapids and whirlpools hiding the same rocks.

Opposite the Bolivian Beni region lies Brazilian Mato Grosso in its most remote wilderness. From the Bolivian side at Guayaramerín, I saw hills eighteen miles away where savages keep settlers out of their domain by the simple expedient of killing all who enter. They stay away from the Brazilian town of Guajará-mirim as a rule, but have been known to stage reprisal raids into the suburbs and carry off children. Two rubber tappers had been caught by them shortly before my last arrival there.

When I flew out toward Manáos, the plane circled above the railway station, upstream terminus of the famous and costly Madeira-Mamoré Railway that was said to have exacted a human life for every tie laid. Even there, on the upper shelf of the Amazon Basin, swamps spread beyond the rivers. Human habitation has not advanced to a level higher than the malaria-ridden mud streets of Guajará-mirim and its surprisingly well-stocked stores. There are typical palm huts on a morsel of ground between river and swamp. At best it is a dismal, unattractive existence, shut away from the world except for air transport and slow river boats from Belém and Manáos to Pôrto Velho, southern terminus of the world's most isolated railway.

Not long after leaving Pôrto Velho I began to notice again that searching flashlight of the sun held to the surface of water beneath forest. During nearly two thirds of the flight I saw this evidence of floods. These are not, as in the Missouri and Mississippi Valleys, occasional overflows. They are normal and accepted behavior of Amazonian rivers, however hard this behavior may be on the few inhabitants. Until some turn of fortune makes Amazonia worth the effort, these waters will rampage unopposed. In the drenched wastelands a few courageous communities cling to soggy islands. A half year before, at the height of the dry season, I had seen blue skies and white cumulus clouds over the same territory. Rivers had settled within fairly defined banks. Flood plains had become grasslands. In the rainy season I see earth and sky merge in a riot of the water giants. Under the overcast sky a murky twilight reigns. Puffs of white vapor rise in a mottled pattern like flock-of-sheep clouds on the pasture of a dingy green sky, upside down.

The Brazilian pilot points to a massive thunderhead looming up in our path, and swings wide to miss it.

"Very dangerous, *senhor*," he says. "There is so much water, so much violent evaporation, those clouds can break a plane in pieces."

Before we landed at Manáos, I marveled that jungle could press in such uncut luxuriance to the borders of a city numbering 90,000. Belém with its 310,000 population also has its elbows pinned to its sides by the encroaching wilderness. Some United States Marines told me in 1942 they saw a large snake in a tree at the airport then under construction at Val de Cães on outskirts of the city. In all my jungle travels I never have seen a snake longer than a dozen feet, and only a few of them. Yet the wild is there, and yields only by inches to civilization. Manáos with its domed *Teatro Nacional*, or Opera House, and its floating docks built during the first rubber boom that burst like a toy balloon in 1912, is a well-known landmark, a symbol of the Amazon Basin's briefly glorious past.

The next flight is to take me straight from Manáos across the head-hunters' country. The destination is San José del Guaviare,

Colombia, on the western arm of the Orinoco. At first we fly with both the Negro and the Solimões in view. Then both disappear on the misty horizon. Below spreads the deepest Amazon jungle. League on league unrolls without variation. Soon open savannas break the mottled green roof. These are natural, not cleared. The only man-made clearings are occasional pin points where wild tribes have felled a few trees to make dugout canoes and plant their crude crops. Even then they do not remove all of the cover from their round plots. By instinct and experience they have learned that the land must be left with some protection against the leaching rains.

The vastness of the scene is overpowering as hours pass. Still we fly. No stops are scheduled on this hop of 900 miles. Fuel in the tanks must carry us through, and those motors must go on humming. They do. Rainstorms reach high intensity here, for this is Amazonia of Amazonia, wilderness primeval and almost unchallenged after 450 years of exploration and pioneering. Solitude wells up from those jungled depths. At no point outside of the polar regions is it possible to view comparable areas where human hands and cultures have left so few discernible marks.

Sometimes air currents set up a junction of heat and cold that forms whole networks of cloud-rivers. Above each stream the vaporous counterpart faithfully follows its original. Evidently the water keeps the air a thousand feet above it at a fairly constant temperature, for the cloud-rivers persist. The white Amazon and its tributaries float, ethereal and lovely, high above the mud and muck.

In San José del Guaviare I saw Indians of the *selva*, Spanish name for the great forest. Wherever I have met them—in Colombia or a thousand miles south along the Perené River in Peru, they differ radically from Indians of the high Andes. Noses are flat instead of pointed. Hair is so coarse it looks as though the tail of a black horse had been cut, tied, and the butt end placed on top of the Indian's head. The loose mop falls all around, over forehead as well as neck. Dark eyes peer through. Sometimes crude bangs have been slashed across close above the eyebrows. If the *selva* should be judged by the type of manhood developed in it over the centuries, the *selva* would rank low as a human habitat. No specimens I have ever seen hint a race of forebears to match the mythical and redoubtable women for whom the Amazons were named. *Selva* Indians are generally of low stature. An average North American could pass most of them under his outstretched arm. Heads appear large and blocklike above unimpressive bodies. Emaciation is more in evidence than the vigor usually expected of people who live outdoors. Clothing, when used at all, is limited to a sack thrown over the shoulders and sometimes reaching the ankles. The color is usually drab— a dirty brown or nondescript mixture. Some tribes wear G-strings. Others omit the formality. Engineers who work with them report a low mental capacity that does not show initiative, and responds slowly, if at all, to education. Such is the native human material—literally raw—of Amazonia.

The *caboclo,* or peon, results from fusion of these *selva* peoples with the Portuguese or other strains from beyond South America. They are shadowy people, pale, thin, hatchet-faced, pinched, furtive, kindly and pleasant, orderly, meek, melancholy, and subdued. They seem never to escape the weight of the jungle, even on paved city streets or in luxurious houses where they serve as domestics. They laugh seldom, and then with that unspoken restraint, that feeling of an environment beyond their powers to conquer. City capitalists dwell on the laziness of the *caboclo.* They say he will not work more than enough to earn his handful of *xarque,* or sun-dried meat, and his *mandioca* meal, a sawdustlike food ground from a native root tuber.

The Pará pallor is a common expression in Belém. Even husky young athletes from beaches of California or Florida do not tan here as they might expect to do on the Equator. The sun is hot enough, but the rainy season hides it for part of nearly every day during six months. In dry weather the relative humidity is still high, from 70 to 90 or more. Heat plus humidity results in a listless, enervating atmosphere. Actual temperature readings are often surprisingly low, and a casual visitor is surprised by coolness where he had expected to encounter insufferable heat day and night. Those who stay year in and year out find the climate lacking in vim, even if not depressing.

San José del Guaviare escapes somewhat from the torrid lowlands. It is typical of the mid-zone where jungle falters before the massed line of Andean foothills. Open savannas are more frequent. Far to the northeast in Venezuela, this mid-zone on fringes of the Orinoco appears as grasslands, or *llanos,* leading up through belts of varying vegetation to barren ridges of the high Andes. Similar conditions continue in Colombia, although jungles rather than grasslands predominate.

Along the inner or eastern curve of the Andes where they enter Peru are dammed the longest tributaries of the Amazon. Every one of them—the Marañon, Ucayali, Huallaga, Apurimac, Urubamba, and Perené, to name only a few—normally should flow into the Pacific. They rise 100 to 300 miles from Peru's desert shore, and then blunder their way ten times as far clear across the continent to the Atlantic, spreading floods and wreckage en route, taking water where there is too much, and keeping it from fertile but parched soils of the Pacific piedmont.

I repeat, it would be difficult to design a continent with more massive natural handicaps.

Natal Bulge: Home of the Migrant

Fly over Brazil from the mouth of the Amazon in any direction, and the plane crosses jungle, swamp, or river lowlands. Fly from Belém southeast and the jungle clearings soon give way to Brazil's land of recurrent drought. Along a fairly well-defined line, some knife-edge of wind and sun cuts wet Amazonia asunder from the Brazilian bulge as it reaches toward Africa.

Brazil's Northeast differs from every other part of South America in its duality of climate. Neither full-time desert nor full-time rain belt, it alternates between the two. During years of normal rains—and there are many—this zone is so desirable that population crowds in. Seen from the air during a dry

period, the country presents evidences of habitation in the form
of roads, fenced enclosures, and many trails. The explanation
is that this semidesert can be delightful. Even in dry weather the
climate is refreshing because of the low humidity, and in wet
weather the humidity is less than in many other parts of Brazil.

Brazil's Northeast occupies the bulge that forms one of the
world's great strategic sea passages. Before the Nazi aggressors
had been pinned down and then driven back from their advanced bases in Africa, the city of Natal in the State of Rio
Grande do Norte next door on the east of Ceará focused tension
over Nazi plans to invade South America. That strategic importance remains for future years, although the tension is
gone for the present. The Northeast has served day and night
as one of the most vital aërial bridges for carrying personnel
and supplies to war fronts. This activity has had tremendous
effects on the internal economy and outlook of the entire region.

On my last trip I saw the Northeast in midsummer of a third
drought year. Eastern Maranhão and Piauí States blanched
rapidly until in the State of Ceará a gray pallor extended to the
horizon. Only occasionally was it broken by spots of green
where some enduring waterhole or new irrigation ditch nourished
a few trees. The drought line runs from Camocim on the coast
just inside the eastern border of Ceará, south and west across
Piauí, and past Floriano on the Parnaíba River. It turns almost
straight south to a few miles past Barra do Rio Grande on the
São Francisco River. From there it swings toward the coast at
Amargosa near São Salvador, capital of Bahia State. It roughly
parallels the coast northward to Natal. The coastal strip from
Natal south is reasonably well watered, and in places has spots
of dense jungle. Such is the paradoxical setting laid by pranks
of hot low winds and moist currents of the upper air. One of
the strangest sights is to see a green mountain range come into
view in the midst of this desolation. At certain elevations moisture is caught, sustaining oases on heights of the Northeast.

In times of prolonged drought men and whole families have
to migrate. Many of them go into the States of Pará or Amazonas. Others move south by way of the São Francisco River into

more fertile areas of Minas Gerais. Thousands crowd into the green coastal plain.

Few regions could resemble each other less than Amazonia in its fetid jungle and the coastal Northeast where free winds blow across dunes of glistening sand. Yet both are Brazil.

At Natal the sea rolls in clean and blue. The Great Barrier Reef takes the full force of the surf, throwing spray high. Through open spaces in the volcanic and coral formation, combers break. Sea fowl rest in quiet lagoons between reef and shore. Stretches of marvelous beach hundreds of miles long make a swimmer's paradise. On the bulge and southward, Brazilians of the coast are children of sun and wind and the open sea.

Beaches of the Northeast are homes of the *jangadeiros* and their colorful sailing rafts. The *jangada* is made of solid logs lashed together and shaped to skim over the surface. A single palm trunk serves as mast for the triangular sail. Bare feet of the fishermen are awash as they set forth at dawn or dusk. Sometimes they remain at sea for days. They return with their catch in large jug-shaped wicker containers. Buyers gather around as the *jangadas* are beached. Crews help each other shove their heavy craft beyond high water. Short logs are used as rollers.

A Mediterranean atmosphere prevails along these coasts. Recife, meaning Reef, and Bahia, or Bay, are the Venice and Naples of Brazil's Northeast. Smaller than Italy's cities and less flamboyant, they share the indefinable Mediterranean flavor. It is compounded essentially of sun, blue sea, and breezy people in mellow-roofed cities that perch on steep slopes with the abandon of boys whose bare feet dangle in the surf.

Bahia crowns steep hillsides that lift the main city above its lower level where coastal craft and large ships weave through the blue harbor. Brazilians still prefer the traditional name of Bahia, dating from colonial times when the metropolis of a distant region became synonymous with the region itself. Properly, the city is São Salvador, capital of Bahia State. Rich with colonial art and memories of years when Bahia was the capital of Brazil, this glory of the northern coasts is also modern. Brazil's first significant oil deposits have been located near by. The most prominent landmark is an elevator tower rising with skyscraper proportions from the water front to a connecting bridge that is level with the upper streets.

Seldom will a more seagoing city be found than Recife. Like Venice, Recife makes little if any distinction between whether its foundations are laid on land or in the water. The main business and shipping district occupies an island between the deep, narrow harbor and the wider bay formed by the Rio Capibaribe. Four bridges lead to other larger islands. The two central bridges come straight out from streets that start at the same point and spread to form a large V when seen from the air. Other waterways meander through Recife, and there are many islands, so that bridges abound. Small sailing craft of rakish rig are met at frequent intervals where most cities would have ordinary street intersections. That is another Mediterranean characteristic of Recife, this city so unlike Belém with its heavy tropical atmosphere, or Natal with its dunes of sand and its moorlands.

People of Recife fit into the picture naturally. Visibly they respond to the sea. Many of them live along the fine beaches, including Boa Viagem. A definitely Mediterranean touch is given by triangular sails of *jangadas*.

Along the water front in Recife are boats of nearly every description. Coastwise sailing vessels tack their way through rows of steam merchantmen. Stevedores unload and load exotic wares beneath the long line of modern cranes on rails for movement parallel to the dock.

In Recife I met the *manga rosa*. This queen of the mangos, spelled with an *a* here, is especially large—from five to six inches long—pink cheeked, and makes exceedingly fine eating. That is, if you eat a mango. You don't quite drink it, but certainly it can't be entirely chewed.

My first experience with such a large one came at the Recife dock. Peeling back the rich orange-pink skin, smooth and clean, I began, leaning over the parapet. Little did I know the size of the undertaking so blithely entered upon. With every *manga rosa* should be furnished the following: one large towel; one

washbasin with running water; much elbow room; dental floss
to remove the fine threads that are inserted, as through the eyes
of needles, between every two teeth before the fruit has yielded
all its delicious juice, leaving a hard flat oval seed matted with
those threads. Later, taking some of the above precautions, I
enjoyed several *manga rosas,* but never again have such good
ones been found as at Recife.

Adding to the Mediterranean aspect of Recife is the old city
of Olinda, perched on a hill slightly to the north in full view.
Its history is tied in with the Dutch, for the Marquis of Olinda
held forth here when the stout seafarers of the Lowlands extended their domain to this part of the South American continent. The town of Olinda glows in the sun, its towers and
spires and terraces set above distant groves of coconut palms,
just at the edge of the sea.

Those coconut groves extend for hundreds of miles along the
coast. From the air they appear to be planted in rows, but
actually they grow wild. Recife enjoys the coco milk, one of its
most popular beverages.

Such beauty as this portion of the Brazilian coast offers to
an eye aloft can only be hinted in words. The Great Barrier Reef
which gives the city its name refracts lights and colors that play
in the water as it alternates between deep and shallow. White
sand beneath the surface sends turquoise fountains glistening
to the top. Bays and islands weave patterns of ever-changing
line and curve around Recife, city of the Reef.

When I turned my back on Recife and faced inland, I sensed
great social gaps and chasms. The first part of the journey was
by train. In the station, several incidents occurred to pull back
the veil from human suffering that ravages the interior and beats
against the prosperous coast. A little girl, shaking with illness,
wandered about the station. She had been sent in from the
country, alone, for medical treatment. With a dignity and fortitude beyond her years, she tried to locate her destination. On
the telephone she was told there must be some mistake. Alone
in a strange city, her lovely face prematurely aged, she at last
fell into the hands of friendly travelers who started her on the

way to competent care. The parents may have been either too poor or uneducated to spare the child this ordeal. As I traveled inland I saw more indications of deep social needs. There were incomplete bodies of children and adults whose mothers simply didn't have enough nourishment.

It is hard to reconcile these lacks with the rich scene that unfolds immediately back of Recife. The State of Pernambuco extends inland from its metropolis on the coast and meets the São Francisco River just above Paulo Afonso Waterfalls. Pernambuco then follows the river to a little beyond the city of Petrolina, on the western river bank opposite the port of Joazeiro. Coastal Pernambuco, or the *mato*, gives way to the *caatinga*, an intermediate climatic belt extending beyond the mountains. Then comes the *sertão*, or semiarid interior. The driest *sertão* embraces in all some 242,000 square miles in Pernambuco and the neighboring States of Piauí, Ceará, Rio Grande do Norte, Paraíba, Alagoas, Sergipe, and Bahia. The coastal zone often experiences booms. Its sugar and cotton are in demand. Droughts of the interior do not appreciably affect the coast, which is watered by rains from the sea. But, as so often occurs in South America, a narrow coastal strip quickly dries the winds.

The transition is striking, whether viewed from the air or from a train window. I saw it both ways, flying into Recife from Fortaleza and going out by train to the interior. From the air I saw dusty *sertão* yield to green mountains that quickly are clothed in tropical forest as thriving as exists anywhere. I also saw reservoirs and works of irrigation, for the wise people of the coast husband their abundant water. By land I saw magnificent terrace farming of sugar cane. The rows follow level contours across a hilly land. Again, the coastal farmers are conserving their soil instead of opening ditches up and down hill to become canyons of erosion under heavy rainfall.

This green doorstep of the Northeast unfolds with a beauty that can accurately be called idyllic. It approaches the charm of rural Japan. Richly forested hills surmount valleys where clear streams run among polished rocks. The whole land is a garden.

Sugar cane in symmetrical rows spreads a green tapestry up the slopes. The forest remains on the tops of many hills, giving a characteristic contour to the horizon where the even texture of the cane meets the bold outline of tropical trees. Fine, modern sugar mills complete the picture of intelligent organization. On this rail line also stands a large preserving plant where tomatoes are canned as juice, cooking sauce, and various other products. Diversification extends into other fields, such as cotton textiles. So the watered coast prospers.

Too soon the train turns a corner into lands of poverty.

More than a change of climate has occurred. The human factor declines. On slopes of thinning greenness and thinning fertility cultivated rows run up and down hill, not along the contours. As in parts of the United States and wherever soils have been recklessly washed away by failure to farm on the contours, here the gashes of erosion are being opened to unproductive rock. Dust swirls into the train coaches, and I see why the travelwise Brazilians started this trip, even on the green coast, wearing linen dusters of the kind made famous in early days of the automobile. Soon full *sertão* is reached as the wood-burning locomotive spouts red sparks into the gathering darkness.

The *sertão* cannot be classified as desert, although, after prolonged drought, it looks like desert. The growth of trees is generally not much higher than twice a man's height, with a few groves of tall timber along watercourses. The trees stand bare, bleaching in the sun. They form the shadow of a scrub forest. Yet even a passing shower will top this desolation with promises of spring. When rains return to normal, this part-time desert bursts forth with flowering trees of pale yellow and magenta. Parrots and some of the earth's most vivid varieties of small birds thrive. Even in drought time many of the birds are seen. Their colors range from brilliant crimson to the most delicate pastel shades of blue and pearl gray. Doves of many sizes send their nostalgic call throbbing through the land from afar. In such an environment the human economy alternates between comparative well-being and stark want. The problem of the Northeast is to bridge that gap.

Set in the midst of this periodically drought-seared zone is Paulo Afonso Waterfalls, one of the marvels of South America and of the world. Reaching Paulo Afonso requires days, and sometimes nights, of pounding over corrugated and rutted roads in trucks—unless fortunately part of the journey can be made in a small omnibus or private automobile. I arrive in a dilapidated taxi early one afternoon and cross by railway hand car to a central vantage point. The whole São Francisco River wedges into a narrow gorge and drops away below my feet to grind and carve the red stone far below with terrific concentrated power. Three of the seven distinct cataracts are higher than Niagara. The river falls 264 feet. In flood season, the upper walls are overrun.

From Paulo Afonso my approach this time to the most highly developed portions of Brazil and its incomparable capital, Rio de Janeiro, is by stern-wheel river steamer on the São Francisco. In a seventeen-day voyage upstream we average two miles an hour from Joazeiro near the center of the drought zone to Pirapora, railhead for Brazil's main traffic network. This is rolling down to Rio the hard and informative way. The stout ship *Octavio Carneiro* on its flat-bottomed iron hull is tied, without benefit of dock, against the sloping river bank at Joazeiro. An impressive water-front wall leads down to the shore by flights of well-worn steps. It is odoriferous. The gangplank begins among piles of dried fish and fresh hides tied in bundles. A few uncertain planks lean on the barge *Rio Verde*. She is lashed alongside the *Octavio Carneiro*. Power is so scarce that every engine gathers around it a cluster of miscellaneous river craft. I have seen one small launch at the center of a dozen boats, its single smokestack puffing wood smoke to maintain a crawling pace. The *Octavio Carneiro* could make as high as six miles an hour in calm water, but we are against the current and must stop frequently to take on firewood or put in at small ports.

Passengers are a cross section of Brazil in some of its most important aspects. Naturally such a small ship could not serve even as a microcosm for a land of such diversity. Yet it makes a good start. Housed between the stubby prow and the pair of stern paddle wheels driven by a single-cylinder steam engine are thirty-two first-class passengers. Available beds in twelve staterooms number twenty-four. The eight people for whom there are no beds sleep in hammocks on deck. This is not a heavy run, either. Nor are there only eight hammocks at night. The cool deck space quickly fills.

I first met the hammock as a vehicle of travel on the Beni River in one of the fastnesses of the Amazon Valley. Early that morning our party shoved off from Riberalta, Bolivia, on two diminutive river launches. Uninitiated as most of us were, we did not notice the iron hooks facing each other across the open pit where a temperamental engine occupied most of the deck space. A veteran of river travel soon showed us the ropes, figuratively and literally, by pulling his hammock from a duffel bag and slinging it across the launch. Some idea of dimensions is given by this: The hammock had to be slung on the bias and with ropes tight-hauled at each end, to fit the narrow deck. There was room for three or four hammocks. At least that is what we thought at the time. Later we were to learn that the Brazilian genius for hammock-rigging could easily make twenty fit into such a space, or more if really pushed to find room. For the hammock in Brazil is bed and couch to millions, whether traveling or at home. Some say the hammock originated in Brazil. That would be hard to prove, but early European voyagers found it here and reported it as a discovery, with sketched illustrations. The English explorer Roger Barlow in an edition dated 1526 writes of the Amazonian Indians that:

> *Thei be called bohiros and ther beddes thei calle hamacas, thei be made of coton after a net facion, and the one ende is tied with a corde at a post and the other ende at another post and so hangeth above grounde.*

In Amazonia to this day the Brazilian word is *hamaca*. In the Northeast, a hammock is a *rede*, pronounced with a strong *hrrr* sound at the beginning. The Northeastern State of Ceará exports 250 tons of hammocks a year. We modern inner-spring softies generally look upon the hammock as something to loll in occasionally during summer holidays. Only the sailors among us use their hammocks as daily necessities. Yet all through the Amazon Basin of Brazil, Bolivia, Peru, Ecuador, Colombia, and Venezuela, the hammock has been replaced by beds only in part, mostly in cities. Rare is the hotel room in back-country towns that does not have hammock hooks on its walls. Boats also are prepared for nocturnal unfurlings that crowd the decks, only to disappear soon after dawn. Sleeping in a hammock is an art. The first night I tried it, all went well until I tried to get back into the thing in the dark. One instant I had hold of the edge, and the next I landed in a surprised heap, backward, on the tile floor. For security and comfort, the approach must be respectful, and the final posture slantwise to flatten out the deep bottom of the crescent.

To the initiate, hammock-snoozing has some points in its favor even compared with an inner-spring mattress. There is a feeling of floating, of swaying gently in the treetops, that carries through the night. On a boat, you are suspended in your own semigyroscopic stabilizer. Anywhere, a passing breeze or a bodily movement may impart a pleasing motion to the hammock. Give me one any time in preference to beds encountered in the interior. No wonder rhythm-loving Brazilians like their hammocks. Passing through even city streets, I saw children before their bedtime in rooms that open on the sidewalk, swinging merrily. Easy to keep clean, economical, cool, the hammock no doubt has a long career ahead in South America.

The luxury of lying in a hammock while tropical scenery unfolds along the river bank is made more enjoyable by knowing how few other facilities exist on board. Out of the air, almost, you draw cushions and a reclining deck chair. Then it all folds up as quickly.

What the hammock means to the poor at home or in their steerage travels is proportionally greater. During seventeen days of continuous voyage on the *Octavio Carneiro*, one lad spends most of his time day and night in his hammock, singing and gay, when without the hammock he would have to lie on greasy and smelly cargo.

The scenes below decks present a crowding and interlacing of hammocks that tax even Brazilian ingenuity. Twenty hammocks, holding half again as many people including infants and children, are woven into one small sample space. I counted them. This feat is accomplished in an open-air cube between decks and barely three paces long on each side.

Wedged in with the *Rio Verde* cargo, and on the lower deck of the *Octavio Carneiro*, are 150 second-class *passageiros*. Not to mention sheep, pigs, and occasionally a donkey. Or the appealing *papagaios*, those lovable parrots whose talents, exploits, escapes, hardships, and irrepressible good humor enliven the whole voyage. I have never seen the proverbial barrel of monkeys. I give you instead a barrel of *papagaios*.

At dawn of the first day out, the *papagaios* awaken me with their laughter and chortlings and snatches of song that open the voyage on a decidedly holiday note. There are about eighty of them in a cubical wire cage four feet on each side. They are just astern of my stateroom, across the narrow topside deck of the *Rio Verde* lashed alongside. That there is real talent among the *papagaios* becomes evident at once. They speak Portuguese with deft assurance. Their laughs are particularly effective. Some are high and embarrassed, yet putting on a front in society. Others bespeak gossips at an afternoon party. The range runs from prim propriety to gusty and robust humor. Through the medley comes at intervals a voice so unmistakable that this unnamed *papagaio* easily becomes soloist and star. The very word, *papagaio*, has a Gilbert and Sullivan ring. Our star performer has one song that by sheer nonchalance and an indefinably dry humor brings a laugh no matter how often it is heard. This song floats incisively but airily above the small talk of the other birds. It has in it a puckish drollery, an urbane quality of tolerant amusement and a detached tone that leaves no doubt about how funny human antics look to this *papagaio*. He serves as court jester and clown, dancing to the music of accordions on board. In mimicry of sound he is so apt that he can reproduce a new whistle almost instantly, to the delight of passengers crowded along the rail.

Across the front of the cage near the top sit nine of the most solemn and imposing *papagaios* on a rod perch which that number neatly fills. Although a tenth occasionally pushes his way in, he is judiciously disbarred with fitting dignity. While the rest of the birds gossip and chatter and clamber around or hang for long periods by their beaks to relieve the boredom of travel, these nine sit with sage demeanor worthy of a Supreme Bench.

A constant preoccupation of many *papagaios* is to get out of the cage through patched places in the old wire, or through holes sedulously cut through the wood frame by persistent beaks. Many times a few emerge and roam about the deck. They make no effort to go farther afield, and of course their wings are clipped. The escapees evidently enjoy the attention they get from those inside, for the rest scream for information on how they did it. One day a *papagaio* escapes toward evening. When the keeper tries to catch him, the bird falls overboard. With excited wings he keeps afloat. It looks doubtful for a while, but the boat is passing an island instead of being in the broad open expanse of the river. Far astern he nears shore, almost out of sight, but his wings are beating valiantly, and he makes it. In mid-voyage the whole cage is swept overboard by a low tree limb as we pass close to shore. The cage falls several feet but catches on the stern of the launch and is saved from the water. Every raucous adjective in the combined vocabulary bursts forth as the surprised *papagaios* land, and are lifted back to their upper perch.

Seldom could caged parrots be observed under conditions so closely related to their native habitat. Flocks of wild parrots at times pass overhead or pause garrulously in treetops. The contrast in manner of the wild and caged birds is striking. Free, the *papagaio*—despite his clownishness—is fiercely independent and swift of wing. Wild birds just caught and offered for sale along the river bank are formidable. Yet the *papagaio* domesticates so thoroughly that the softer side of his character takes almost complete charge in captivity. Coloring of the birds blends perfectly with foliage we pass. Their predominating green matches the trees in varying shades of the remarkably vivid Brazilian forest. Their yellow trimming imitates a flowering tree then in bloom. Dashes of crimson on the shoulder of their wings catch the hues of vine blossoms and wild flowers.

Moods of the *papagaios* range from roaring and sustained bedlam to almost complete silence. They respond to shipboard events, rising to the occasion with any excitement such as the sighting of *jacarés* slithering off sunny banks into the tan currents.

As for the crew, most of them sleep wherever they can on iron decks or in corners of this ship with its beam of 21 feet and its length of 102 feet. *Comandante Pedro José dos Santos* insists on having his cabin kept clean, and at times puts perfume behind his ears. One of the Brazilian popular nobility whose chocolate coloring does not shut off opportunity in this land of racial tolerance, he presides over the Captain's Table with ease and a touch of elegance.

Due to the wartime shortage of coastal shipping on which most Brazilians usually rely for travel north from Rio de Janeiro, many are going by way of slow river boats on the São Francisco. There are faster boats than the *Octavio Carneiro* on this stream, and also slower ones. A few de luxe packets race ahead. Although faster, they lack atmosphere. Several families are moving from the drought-stricken areas, but will return one day. They seek temporary new homes in the States of Minas Gerais, Goiaz, or Mato Grosso. It is an old cycle in Brazil's Northeast, home of the migrant.

Hawkers of wares produced by Brazil's growing industries take occasion to display samples of gingham and ribbon. A man's shoe with elastic in the sides instead of laces, a style once popular in the United States and called the Congress shoe, is in vogue along the São Francisco. Patent medicine venders ply the towns with legerdemain and bottles of miraculous elixirs. An ailing infant fails to survive such doses after its mother visits a village drug store. The little body is prepared on board for burial and taken ashore at a remote town. Sickness, most of it due to plain filth, is rife. An encouraging sanitary advance is the toothbrush. Men use it with vigor on deck each morning. Refined ladies adapt themselves to conditions as they find them. That, too, is typical of Brazil. Babies and young children abound. Of privacy there is almost none.

So we journey on together—the Brazilians and the lone North American. Since there is only one, he is known simply as Mister, pronounced Meé-ster. Toward the end of the trip my last name is added, with vast amusement when the *Comandante* and others pucker their lips and try to make their tongues form the sound. *Skahrpay* is about as close as they come to it. Sharp is definitely an un-Brazilian name.

The broad valley gradually becomes greener as we sail south. A flat plain upholds mesas and ridges that only occasionally come close to the alluvial banks. Much of the land is flooded in time of high water. Constantly crumbling, the shoreline dyes the river ocher. *Jacarés* lie in the sun and splash for cover as we approach. Egrets and long-legged tropical birds are abundant.

On the night we reach Pirapora, railhead for the trip to Rio de Janeiro, that one unforgettable parrot song comes rollicking up from somewhere below decks. There the barrel of *papagaios,* washed and sleek for the market, carries on. The song seems to say that captivity, however distasteful, will be borne with good humor and turned, as far as possible, into a carnival.

Brazilian Plateaus and Perverse Rivers

Although Brazil is as large as the other nine South American countries together, Brazil has few mountains, and these interpose their bulk precisely where fluent transport is most needed. Rio de Janeiro's Sugar Loaf at the entrance of Guanabara Bay is a signpost set to warn with its rounded precipices that access to the interior will be arduous.

The usual approach to Rio is by sea or air. A more revealing way, in terms of understanding Brazil, is to see the interior before emerging among the glories of a city that escapes all efforts

to portray it in words, oils, or color photography. I have entered
Rio many times and by all available means of transport, but no
single trip taught me as much as the slow trek overland from
Recife.

Scenically, Rio's peaks are indispensable. Sugar Loaf guards
the entrance to a bay of iridescent blues shimmering twenty
miles inland toward pinnacles near the cities of Petrópolis
and Teresópolis. There, in high valleys, *Cariocas* find relief
from summer heat. At Rio's center the thin rock needle of
Corcovado holds high the luminous 130-foot statue of *Cristo
Redentor* with arms outstretched over the city. Tijuca Peak
rises above a waterfall known affectionately as Cascatinha, or
Little Cascade. Copacabana Beach and others are looped in a
series of crescents where surf glistens on white sand. The sea
beyond is clean blue and graced by the first of picturesque
coastal islands. Some of those islands also have served as concentration camps of the Vargas dictatorship.

By territorial area and population, Brazil constitutes half of
South America. The Brazilian people merit close acquaintance.
Watch a group of Brazilians in conversation, whether at the
market place or at the Foreign Office, and you soon discover
that the language of gestures plays a more colorful, intriguing
part than the language of words. Someone ought to do the subject justice in print. The most this sketch can do is to catch a
few of the broader gestures and their more obvious meanings.
Only a Brazilian could fathom the subtler nuances.

One of the first gestures to attract my attention was a rapid
movement of both hands. They are held about waist level and
whisked past each other, alternately stroking the inside and outside of the other hand. The palm of one slaps the knuckles of
the other, and this is kept up until the desired meaning has been
conveyed. As for the meaning itself, these Brazilian gestures
evidently are as versatile as Chinese pictographs. In China, a
novice is likely to have a taxi brought to the restaurant door,
after he has ordered chicken, unless he prefaces his order with
explanations to make his meaning clear. The same Chinese sound
means taxi and chicken. Also, each Chinese pictograph has sev-

eral sounds. The most frequent meaning of the Brazilian two-hand gesture appears to be that the subject under discussion doesn't amount to much, or has taken an unfavorable turn. With this gesture they toss off an opposing political argument, inform their neighbor that the crops are bad or that the market is falling. It is the quickest way to dispose of unpleasant or dubious topics. As performed by Brazilians, with accompanying facial expressions and tones of voice, this gesture takes on diverse and exact shades of meaning.

For superspecial occasions the Brazilian reserves this one: He lifts his right hand, reaches behind his neck and pinches his left ear lobe. This means the ultimate in approval, delight, admiration. For less demonstrative occasions, the Brazilian pinches lightly the lobe of his right ear.

Also, there are rhythms and dance steps that originated both abroad and in Brazil, but have fused in characteristic Brazilian folk movements. Watching Brazilians sing and dance in the streets, I recall with considerable regret how hard it is to advance community singing in the United States. Brazilians sing for sheer joy of singing. They dance because it is in them to dance. They sing and dance in public without any evidence of self-consciousness or of self-display. They do it as naturally as the wind blows, or as Fuchsias grow wild in profusion throughout the lake district of southern Chile. Carnival is the focal point for this Brazilian folk music and folk rhythm. Intricate steps and pirouettings spring forth naturally in street urchins and the wives of Cabinet Ministers when they respond to the call of Carnival. So spontaneous are the rhythms that Brazilians seem to be in perpetual motion. They are untiring for days and whirl into the next upbeat of the music on the exhilaration of the last. Unfortunately, the picture is marred by excesses at times, but in its best expression the sheer spontaneity of Carnival is Brazilian of the Brazilians.

Rio has an indefinable lightheartedness I have not found in any other Brazilian city. It is the kind of outlook described by the Cubans as *alegre,* or gifted with an inner happiness that doesn't depend on the number of *pesos* in pocket. Among the sun-loving and beach-loving *Cariocas* of Rio, their own version of being *alegre* enters importantly into the folklore of Braziliana.

Along the Avenida Rio Branco flows the daily urbanity of the *Cariocas*. Here they sit at pleasant sidewalk tables and watch their fellow Brazilians pass. The human stream is enlivened with laughter. Looking more closely, I see hard furrows set in some of the faces by toil and inward struggle. Those faces, all of them and 44,000,000 more, are Brazil.

Brazil . . . of Portuguese gentleness in contrast with the harsher attitudes of Spanish colonial traditions.

Brazil . . . of racial tolerance where redeemed Negroes walk more erect than they would today, had the slave ships of their forebears put in, long ago, at New Orleans instead of Bahia.

Brazil . . . of elegant ladies whose bearing bespeaks innate democracy of an aristocratic but not snobbish stamp. These ladies and the culture they represent belong in the tradition of Emperor Dom Pedro II. Their memories of those spacious nineteenth-century days are kept fresh by palaces and mementos in Rio and the cool mountain retreat of Petrópolis.

Brazil . . . of a racial mixture that has not yet jelled in one distinct national type, but has progressed substantially toward that goal.

Brazil . . . of Carnival and the carefree beaches, of growing industry and the middle class it brings as an indispensable base for effective democratic government, of iron mountains and the Amazon.

Brazil . . . of Dr. Vargas.

Brazil . . . seething with currents of social and political significance for the world.

So we come to the central highlands of this mammoth country. Plateaus that extend inland from Rio de Janeiro make possible the comfortable climate of cities such as São Paulo and Belo Horizonte. It is on these uplands that Brazil's future, in large measure, appears to be written. Minerals and waterpower are brought close to the coastal cities by an escarpment that drops 2500 feet almost into the sea.

Despite all of these advantages, the mountains in the States of Espírito Santo, Minas Gerais, and São Paulo are so placed that railways and roads must cross them at tremendous cost.

In one of the strangest geological formations to be found on any continent, South America here tips inland from the coast instead of sloping to sea level. Results of this unusual configuration are far-reaching, A Brazilian once commented to me, in a revealing aside, that rivers of the United States run toward the sea. He was thinking of his country's misfortune in lacking a single river outlet of commercial utility along the entire coast south of Amazonia. The arid Northeast depends entirely on more expensive means of transport, although railways and roads are not difficult to build on its level plains. The São Francisco River is cut off from the Atlantic by Paulo Afonso Waterfalls. Smaller streams on the way south are inconsequential. The Rio Doce, back of the iron ore port of Vitória, is small, and soon broken by rapids. From Vitória all the way to Brazil's southern border in the State of Rio Grande do Sul, a series of ranges, cliffs, and plateaus prevents the formation of large rivers on the coastal side. Instead, Brazil has to watch its watersheds gather their strength to speed mercantile fleets on great rivers of Paraguay, Uruguay, and Argentina from 1000 to 2000 miles away!

A flight south from Rio along the coast discloses this odd land-tilting. The wind this morning blows in past Sugar Loaf and lines up with the main runway of Rio's centrally located airport. No city known to me can so quickly fold its wings into downtown thoroughfares. The airport is only three or four minutes from the Avenida Rio Branco by taxi. The city cut down a hill to obtain the new ground now extending into the bay. Heavily loaded dump trucks constantly enlarge the airport's borders. Even so, there is not room enough to prepare for large planes of the future. Because of the wind's direction we fly straight out over the bay, then turn starboard with Sugar Loaf falling behind on the port side as Corcovado looms up on the other. That last look at Rio draws the city into focus. The plane wings steadily past the Two Brothers, Gavea and Tijuca.

From this height Rio's rare combination of mountains, sea, bay, forests, and valleys is seen in full perspective. Yet new marvels lie ahead. South of Rio, as north, the sea spreads white crescent sands between the verdant shore and surf-rimmed islands. At this point begins the coastal escarpment. Streams rise within sight of the sea, but flow away from it. They swell headwaters of the Tieté, the Paranapanema, the Iguassú, and other tributaries of the extensive river system that converges in the Rio de la Plata at Buenos Aires.

Soon is seen one of the most interesting among municipal power systems. São Paulo, Brazil's commercial and industrial metropolis, has made ingenious use of the escarpment. The city itself lies on the plateau. By damming several streams, São Paulo has formed a network of lakes. The water is then dropped down the escarpment to power stations near the seaport of Santos.

The region around São Paulo initiates a zone of transition between tropics and semitropics, leading on to the temperate climates of Uruguay and Argentina. Here flourishes the Paraná pine. In one mighty stem this tree shoots up without branches until, near the top, arms reach straight out and then curve upward. When found as virgin forest, the Paraná pine presents one of the most beautiful tree-patterns to be seen in flight. Its vivid interlaced crowns cover vast leagues of southern Brazil and extend into adjacent countries. From Curitiba, capital of Paraná, to the coast at Joinvile and Blumenau in one of the most Germanified regions, the highway presents a fascinating cross section of foliage. Paraná pines stand, on higher elevations, beside tropical trees including varieties covered with large blossoms. Sometimes white and pink occur on the same tree. The white petals stand out like clusters of stars in the dark forest. This is in Santa Catarina, the last State before Rio Grande do Sul and its capital, Pôrto Alegre. We have reached the southern extremity of Brazil, 4000 miles below our entry north of Belém.

Pôrto Alegre means Happy Port, and if whistling denotes a happy people, then the city is well named. This is Brazil of temperate skies, of open cattle country, of long rolling hills, and of the *gaucho*.

In Paraná State are the Falls of the Iguassú and the Seven Cataracts of Guairá. On the way there, flying north and west from Pôrto Alegre, the plane crosses unbroken wilderness with splendid stands of Paraná pine where no ax has rung. My first view from the air discloses a bend in the river, forming a large lake dotted with islands. From this lake the river pours through numerous channels. Dropping 210 feet as compared with Niagara's 160, and extending 9500 feet along a narrow hairpin gorge, Iguassú has no fewer than 275 distinct waterfalls. Panels of dense tropical foliage provide frames. Broad terraces diversify the symphony of waters. Flocks of green parrots, trimmed with blue and a dash of crimson, live in the mist-drenched trees at the very edge of roaring waters. Iguassú is near a triangle border junction of Brazil, Argentina, and Paraguay. It is spectacular scenery, but these rivers would mean more to Brazil if they ran to Brazil's own Atlantic Coast. Possession in Amazonia of the world's largest single river network does not help Brazil solve the many economic problems entailed in that capricious inward tilt of a continent's edge. Unbalance and maldistribution, more than lack, again are found to be characteristic of South America. Abundant water transport flows through a distant Brazilian jungle, while tunnels must be driven in mountains of solid granite to move every ton of iron ore and merchandise at the center of Brazil's industrial activity.

The plateaus of Southern Brazil offer a vantage point for drawing together impressions of the vast South American canvas before taking in the central lowlands and completing the picture in Patagonia. São Paulo's plateau is linked with others that form the second—and last—divide of the South American continent from east to west. The Andes form the only connected north-south divide. From them runs at right angles the low Orinoco-Amazon watershed between 2 and 5 degrees North Latitude. Then comes the Amazon Basin, delineated on the south by Brazil's plateaus between 15 and 18 degrees South Latitude. North from São Paulo are the States of Minas Gerais and Goiaz, while Mato Grosso terminates Brazil on the west where Bolivian plains lead slowly up to the Andes.

Chaco and Pampa: Land of Far Horizons

The brush that paints South America must sweep with broad flat strokes when it reaches the central lowlands of the continent. Here the interior draws in from both sides to form a cornucopia of plains as long as the United States is wide. Draining away from the southern limits of the Amazon Basin into the *Gran Chaco* of Paraguay and northern Argentina, they embrace great rivers including the Paraguay, Paraná, Uruguay, and Rio de la Plata. On the west they roll to foothills of the Andes. Almost at sea level they swing past Brazil's dwindling plateaus and reach the Atlantic. Wide and fertile in Buenos Aires Province, they spread through *pampa* grasslands to southern deserts and end in sheep pastures at the Strait of Magellan.

Chaco in Spanish means an open space, a clearing, and often is applied to a planted field. The *Gran Chaco* emerged into world prominence some years ago when the war between Paraguay and Bolivia over parts of this territory came before the Geneva League of Nations. That war finally ended in 1938 with a boundary accord reached through arbitration by other American nations. Paraguay gained at Bolivia's expense.

Sailing down the Paraguay River from Corumbá in Brazilian Mato Grosso I saw buildings still marked with signs of battle. In that war it was standard practice for writing about the *Chaco* to be couched in such phrases as steaming jungle. Rare was the story or speech about the *Chaco* that omitted this particularly misleading description. There is some jungle in the *Chaco*, and it can steam. Part of the bitterest fighting took place there. Yet the *Chaco* in most of its extension is open country. It is wooded, if at all, with scattered palms. In some sections it is almost desert. Nor are these plains confined to Paraguay and Bolivia. Argentina has the *Chaco Central* and the *Chaco Austral*.

This is South America of the inland riverways. It is a counterpart of the watershed drained by the Mississippi and its far-ranging tributaries, the Ohio and Missouri. Here the arteries are the Paraná and Paraguay and Uruguay, converging in the Rio de la Plata. Because of the strange inward tilting of the South American continent, which we first noted on the coast south of Rio de Janeiro, this river basin begins within sight of the sea, but its waters travel a full 2000 miles to reach their deltas. All of the large rivers run roughly parallel with the coast. Their headwaters rise deep in the interior of central Brazil. The Iguassú, one among many tributaries, begins near the city of Curitiba and flows away at right angles to the coastline before merging in the Paraná. Within this river network the country of Paraguay is suspended. Possibly no other country in the world is so completely a land of rivers. The Paraná swings along its borders on the east and south to the point where the Rio Paraguay rolls southward as the main stem of these many waters.

Nudging a mud bank of the Iguassú River one night without benefit of pier or quay at the Argentine port of Puerto Aguirre, a sturdy little craft with its few brave lights confronts the vast land and vaster darkness. A few rays ripple on the current as it flows silently to its junction with the Paraná. Here is no hint of thunderous mists where the Iguassú tumbles into its terraced gorge only twelve miles upstream. Moths and whirring insects of the jungle night make deck lights flicker with beating wings. My river steamer on the Iguassú this night is headed south toward the Paraguay. When the last bale and barrel have been loaded, it slips away into the night toward distant Buenos Aires. As we journey, other boats whistle 'round the bend on their way to the Paraguayan capital, Asunción.

Quite close to Asunción, the Paraguay is fed by another sizable river, the Pilcomayo, which forms the long southern boundary of Paraguay westward to the Bolivian line. One railway crosses into Paraguay from Argentina at the port of Posadas on the Paraná. These trains connect Asunción with the outside world. Otherwise, Paraguay depends entirely on rivers or poor roads for its outlets. A factor of prime political significance in this geographical position of Paraguay is Argentina's dominance of the river funnel through which Paraguayan products must flow outward.

In Asunción, the river packet is more in evidence than the railroad. The mellow whistles of approaching boats are as welcome as in days of old Mississippi. Crowds gather at the excellent quays to welcome returning members of the family, or to send others off on a long voyage. The packets slip through channels lined with jungle, or pass cultivated land as level as a table. Asunción itself retains much colonial atmosphere. Many visitors go away to write about cobblestone streets with grass growing between the cobblestones. Such visitors ought to approach Asunción, not from super-modern Buenos Aires, but from Foz do Iguassú. After seeing the hinterland where unbroken jungle knows no trails except those of the jaguar, and where the few settlers still carry side arms as in the Wild West, Asunción seems like a marvel of modernity. After I had battled red mud on the few jungle roads, broad smooth cobblestones of Asunción seemed like four-lane highways. Also, there is paving in Asunción, more each year, smooth and fine. As in so many cities of South America, transport facilities are badly overworked. Small busses, as fragile in appearance as gangling insects, carry an unbelievable volume of perspiring humanity. Larger modern busses and streetcars help relieve the traffic at rush hours, but the ancient conveyances still creep along. Every yard forward is a marvel of resilient springs underneath, and of resilient dispositions inside the narrow cabins.

Remarkably homogeneous and unmistakable as a type among residents of South America, Paraguayans are intensely nationalistic. They pride themselves on being fighters, and have no intention of surrendering their independence, whether to larger countries next door, or to outsiders. Less demonstrative than most Latins, they seldom engage in public displays, and then tend to watch rather than to shout. Yet beneath their quiet exterior broods a temper which can flare hot and quick. With the North American revolutionists of 1775, these people say, *Don't tread on me*. That is a basic attitude of this proud, little-known land encompassed by mighty rivers.

The trail now leads straight into Argentina. Approach this country overland from any direction, and impressions of its advancement—except in present politics—can hardly be missed. I entered at Posadas, capital of Misiones Territory in the finger of land that points north between Paraguay and Brazil. For more than four months I had been traveling through the interior. Most of this time was spent in Brazil. Bolivia's deep interior was also on the itinerary. Toward the end I came through the center of Paraguay from north to south. The Brazilian river boats had ranged from almost the most primitive imaginable to a few quite modern ships. Some of the best Brazilian lines, ranking with the Argentinian ones, were not on my route.

The contrast now being drawn between Brazil and Argentina is not necessarily uncomplimentary to Brazil. It is simply a situation brought about by differing conditions in the two largest countries of South America.

Brazil is gangling, disjointed, poorly organized. The enduring unification sought through dictatorial methods of the Vargas regime has not been achieved. Possibly it cannot be achieved by any form of government until the country has been drawn more closely together by improved transportation and education. Argentina already has a highly developed network of railways, river fleets and highways joining every important part of its national territory. When struggling with nonexistent travel information and sometimes nonexistent travel means in Brazil's interior, I was told by an Argentinian that in his country I would have no further troubles of that kind.

"There is plenty of transportation in Argentina," he said.

At Posadas the fact became agreeably apparent. Already at Pôrto Esperança, a Brazilian port on the Paraguay River, I had seen the pale-blue-and-white ensign of Argentina flying on smartly painted cargo ships. Even at that distance, in a Brazilian port, Argentina took pride in excelling. The Brazilian boats were dingy by comparison. Later in Asunción, capital of Paraguay, I saw sleek Argentine river ships, not paddle-wheelers but tall ships driven by powerful screws.

The *Guayra,* as she lay at the Posadas dock the morning after I had come from Asunción by car, rail, and ferry bridge across the river, seemed like a vision. Built in Glasgow, the

Guayra and her sister ships are fully up to transatlantic standards. More significant than the original workmanship, which is native to Scotland, was the upkeep.

One look at the officers told the story. They were immaculate, cultured, erect and self-respecting, although a bit haughty. And they were Argentines, not representatives of some foreign firm. The ride up the Paraná River to Iguassú and back was sheer delight and relief after months in the Brazilian wilderness. Moreover, this was still wilderness. Across the river lay the most remote parts of Paraguay. Ahead loomed Brazil. The difference is that Argentina withholds no effort to reach its farthest confines with transportation and culture. Soon after entering Argentina this time, I found many railway stations of the interior so swept and clean that passengers do not even drop peanut shells on the outdoor platforms.

Uruguay also is a country of advanced development on the plains of southern South America. Small in numbers, but great in character, the Uruguayans stand out, not only along the Rio de la Plata, but in Latin America as a whole. Whatever the background for their present mental attitudes, those attitudes are instinctively on the democratic side. Courage to act accompanies their convictions. Their decisions in the world struggle against Nazism have savored of allegiance to principles rather than calculation of material interests. During each recurring stay among the Uruguayans I seek to understand more of their character. Seen promenading in Montevideo, alert and smartly clad, or met in humbler circumstances, they manifest something different, something direct and heartening for the present and future of South America.

On the trip from Buenos Aires to Montevideo, the overnight boat crosses slantwise down a long river estuary between two worlds. The difference is not visible in geography. Much the same terrain, level except for a few low hills, appears in the early morning light. Blue water, however, begins to hint the deeper contrasts. Mud in suspension flows past Buenos Aires where the Rio de la Plata spreads thirty miles wide. Under conditions of Argentine politics, those opaque currents accurately portray what has been going on. The course of government is roiled in the proud land of this tawny river. The Rio de la Plata is named silver without ever gleaming gray-blue in the sun. By the time seaward Montevideo is reached, much of the mud has settled. The South Atlantic rolls in, clean and refreshing, against white beaches. Argentina, too, has that kind of shoreline at Mar del Plata on the open sea, some six hours by train from the capital. Yet this aspect of Argentina is not seen by boat from Buenos Aires to Montevideo. There the contrast between muddy river and clean sea is sharp and symbolic. For Uruguay runs as a clear current in a straight course. People and Government are united in their allegiance to the principles of human freedom.

Why these two neighbors of the Rio de la Plata differ as they do is partly apparent by comparing certain broad characteristics. Deeper causes for these differences are not easily distinguished. Size alone is an over-all influence within the two countries. Argentina is large and aspires to leadership in Latin America. Uruguay is small and makes no effort to be more than it is. Yet size does not account for the basic differences. A smaller country might be expected to fall more easily under the dominance of a landowning oligarchy. Instead, it is Argentina where a relatively few families hold the instruments of economic power, and use this power to maintain their grip on the Government. Among the everyday people of both countries, democratic sympathies prevail. For numerous reasons, present-day Uruguayans do not have to resist their own Government. The nation moves forward without serious internal wrenchings. One explanation for the democratic attitude of the Uruguayan Government is that this small country for some time has consciously been declaring independence from being dominated by the Argentine. Uruguay, instead of being subjected by geography to its larger neighbor of the Rio de la Plata, shares with Argentina the sea approaches to that influential river. Headlands of almost equal strategic value in both countries command the delta.

Low-lying and broadly curving, these coasts terminate the *pampa* after its seaward sweep of 1000 miles from foothills of the Andes in northwestern Argentina.

This is South America of far horizons. On plains of southern Brazil, Uruguay, Paraguay, and Argentina have been written the sagas of the *gaucho*. In Montevideo are two impressive bronze monuments, one to the individual *gaucho*, and the other to covered-wagon pioneers. Properly speaking, the *gaucho* is an historical type no longer found in South America. The name does not belong to any cowboy in *bombachas*, those long and full riding pantaloons of swashbuckling lines flopping over boots of limp leather that gradually settles into accordion pleats around the ankles. To the Argentine, an ordinary cowboy is a *criollo*, or a *paisano*. The true *gaucho* lived in the nomadic and adventurous period before the *pampa* had been fenced. He rode with armies of liberation in colonial wars against Spain. Around his name have clustered the nostalgic folklore and music of the *pampa*. Only in Brazil is the name of *gaucho* still used as synonymous with cowboy.

A lone *ombú* tree, its rounded top and sturdy central trunk standing in a pool of shade on the sun-drenched grasslands, is a one-stroke portrait of the *pampa*. A lone *gaucho*, strumming a love ditty to his distant *China Girl* while his pony grazes near by, is *pampa* replete.

Patagonia: Windy Promontory

Wind was my first pervasive impression of South America's southernmost plains where they narrow toward the Strait of Magellan, leap to the large island of Tierra del Fuego, and yield to rocky forerunners of Cape Horn.

Wind that tugs at everything in its path . . .

Wind against which a man makes headway only by strenuous exertion . . .

Wind that whips up ice particles from glaciers hundreds of

miles long between Andean ridges far to the west and drives in undulating lashings across huddled plains-grass . . .

Wind freshening through the half-light of some days when even at noon every familiar outline is transmuted into a realm of pale dust-blown shapes with earth and sea and sky fused in one taut and roaring whole.

Anywhere south of Bahía Blanca in the lower corridor of Buenos Aires Province, the winds can blow with seemingly inexhaustible reserves. In Patagonia a plane in flight may suddenly be pummeled as by hundreds of crackling whiplashes.

Numerous surprises await anyone who approaches land's-end expecting to find a savage wilderness. The trip itself is comparatively luxurious. De luxe trains on the way to San Carlos de Bariloche and the Argentine lake district leave Buenos Aires. I boarded in early evening and a day later reached San Antonio Oueste, junction point for busses south. The train to Bariloche trailed its black smoke out of sight on the windy horizon as we waited to be shuttled on a spur track to the port. There a fleet of five large busses, blue and shining, stood at the station. They are called "Pullmans," although they have no sleeping accommodations. With Argentine efficiency the passengers and luggage are loaded. We find our numbered seats as twilight falls.

Through the night we push ahead as ships buffeted by a storm. The heavy and powerful bus trembles under the impact of Patagonian winds. Inside, the only light glows from the illuminated dashboard. A feeling of adventure runs through the bus. Young Argentines are off for their first military training at Gallegos on the threshold of Magellan's Strait. Chilean businessmen resident in Buenos Aires are on the way to Punta Arenas, southernmost city of their country and of the world. Everyone among us with any feel for the open road and the call of the seven seas has wanted someday to follow in Magellan's course. The rapidly falling temperature reminds us we are approaching polar seas. From fathomless reaches of the midnight sky when we stop at wayside inns to refuel, the wind has swept all cloudiness, all mists, even star dust, leaving only diamond points of icy constellations.

It is a journey of five days and five nights. We do not always travel after dark. There are substantial towns with hotel accommodations. Trelew, Comodoro Rivadavia, and San Julián lead on toward Gallegos. Broad and smooth is the gravel highway, maintained in excellent condition by the Argentine Government for military as well as economic reasons. The road follows the coast at a short distance inland. Occasionally we dip down along beaches where boulders glisten with dried salt-water spray far back from the line of frigid surf. Sea birds of stout and swift wing flash through the spume. We are nearing penguin coasts. The southernmost extension of Africa had been left behind even at Buenos Aires, and now ahead lies Cape Horn, 1500 miles below the latitude of the Cape of Good Hope.

The road traverses a landscape that hardly changes as the days pass. A bunch grass called *coirón* spreads to the level horizon. Fences are constant reminders that this is developed land. For at least a decade it has reached capacity in its principal commodity—sheep. These grasslands unfold between the sea and the distant Andes with only slight undulations and a rare outcropping of rocks. There are a few shallow lakes, and others that have dried to form salt flats. Stripped of grass cover, these are whipped mercilessly by the wind. In such vast monotony, little things drive home the country's essential character. One fence, stark on a rolling skyline like some Rockwell Kent drawing, summed up for me the loneliness of Patagonia. At a wayside stop I walked a short distance into the open. What happened to the ants on a few bare spots made me feel the searching nature of this wind. One instant I would see several ants proceeding with antful might and main toward their flat holes. No anthill could stand. Neither can the ants when some invisible gusty blast descends upon them. They simply disappear.

Wind-wise dwellers in this almost treeless land have sealed themselves in metal-sheathed houses, there to enjoy whole rooms lined with potted plants. Often the ceiling of such a room will be covered with climbing ivy. Inside, a warm hush settles over us. The piercing blasts shrill outside as echoes.

Such are impressions in midsummer. The season is betokened

by a vigorously supple and resilient evergreen shrub. On an unusually windy day there seems to be color among the thrashing green branches. Sure enough, at the tips are blossoms that must rank among the hardiest in the plant kingdom. Lavender and delicate though they are, they snap gaily and come back for more. They hold the end-spot in this game of crack-the-whip.

At Comodoro Rivadavia, oil derricks and tanks are kept spotless with aluminum paint—another evidence of Argentine pride in efficiency and appearance.

No other significant change occurs to break Patagonia's monotony until the plains have begun to meet southern outposts of the Andes as they curve in from the west. Argentina's grasslands become drier and less fertile as they near the Chilean border. For reasons of its own, Chile leaves this part of the international highway in miserable condition. After the smooth gravel of Argentina, the bumps make hard riding until Chile's better roads have been reached.

My first sight of Magellan's Strait discloses a wide channel swinging in from the Atlantic. Calm this day in a respite from usual winds, the water is gray-blue with a sheen as of just-melted ice. For the eastern 130 miles of the Strait my passage is the landlubber's way—by road. The car comes down to water's edge at times. Nearer Punta Arenas the route threads among lakes and lagoons.

The land steadily improves as we advance. Chile has the best pasturage in the transition between aridity of the east coast and rains of the west. Large herds of sheep are being driven along the road toward market. Beside a lagoon in the distance, hundreds of flamingos rest, their plumage showing pale crimson in the slanting sunshine. Trees bent into fantastic patterns show how the winds blow.

So Patagonian plains merge with the Andes. At the crossroads of seas and mountains stands Punta Arenas, companioned on its latitude only by oceans and winds that beat from around the rolling globe against South America's windy promontory.

IN SEARCH OF FRONTIERS

Frontiers: Andes

WHAT, THEN, DO the Andes offer for modern pioneers?

Anyone who has flown, ridden, or hiked in the Andes can see at a glance that food production and transport involve staggering difficulties.

Mineral production, while costly, has poured down from the Andes since early times to swell treasure chests of Indian chieftains, Spanish courts, and modern capitalists.

The Andes for South America are both a colossal storehouse of mineral wealth, and a colossal deficit. Minerals, although still substantial after nearly 450 years of colonial and industrial exploitation, have worn thin in spots. The deficit is written in stone so massive that to cut through it is beyond foreseeable economic possibilities, if not of mechanical genius. The wealth, being almost exclusively mineral, will someday be drained to its dregs.

Already Bolivia faces a crisis that could grow to national bankruptcy. Declining richness of Bolivian tin mines, previously reported in a chapter on Bolivia, caused a mine owner to offer me, in all seriousness, title to a tin mine with surveyed reserves worth $10,000,000! He had ceased operations in the midst of wartime demand for tin when Japan still held the Malayan and East Indies mines. He simply couldn't make it pay, and he was an old hand at tin mining in Bolivia.

The thing to remember about mineral wealth of the Andes is that, long before the Spaniards came, native miners had been working for centuries. Gold was extracted to be hammered into thin sheets and shaped as images of sun-gods. Tales of rooms half-filled with gold may be explained in part by this art form. There is more air than gold inside an image a foot long. Yet the Incas and their predecessors made a substantial beginning on the extraction of Andean gold. Greedy Spaniards, who matched avarice with technical skill, did such a thorough piece of surveying before the *Mayflower* reached Plymouth Rock that few gold or silver veins, and none of great consequence, have been discovered in the Andes since colonial times. As I dropped down from Cerro de Pasco in Peru toward Tingo María in the jungle, I soon passed on the road a series of circular stone enclosures about four feet high. Beside some of them lie heavy millstones. Here the Spaniards crushed ores brought in from great distances by herds of llamas. Inside the enclosures, other animals paced their monotonous round as blindfolded donkeys still do in primitive industries of China.

Modern industry has sought copper and other minerals, in addition to gold. Two thousand five hundred feet deep in a Peruvian mine shaft at Cerro de Pasco, I stood in what the mine superintendent called a "jewel shop." Disney's seven singing miners were nowhere in sight, but the walls glistened with microscopic gems. They were not diamonds or rubies, but crystals of silver and copper with some gold to add warmth to their flame. It was strange to think where we were. Even after descending half a mile in an elevator shaft we still stood two and a half miles above sea level.

Similar experiences may be had at key points along the Andes. At Oroyo, south of Cerro de Pasco, the air is heavy with fumes from furnaces where copper ores are melted to form flat ingots. These are loaded on freight cars for the steep descent to sea level. From Callao, seaport of Lima, they are shipped to refineries in the United States. Other mines in Bolivia and Chile yield not only copper and silver, but antimony and numerous other indispensable sinews for industry. Far to the south along the Andes, Argentina has hardly begun to explore or utilize its own minerals. The reason is that Argentina's soil has been its wealth.

Oil is one of the truly great resources of South America. Venezuela and Colombia have extensive pools, as does Peru in its northern coastal territory near Talara. Oil also is known to exist on eastern slopes of the Andes. Bolivia has producing wells.

Other oil deposits have been located and are being worked at several points in Argentina, including Comodoro Rivadavia, Salta, Mendoza, and Neuquén.

Unquestionably there are opportunities in South America for further mineral discoveries and development. The field, however, is by no means virgin territory. Nor is it one in which lone prospectors can usually hope to strike it rich. Highly capitalized mining enterprises have gone far toward surveying reserves, and staking claims.

A growing tendency that springs directly from the nationalistic wave in South America is for governments to assert as much control as possible over present and future mineral exploitation. This is only natural, but in the process there have been some unfortunate blightings of productive enterprise. South American attitudes toward foreign capital in their midst were frankly summed up by one outspoken diplomat in a group en route to the Eighth Pan-American conference at Lima in 1938. As they promenaded in the cool of evening on a terrace overlooking extensive railway yards owned by a foreign firm at Mollendo in southern Peru, he stopped. Waving his arms toward the yards below, he exclaimed:

"Look at that! It is on our soil, but it is not ours. Someday we will own these things ourselves."

The process of economic independence is actually under way, even in the mining industry. In the natural accumulation of capital by citizens of Latin-American countries, it has been possible for whole enterprises to be founded on native money. There are several growing mines of this kind in Peru and elsewhere.

At times there has been friction and even legal conflict that ended in virtual confiscation of foreign properties. Such was the case of the Standard Oil Company of Bolivia. Without entering into the merits or demerits of this dispute, it is plain that the net result was the ousting of a foreign firm and nationalization of the oil fields. Signs of similar tension have appeared in Chile and Peru. It is understandable that when South Americans see their mineral or other wealth being carted away, as well as most of the cash proceeds, they inwardly rebel. One method they adopt to keep some of the cash proceeds in the country is to levy high taxes. Bolivia has done such a thorough work in this unpopular field that during my 1943-44 trip I found mine operators complaining loudly. This particular country lives from taxes imposed on its minerals, chiefly tin. The present danger is that such an unbalanced economy, forcing mineral taxes beyond levels that permit profitable operation, may weaken or destroy the tax source itself. There comes a point beyond which mines of dwindling tin content cannot meet world competition and at the same time sustain Bolivian taxes.

Because of these and other problems that arise in a mining region where digging has proceeded continuously for many centuries, it is evident that Andean minerals do not offer many new visible horizons. They offer instead the kind of marginal operations that require costly technical skills. In the large San José Mine of Maurice Hochschild at Oruro, Bolivia, I saw a dragline scooping up mine tailings to be sifted. Now it pays to reclaim the wastefulness of an earlier and richer period.

Apart from mining, the Andes hold forth little that might attract pioneers in this period. Even mining is a hard, lonely, artificial existence in the Andes, more than in many other regions. The altitude alone is such that mine officials and their families have to come down every so often to take some deep breaths of the kind of air to which they have been accustomed. I saw these people spending long evenings on the desolate *altiplano* in the exotic cheer and comfort of their American or English surroundings that have been imported, sometimes by muleback. Of cultural diversions there are almost none. The motion picture houses, where they exist, are small, and usually filled with Indians who may be admirable characters, but have not succumbed to the blandishments of soap and water.

One odor of the Andean highlands that is particularly offensive to most outsiders is the *coca* leaf after it has been chewed, as the Indians do regularly for its narcotic effect. Awareness that this leaf is a social scourge does not speed the process of adjustment. All along the upper Andes dried coca, containing cocaine, and alcoholic drinks of particular violence keep the mass of Indian inhabitants saturated and befogged much of the time. They work enough to buy a few crude foods, and squander most of their pittance on enslavements.

In mountains of such height, human habitation necessarily seeks the lower slopes and valleys. Of all the northern Andean countries, Colombia is most favored with valleys of moderate altitude—4000 to 8000 feet—pockets of reasonably fertile soil, and pleasant climate. Quite naturally such valleys long ago were settled almost to capacity, until new developments enlarge their possibilities.

The Magdalena River in northern Colombia is a curious phenomenon. While it cuts a deep valley, provides a navigable waterway, and heads straight north to the sea, it does not actually provide a pass through the Andes barrier for purposes of land transportation. That is, a road following the river from north to south would end at high altitudes. Feeder roads east and west would have to scale slopes at uneconomic costs. This helps explain why the Pan-American Highway at present skips all the way from Panama to La Guaira, seaport for Caracas in Venezuela. Drivers headed south as pioneers on the eventual through route from Alaska to Magellan's Strait must ferry their cars 800 miles by sea. The journey continues over a roundabout route from Caracas to Bogotá, capital of Colombia. Another reason for this gap in the road that someday will directly link North and South America is the low-lying Chocó jungle and its hostile tribesmen. Joining the Darien jungle of Panama, the Chocó as I have seen it from the air would be a matted, soggy, difficult terrain for road-building engineers even if they didn't have to contend with sudden secret arrows.

Colombia funnels its economic activity on a north-south axis through parallel valleys of the Cauca and Magdalena Rivers, and so by-passes the Chocó. Bogotá is reached quickly by air, unless a traveler has plenty of time. The Magdalena is temperamental and may exact two weeks or more along its mosquito-infested banks from Barranquilla to La Dorada. Then the trip is completed by rail and road through a jumble of mountains to

Colombia's capital in its broad level valley 8660 feet high. Not so long ago part of this journey had to be made by mule. Such backward travel conditions after 450 years of European settlement in the region of South America closest to the Panama Canal, the United States, and the main arteries of world trade, are due to the nature of the terrain more than the type of people who have settled here.

Many upper valleys of Venezuela and Colombia are open, as well as endowed with soils well suited to specialized agriculture. Available hillsides are cultivated intensively in Colombia, mostly for coffee plantations. Rains do not have the leaching thud and suction they exert in the near-by Orinoco Valley and the more distant Amazon. Venezuela depends on petroleum income to such an extent that agriculture is neglected. Serious results occur in high prices of foodstuffs and of living costs generally. Venezuela has undeveloped food possibilities in some of its valleys at elevations of 2000 to 4000 feet. Also, the Venezuelan forerunners of the main Andes Cordillera are more liberally supplied with viable passes than are the central ramparts. It is possible to cross from Caracas, situated at an altitude of 3000 feet and almost on the coast, to the valley of the Orinoco by passes of comparatively moderate height. Roads, however, are few. Airplanes provide much of the contact between Venezuela's capital and settlements of the interior.

One of the few reasonably thorough projects of soil research in South America has been carried through by the United States Department of Agriculture in the northern Andes. Venezuela, north of the Orinoco River, was surveyed in 1941-42 by competent soil technicians including Hugh H. Bennett, now chief of the Soil Conservation Service. Promising strips were located, although much of the soil would not produce enough to overcome transportation costs. An extensive report was published by the Soil Conservation Service at Washington in 1942.

In an earlier field study of soils in western Ecuador, Mr. Bennett discovered in 1923 one belt of soil on the Pacific side of the Andes that filled him with enthusiasm. It is in the Guayas River valley of Ecuador. This land is already largely planted to cacao, from which cocoa and chocolate are made, but it could be cultivated more intensively. Ecuador's coastal plains are broken by outcroppings and enriched by recent volcanic deposits. Heavy rains have not yet dissolved and carried away this comparatively new plant food. In some areas a long dry season enables the soil to recuperate from too much drenching. Yet these are only small fingers of agricultural promise in relation to the whole of South America.

Peru, through its Agricultural Experiment Station in Tingo María on the Huallaga River, is increasing soil research that also extends to other parts of the country.

A Colombian, Dr. Jorge Ancizar-Sordo, issued a brochure in Spanish at Medellin in 1941 on *Impoverishment of the Soils of Colombia, and Its Repercussions on Cattle Growing*. This serves to fill in data on part of the Colombian area. After 10 years of research on Colombian soils, Dr. Ancizar-Sordo found general deficiencies of phosphorus and calcium.

So, while the northern Andes have some food prospects through careful development, minerals are still their major reliance.

On a population map where concentrations of people are shown by dots that merge in black lines and masses, or barely fleck the white paper, it becomes quickly apparent that the northern Andes are one of the most heavily settled areas in South America. In contrast, the low-lying Orinoco and Amazon Basins thin out until the map might almost be that of some uninhabited planet. All of the advanced cultures known to have existed in the northern part of South America sprang to flower along the valleys, plateaus, and ridges of this massive mountain homeland.

Nothing approaching the architecture of Cuzco and Machu Picchu, to mention only two examples, has ever been found among ruins of the tropical lowlands. Using materials at hand, the mountaineers built with enduring rock, while the forest dwellers have moved in the green exuberance of an ever-changing world where palm fronds and wood have not preserved their story. Only at a few points, such as the island of Marajó in the mouth of the Amazon, have the wet tropics left relics to indicate more advanced stages of culture. Otherwise, the Amazonian forest with its wandering rivers and rapid cycle of change wipes out even the high-water marks of human penetration, unless towns are preserved by continuous habitation from century to century. As for temples or other ruins of the kind discovered in the Mayan country of Yucatán or overgrown by the jungles of Burma, Amazonia has yet to bring them to light, if any exist. With a persistence that could not be explained by some passing breeze of human whims, pioneers have gravitated during the centuries from inhospitable coasts and jungles to the highlands of the Andes. After nearly half a millennium of European colonization, the mountains remain the seat of civilization and culture in the whole northwestern half of South America.

Earliest inhabitants of the Andes sought to stretch meager soil to cover food needs of their communities. Stone terrace walls may still be seen, some of them intact and in use, where the Incas and peoples before them pushed their farming up the steep slopes of barren ridges. Soil and water were gathered and husbanded. It is a less-than-complimentary phase of present farming methods that modern governments have not proved as foresighted as the Incas. Descending steeply by car from Cerro de Pasco in Peru on the way to Huánuco and Tingo María, I found that it is not unusual to be stopped by sudden freshets. No rain is falling on the road, or in sight, yet from the high ridges roars a deluge that fills every gully. Great boulders crash along in the flood. The rubble of rocks and gravel covers hundreds of yards of the road in a few minutes. Emergency crews stand by to clear a passage when the water has subsided sufficiently. I saw adobe houses swept away without warning.

In this part of Peru such recent erosion could have been avoided in large measure. The steep slopes were stripped of their natural forest and other cover. In a zone of heavy rain, the ensuing floods are devastating. These conditions occur on the famous road from Lima to Pucalpa on the Upper Ucayali River, where river steamers set forth on the Amazonian network to the Atlantic nearly 3000 miles distant. The road has been open to traffic all the way only for a short time. On this road rest Peru's hopes for opening a large part of its tropical empire. Tingo María is an important center of agricultural research. At an altitude of 2200 feet, it is in land typical of lower eastern foothills of the Andes, a belt of forested ranges and valleys forming the transition between jungled lowlands and barren peaks. It is still one of the most remote regions in the world, although throughout most of its length it lies only about 150 miles from the Pacific Ocean. In that narrow strip rises one of the world's most formidable mountain barriers. The road to Tingo María crosses, by way of Oroyo, a pass nearly 16,000 feet high. Soils of the eastern Andes region are generally not as rich as might be expected. Heavy rains leach them. Although Peru has hundreds of square miles suited to banana cultivation, for every one in Ecuador, the Andes again write a heavy deficit. Bananas are exported from Guayaquil to Peruvian ports. Coastal Peru cannot draw from its vast tropical hinterland on headwaters of the Amazon River, without climbing the central Andes. It is being done by the building of truck highways, but the traffic is expensive.

Valleys of the central Cordillera in Ecuador, Peru, Bolivia, Argentina, and Chile are too high and cold for profitable agriculture, even when they have enough rain. Some excellent soils exist in isolated pockets there aloft. Soil experts in the United States Department of Agriculture have told me they wish those lands of the *páramos* could be utilized as their deep fertility deserves. On the whole, upper Peru and Bolivia are rock-strewn tablelands without a tree in sight, for they are far above timber-line at 13,000 to 16,000 feet—on the level ground! Other valleys appear at intervals along the entire Andean chain, but their total of arable land at altitudes where most people would want to settle is in the proportion of a few pencil marks on an ax handle.

The Andes south of Uspallata Pass are a storehouse of minerals not yet fully explored, particularly on the Argentine side. One hindrance of continuing economic validity is the distance of these southern ores from potential markets. Chile, lacking extensive farm areas of the kind that have made Argentina a leading world exporter of corn, meat, and wheat, has been compelled to develop its mineral resources. Argentina's growing industrialization is turning attention to the country's mineral reserves. Unlike those of Chile, they are shut off from easy access to the sea. When mines are opened in Argentina's southern Andes, the ores will have to be carried out of mountains as yet unprovided with adequate means of transport, and then moved through Patagonia's plains. Argentina's rail network ends with the line from San Antonio Oueste to San Carlos de Bariloche. South of that, everything is by road except for a few short rail spurs. Many new roads will be needed as mines are established.

Agricultural possibilities of the southern Andes are slight, although soils are good in many valleys. The existence in Argentina and Chile of far more accessible plains, and Argentina's ability to produce a surplus of low-priced foods, lessen prospects of important farm exports, except sheep, from the mountain areas. Most of the sheep lands already are loaded to capacity. An enterprising pioneer still might carve himself a ranch from virgin territory, but he would have to do so against the competition of highly capitalized firms such as the *Sociedad Explotadora de Tierra del Fuego* at Punta Arenas. The *Explotadora* has 1,250,000 sheep on 4,481,865 acres. It and other large operators have long been searching for suitable sheep pasture.

In summary, I should say that the Andes hold definite mineral prospects in the south to make up for declining veins in Bolivia and Peru. Agricultural frontiers are more promising in the north, where fertilization and soil management could greatly aid in balancing Venezuelan economy, as well as Colombia's in lesser degree. The lone pioneer does not appear to face in the Andes very many golden opportunities. Capital and organization on a large scale are required. Without them it is impossible to surmount the hurdles of distance from market, faulty or nonexistent transportation, unsanitary food, water, and the lack of other community facilities. Even colonies of pioneers who set forth hopefully with pooled capital find themselves in a hard environment. Hiram Bingham of the United States, who brought

Machu Picchu to light in 1911, became fired with enthusiasm for sending pioneer colonies into Bolivia. He tried, and the venture had to be abandoned. William H. "Alfalfa Bill" Murray of Oklahoma had a similar experience. I have seen the broken remnants of colonies where a few poverty-stricken survivors carried on, largely because they couldn't earn enough to pay a passage out. There have been a few successful colonies established in recent years, usually by refugees from Nazi Europe to whom any new home was welcome. Such colonies are small, amounting to little more than places of refuge. Whether they leave a permanent mark on the Andes remains to be seen.

Two personal experiences summarize what the Andes mean to me as a pioneer field for individuals.

On the train one day from Juliaca to Cuzco I met a young North American whose face was turned toward gold fields of the Madre de Dios region in Peru. He had been for some time in northern Peru, and said he had contracted malaria there. Recovered, he was plunging with youthful enthusiasm toward a wilderness more remote than anything he had seen previously. The men who had induced him to join their venture told him tales of orchids which, if true, would have done justice to the orchid nursery I saw another time in San José, Costa Rica. He regaled me by the hour with descriptions of waterfalls and natural beauties, of gold nuggets and the jungle. At first it sounded as though he had already seen the Madre de Dios region, so vividly engaging was his account. It took me a while to discern that he was repeating what he had been told. To reach this highly colored pioneer land, he would ride by truck after leaving the train, and finish the hardest part of the journey by muleback or afoot. The last I saw of him, he was swinging aboard the truck, headed for possible rich strikes of gold—and for inescapable disillusionments. The Madre de Dios is about as shut-in and unattractive a place, apart from the natural beauty of the jungle, as anyone could imagine. It slips from the Andes into upper reaches of the Amazon Basin. Conceptions of ordinary cleanliness are so lacking that towns draw their water from wells placed at the lowest point of seepage from all of the settlement's latrines and stables. Such handicaps can be removed by people with elemental know-how, but the terrain is difficult at best. I have watched United States sanitation officers struggling to educate natives in the unaccustomed art of being clean.

The other experience that has stayed with me is the conversation I had with a North American engineer who had given more than thirty years to the development of an Andean country. When I met him he had been broken, professionally, by the growing nationalism of that country. Native engineers whose path he had prepared were being given all the contracts. He sincerely liked the country, and would have gladly gone ahead serving it. So deeply had he identified himself with the people that even his resources were almost exclusively invested among them. With no future there after years of unselfish service, he had no alternative except to leave. Yet his funds were difficult to liquidate, and he had to stay in the effort to save something from the wreckage of a career.

Those are only two incidents, yet anyone considering the Andes as a pioneer field ought to know about the human as well as natural hazards. The usual pattern of Andean development is a foreign firm staffed by men who do not settle permanently, but stay as long as they want, usually with their distant homelands made more attractive in memory by the harsh world around them. The environment will not change, and so the basic development pattern is set. Its most important variation is the increasing entrance by South Americans themselves into the capitalization and engineering of Andean resources.

Frontiers: Amazonia

It is popular, especially just now, to speak of South America in glowing terms as the "continent of the future," as an "untapped storehouse of food and other natural resources," as offering "new roads to riches," and so on. Without discounting the parts of these statements that are true, we need to shift the emphasis, and stop all this romantic nonsense about South America. The South Americans will respect us for being more realistic.

Someone well versed in Amazonian conditions heard that Mrs. Eleanor Roosevelt had proposed sending thousands of refugee European families into the Amazon Basin.

"That would be murder," he said, "slow murder."

Moreover, he meant it. Not that the Amazon Basin is incapable of absorbing pioneers in search of new homes. But Foreign Minister Oswaldo Aranha of Brazil put it neatly when he quoted to me a writer who said that men had come to Amazonia before the slow processes of land formation had made it ready for human habitation. This is just one instance of difficulties faced by South America, difficulties that are built into the geographical make-up of the continent.

The Amazon Basin is South America's most extensive frontier. Wartime demands for wild rubber sent new waves of activity through the slumbering valley after Far Eastern supplies had been cut off by the Japanese. Already this second boom in Amazonian history is flattening at the top and slanting downward. The emergency wild-rubber program barely holds its own, instead of building permanent prosperity. This is another way of saying that nearly half of the South American continent is slipping back from the threshold of a rare opportunity. As yet no key has been found to unlock this natural storehouse on an enduring, large-scale and progressive basis.

North Americans have to revise most of their Temperate-Zone conceptions of pioneering before they begin to grasp what they would find in Amazonia. Europeans are even less prepared to assess Amazonian possibilities, unless they have had direct experience with other regions of the tropics. Darkest Africa has become an open highway by comparison. India's jungled areas and the densely populated equatorial Far East long ago left Amazonia behind in the march toward incorporation by modern civilization.

Why does this tremendous valley lie under the sun and rain

in an exuberance of vegetation, including the world's best rubber trees, and yet support an average of only one person on two square miles? This is so over a territory nearly equal to the United States. The explanations are deep-rooted and long-range. Expenditure by the RDC of some $60,000,000 here during the past two and a half years has only rippled the surface of the jungle at its edges. The first Amazonian boom, from the late nineteenth century to 1912, exceeded this one in changing the face of Amazonia. No public work executed during this current boom equals the marvelous floating piers at Manáos. They rise and fall as much as fifty feet when the Rio Negro fills and slackens its currents under a surface of black patent-leather sheen. The piers were completed just before the bottom fell out of Amazonian rubber under the borings of low-price competition from plantations of the Far East. During three decades Amazonia sank back toward a primitive condition that apparently has prevailed with little variation during recorded history, and beyond. From the "Black-Gold-Rush" days when opera stars from Europe sang in the ornate *teatro* at Manáos with its three galleries and Hall of Honor, Amazonia became again poor, shabby, largely forgotten and deserted. Manáos in the center of the basin, and Belém near the river's mouth, lived in memories of faded grandeur. Their expansive public squares and ample housing made new building unnecessary until recent years, when the airplane began to stir their weed-grown solitude. Far up the main stream in Peru another city, Iquitos, held its own as the metropolis of the remote lowlands just before they rise to meet the Andes.

Apart from those three cities, Amazonia in its whole span has not produced significant centers of culture. There are a few sizable towns, such as Santarém at the junction where the sandy-banked Tapajóz flows broad and clear into the muddy Amazon. Beyond those settlements the cultural level declines rapidly to the dugout canoe, the clearing in the jungle, and a few huts clustered together for mutual protection. Such conditions do not prevail over thousands of years unless the land itself raises stubborn barriers in the path of human advancement. Of barriers

Amazonia has many. This does not mean the barriers are insuperable. However, any realistic approach to the possibilities of this vast region for a war-depleted world must weigh advantages and disadvantages in the same scale.

As in any pioneer land, there are three interlocking forces of development. One is the individual pioneer and his family, setting their faces toward a new home, new frontiers to conquer, new fortunes to be made, new civilizations to be founded. Another is organized private capital on a larger scale, ranging from partnerships of two or three, such as began with the rugged Suarez Brothers of the Bolivian Beni region, to billion-dollar firms such as Henry Ford with his rubber plantations on the Tapajóz. Often determining the success or failure of these private enterprises, and sometimes engaging directly in Amazonian development, are the various interested governments. Since most of the Amazon Basin lies in Brazil, that country has the largest stake. Peru, Bolivia, Colombia, and Venezuela come next in about that order. Ecuador had its claims to parts of the basin pinched off by Peru a few years ago. Three European colonies occupy nearly half of the area between the lower Amazon and the shelf of South America as it slopes northwestward toward the delta of the Orinoco. These peoples and governments are moved by daily necessities to draw from the Amazonian land whatever it has to offer. Washington, working with them from a distance of 5000 miles, has devoted some of its best technical skills to the task of producing more vital war materials. So came a tremendous spurt for Amazonia—one not likely to be repeated until some throe of world affairs again causes men to reach out into this wilderness.

From experience to date it is generally agreed among those who have taken part in the second Amazonian boom that such gains as have been registered are not greatly promising. There have been permanent results emerging from both rubber booms, but they consist in relatively small-scale rubber developments, as well as sawmills, export of woods and other natural forest products, retail trade, shipping, and related activities.

Wild rubber probably will continue to be moderately profitable until plantations in the Far East can be restored. After world production has again been normalized, there is no indication that Amazonia will be able to gather and ship its rubber at prices low enough to meet the competition of plantations and synthetics. Brazil and other rubber countries no doubt will try hard to supply needs of their own rubber factories. That is one outlet in a growing industry. Some encouraging progress also is reported on the long, slow road toward successful rubber plantations in Amazonia.

Apart from these still unproved rubber prospects, what does the great valley offer?

For some time now this question has been under intensive and qualified examination. It is not necessary for anyone to take the observations of a traveling news correspondent on such questions as soils, minerals, climate, or resources in general. Experts of the United States Department of Agriculture and other authorities may differ in some details, but they concur in deflating notions that the Amazon is a rich frontier region beckoning to settlers. It doesn't take a soil expert to tell people they will have a hard time making a go of farming in Amazonia. For centuries, thousands of uneducated Indians and hopeful immigrants have learned that—the hard way. All the experts do is to explain why, and open doors toward possible solutions.

Looking at the luxuriant jungle, the uninitiated almost invariably says: "What rich soil!" Any Amazonian farmer knows better. The jungle has set up during centuries a cycle of growth that maintains the lush vegetation as long as the cycle is not broken. Roots lie mostly on the surface. They literally sponge all available plant food. Here enters the termite. A byword in the Temperate Zone for destruction of wooden houses, these insects actually perform an indispensable function in the tropical jungle. They are part of a cycle that must be grasped before Temperate Zone farmers can see that their kind of cultivation does not work in Amazonia. By boring through the trunks of trees the termites speed the change of wood back into easily accessible plant food. So they are useful members of the jungle community.

Walking through the Amazonian forest I found it surprisingly open. Impenetrable mazes are the exception rather than the rule. Fallen logs of the sort familiar in Temperate Zone woods are seldom encountered. Once a trunk falls, it quickly goes to pieces. So hungry are the giant trees, palms, and vines that they quickly devour surface fertility. In many places they leave nothing to build a humus. Field investigators of the United States Department of Agriculture confirm that surprisingly little soil suited to general farming exists under this forest. Along the rivers are fertile levees, but most of these are flooded during many months each year.

The result of these and other well-established facts is that the Amazon Basin as a whole does not offer prospects of large-scale agricultural development, without expenditure of more capital than most immigrants possess. Even business firms and governments have yet to come forward with programs able to conquer the Amazon. Brazil at present is sending an expedition through lands on headwaters of the Xingú River. They will need some soil experts along. Even on highlands of the Amazon Basin where better soils might be expected, they do not always exist. In the Beni region of Bolivia, large enterprises such as the House of Suarez have experimented with planted crops, but come back to gathering Brazil nuts, rubber, and other natural products of the forest. Others who have tried, for many years, come to this vital conclusion: *That the future of Amazonia lies in exploitation of the forest itself, not in cutting it down. Rubber, woods, nuts, vegetable oils, chemicals—these are the riches of the Amazon Basin.*

Minerals, including oil, are known on fringes of the basin. It is held unlikely that minerals lie close enough to the surface for profitable mining in the main valley.

Amazonian weather is surprisingly livable. H. G. Baity, one of the sanitation engineers sent from the United States to speed rubber gathering in the Amazon Basin, told me he "arrived clad in a pair of shorts and an umbrella," and during his first night in Manáos he "nearly froze."

Mr. Baity's unexpected comment on Amazonian weather was

confirmed to me by a score of people—North Americans, Colombians, Brazilians, and others. When sixteen of us came into the Amazon Basin during October, 1943, in a party of news correspondents invited by RDC to look over wild-rubber production, one of our first impressions was that this might be the steaming jungle, but we weren't steaming, and neither was the jungle at that moment. We later ran into some hot days on jungle trails. Few experiences in that brief tour during the dry season upheld the bad repute in which Amazonian weather is generally held outside the basin itself. It was hot and frequently humid, but so are Georgia, Louisiana, Washington, D. C., New York, and Kansas City. Returning alone through the same Amazon regions nearly six months later during the rainy season, I found the jungle steaming, but sometimes it was cool steam.

In Manáos the daytime temperature was moderate and the nights a bit chilly. Whenever the awning of the overcast sky is rolled back and the equatorial sun burns through, the Amazon makes hot steam. Even so, there are compensating factors. The jungle spreads its leaves to absorb sunlight from above. Covering most of the Amazonian country, this protective green roof shuts out the worst heat. Humidity is high, but the air is usually in motion. As soon as the sun goes down, the evening cools rapidly. Before morning, many people often need some bedcovers. The only thing about Amazonian heat that makes it disagreeable over a long period is its uniformly high level. While other places are hotter for short periods, Amazonia seldom falls below 60 degrees Fahrenheit, and ranges on the average in daytime around 80 to 85, with occasional spells when the thermometer tops 90. During this trip I carried a small humidity guide. The day I left Boston the temperature was 85 and the relative humidity 60. In the Amazon Basin I sometimes had readings of humidity up to 78 and in the low 80's. More frequently it was between 60 and 70. Readings in the 90's are usual in the wet season. The purpose of all this meteorological comment is to show that climate as such does not forbid habitation in the Amazon Basin, even at its lowest and wettest.

Among the established residents who assured me they live in reasonable comfort along this river is Luis A. Payán, Consul General of Colombia in Manáos. A native of the cool Colombian highlands, he has lived eight years in the Amazon Valley, and four of these at Manáos. Several Brazilians said they find Rio de Janeiro hotter during the summer than Amazonia at any time. That has been my experience.

There is no need to assemble more evidence on climate in terms of human comfort. More significant is the effect of Amazonian climate on the land. After years now of intensive searching up and down the Amazon, United States soil experts have found very little to encourage general agriculture. This does not mean that nearly half of the South American land is useless. It means that the riches of the tropical forest must be more highly utilized. That again takes hard work, capital, time, and organization.

Committing what has aptly been called "plowman's folly," Europeans took the plow to the humid tropics of Malaya, Ceylon, and other Far Eastern areas. They cut the jungle, exposed the soil to rain and sun, plowed, and before they realized their mistake had lost most of the soil's fertility. In South America the same mistake is being made. Even Henry Ford appears to have relied on North American engineers more than on the counsel of tropical soils specialists when he first tried his rubber plantations on the Tapajóz River. With methods better adapted to the Temperate Zone they set about leveling the jungle. Rubber saplings then were planted in neat rows. It wasn't long until the engineers discovered something was radically wrong. Out of the recesses of the jungle came spores of a leaf fungus. The unprotected rubber trees did well until they reached a height where the winds reached them with large quantities of spores. Then their leaves wilted. Fordlandia had to be abandoned. It still is used for some experiments, but Mr. Ford's hopes of success in developing plantation rubber rest on the newer groves at Belterra.

Even there, Ford engineers are said by some tropical experts to be making mistakes. Although the rubber tree is a forest plant, they strip the land and compel the saplings to grow in the unaccustomed glare and heat of the full tropical sun. Such methods succeeded moderately well at first in the Far East, although the more experienced plantation founders there have gradually adopted ways long familiar among the natives. When they want to start a new forest crop, they leave enough of the old trees to provide shade, at least for a while. In Amazonia, such protection is far more urgent. The leaf fungus does not exist in the Far East. Neither is it devastating in Amazonia when rubber trees are given enough space and surrounding vegetation. Out in the uncut jungle I saw many rubber trees without a trace of the blight.

Ford botanists are concentrating on development of clones, or rubber strains, with leaves that resist the fungus. They say they are over the hump in their experiments. I saw splendid young stands of clean trees. Six to eight years will be required to find out whether high yielding strains can successfully be grafted with the resistant tops. Also, the open plantation method has yet to be proved feasible in Amazonia. Since this has been the outcome of a pioneer rubber project backed by Ford millions over a period of seventeen years, what about other forms of agriculture in the Amazon Basin?

It is apparent to anyone who flies across the region that large-scale farming such as a traveler sees in Iowa, Kansas, or the Province of Buenos Aires in Argentina, does not exist here. There are clearings in the jungle, but these are generally small. Food production after more than four centuries of colonization by Europeans does not feed even the sparse population. Rice, one of the few foods that might be grown in large quantities, is still imported. The *caboclos*, the Brazilian peasants of the forest, subsist on a diet that can be endured, but no more, by North Americans or Europeans. They could not be expected to like dried *mandioca*—a food resembling sawdust—and sun-dried meat when it can be obtained, buttressed by some rice and occasionally some thick pumpkin-type vegetables or tropical fruit. I saw North Americans attempting to grow lettuce, or radishes, or even the lowly onion. With great pride a hostess one night in Manáos produced several leaves of lettuce grown in the garden of a lady who devotes herself assiduously to overcoming the unbalanced diet. In Riberalta, Bolivia, onions will not form. Nothing comes but green tops.

Ants of Amazonia also like green vegetables. A garden planted in the ground may be stripped of every leaf overnight. Boxes on stilts are filled with dirt as people try to grow a few table vegetables. One morning a North American resident in Manáos came out to look at a young tree he was nurturing in his front yard. Every leaf had been carried away during the night by cutter-ants. I flew over savannas where anthills up to six feet high form whole cities. Of the ants it has been said that unless they are conquered, they will conquer South America.

From the standpoint of obtaining a more complete picture of the rubber work, as well as the Amazonian land, my trip turned out admirably. I saw the height of the dry and wet seasons. In the Amazon Basin, the year rises and falls with periods of transition between those two extremes. On the homestretch, my path re-entered the Amazon River country from the region where its longest tributaries start as mountain springs in the high Bolivian Andes. At La Paz I again stepped into an airplane, the first since leaving Recife in northeast Brazil five months before. Meanwhile, the trip had proceeded from the Amazon Basin to Magellan's Strait and back.

Amazonian wild rubber is excellent. Some of it exceeds in resilience and wearing qualities even the cream of Far Eastern plantations. After all, Amazonia is the home of rubber and gave it to the world. Synthetics developed to date fall far short of Amazonian rubber for certain important uses. Even so, the wartime stimulus to production has neither come up to original expectations, nor held out as much promise for the future as had been anticipated. A fair summary is that wartime rubber production in Amazonia has helped to fill a gaping hole. RDC has not failed miserably, as is sometimes charged. Neither has it realized early expectations, but it has performed some indispensable services.

All of the Latin-American countries that produce wild rubber have made a substantial contribution to the war effort. Brazil particularly, as the largest producer, has sacrificed hundreds of millions of dollars by binding itself to sell all of its export rubber to the United States at a fixed, and low, price.

Brazil's part in the rubber program has been characterized by an evident desire to do all the country could to meet one of the most urgent war needs for a raw material that had suddenly been cut off from the United States by Japan. Such difficulties as have developed on the Brazilian side have sprung from residual economic and social conditions rather than from deliberate intent to hinder the war progra.. . The difficulties have nevertheless been serious. Several field workers of RDC told me at widely scattered points about experiences they have found disturbing and disappointing. One technician had spent months deep in the interior. A veteran who lived with the people, eating their *xarque* or sun-dried meat and trekking alone through the jungle, he spoke out with startling frankness. Speaking of some Brazilians he said: "They aren't our allies; they are saboteurs of our war effort."

Allowing for the strong language and overstatement in which men of action sometimes indulge, there still remains a sobering weight of human attitudes that must be measured in assessing how the rubber program has affected the Good-Neighbor Policy.

This technician told of single-barrel shotguns sold by RDC for 200 *cruzeiros*, written Cr$200,00, or $10 U. S., to boss rubber gatherers, or *seringualistas*. These guns have no purpose except to be sold to tappers, *seringueiros*, so they can protect themselves against wild animals and savage Indians. Yet the bosses were fattening on this human necessity to the extent of charging Cr$600,00 and sometimes Cr$1,000,00. This means a price of from $30 to $50 on an item that cost the distributor $10.

When prices for rubber are raised, it is problematical how much of the rise will go to the lower levels of rubber workers. I found the House of Suarez in Bolivia counting on keeping half of the gain for itself when the price was effectively raised by RDC from 45 cents to 60 cents a pound through a price premium. It is easy under Amazonian methods for the *seringualista* to take back large parts of the *seringueiro's* new income merely by raising prices on his supplies, which usually come through stores operated by his boss. This is a harsh social scene, far removed from many romantic notions still widely entertained about South America. Such things have a direct bearing on decisions by idealistic young men and women who say they want to go to South America after the war and carve out a pioneer career for themselves. South America has opportunities, but they should be approached with as much knowledge as possible of the whole picture.

RDC officials made much to me of their achievement in moving supplies into the deep rubber country. It has been done, evidently to the satisfaction of most producers. Along the way have been strange, war-born oddities in this transport development. Sports cruisers totally unfitted for river work have been sent as far inland as Bolivia. Higgins boats, although admirable for landing troops, have proved impractical in the rubber war. They burn eight or more gallons of gasoline per hour, and transport of gasoline to distant river bases is one of the bottlenecks. Few boats sent to the rubber technicians have had any protection for their propellers against floating debris and submerged rocks. The ideal is a tunnel stern, with shaft and screw set in the boat's hull above the reach of passing obstructions.

One morning at the Mamoré River port of Guayaramerín, or Puerto Sucre, on the Bolivian side, an awareness of what it takes to bring out wild rubber came into focus for me with sudden dramatic impact. We were in the shadow of hills only eighteen miles away where savage Indians of the Brazilian Mato Grosso lately had killed rubber tappers who ventured into their domain. H. H. Munro, Manager of RDC in Bolivia, had flown from Cochabamba to arrange for a trip up the Guaporé River along the remote western borders of Mato Grosso. I was to accompany him. Before leaving Cochabamba, Mr. Munro sent a radiogram to Manáos on the Amazon River, requesting that a Catalina flying boat be sent to Guayaramerín.

A few days before Mr. Munro left his office, Pancho Ramsey,

Chief Pilot of RDC, came through Cochabamba. Pancho, a onetime American cowboy and barnstormer, had flown our party through the rubber country nearly six months earlier, aided by Captain Frank L. Sage and other pilots. Chief Pilot Ramsey assured Mr. Munro that he would follow through and see that a Catalina arrived on time. Then he took off in a fast Lockheed for Peru on an inspection flight that was to return to Manáos eventually by way of Colombia. I had flown a day earlier from Cochabamba to Riberalta on the Beni River. From Riberalta the overnight river launch brought me to Cachuela Esperanza. A truck of the House of Suarez pounded a dozen of us across the muddy road to Guayaramerín.

It is a region known for its massive water snakes—the *sucurí*— for unusually large *jacarés* and for weird insects. We were bouncing around on our gear in the open bed of the truck when in hopped a branch about six inches long. The branch was gray, dry, broken off at one end, and at first glance had no visible means of locomotion. Yet it could jump, and did, to the discomfiture of Bolivian passengers who wanted to have nothing to do with it. They called it *matacaballo*—horse-killer. Horses were said to get in trouble by eating the things. Some people in the truck did not take this belief seriously. Others did. The insect—for it was no branch—had two thin legs on either side. When closely watched, it could be seen moving slightly near the tail. The head was that funny part where the branch seemed to have been snapped off. There were even bent fibers at the end. No eyes or antennae were visible. It moved with forward thrusts like a torpedo being launched from the deck of a subchaser. After landing on a few knees it was escorted overboard.

A little farther along the road we saw a marvelous flight of macaws. Their long tails, white faces, beaks, and vivid red, blue, and yellow feathers were clearly visible as they landed in a bare treetop. With such evidences of wilderness encroaching along slender lines of human development even in this center of the Suarez domain, we rode through tropical downpours during the last half of the journey to Guayaramerín. Our truck crew hastily covered the passenger section with an old canvas. It was drawn tentlike over a ridgepole. Inside we had a circus, becoming hilarious as we landed in each other's laps and dodged the hurtling luggage.

At the RDC Staff House in Guayaramerín, I found the rubber battle going ahead against dangers sometimes comparable to those of war fronts abroad. Sixty-five per cent of the town's 1500 population had malaria, according to United States sanitary officers. More than 700 cases had been treated in the overworked hospital during the past few months. Within my first three days in town, four members of the RDC staff left work and went to bed. The Sanitary Mission had spent $29,000 of Good-Neighbor money to fill pestilence-holes in the streets and dig drainage ditches. Yet they admitted they had hardly scratched the surface of malaria prevention. Ditches already were filling with weeds. Bolivians had to be coaxed into keeping up this valuable work. Within fifty feet of the Staff House, a large pool in a cow pasture was full of stagnant water. The house itself was screened, but it might as well not have been. The job was so carelessly done that mosquitoes made sport of it. My roommate, the young Chilean assistant to the local RDC manager, was among the casualties under that roof.

With a soldierly disregard for danger that was not always matched by enough common sense to keep them on their feet and fighting, the RDC men carried on. One of the technicians operating out of Riberalta had rushed his companion back from the upper reaches of the river a few days before. If the full story of these rubber technicians ever is told, it will be an epic of American war sacrifice. Soldiers at the front operate in the mass. These soldiers go out alone against the jungle. Sometimes for weeks or months they are out of touch with their bases. They emerge to tell of friendly Indians put to work gathering rubber, or to report discovery of promising new areas. They face the danger of encountering hostile Indians and not coming back. Armchair criticism of such men is unthinkable to anyone who has seen them in the field. Rather, the brunt of valid criticism runs back home to a nation that allowed itself to be caught without an adequately protected supply of indispensable natural rubber. Because foresight was not exercised in Washington before Pearl Harbor, this whole jerry-built and mistake-laden war rubber program became inescapable.

Such thoughts had been gathering momentum in me before that morning when nearly six months of observation and thinking suddenly came into clear focus. The moment of focusing turned out to be arrival of the *RDC I*, a steam launch of 35 horsepower. I was on the second floor, typing, when excitement began to surge up from the river bank. There, from upstream, came a symbol of the whole rubber program. Two trailing snakes of rubber balls threaded on steel cables more than 100 feet long were being swung downstream by the current past the launch to which they were attached. A round raft made of rubber balls floated alongside. Lashed to the tuglike launch on either gunwale were barges loaded to the rails with rubber. It was an occasion that stirred the community even more than the landing, earlier that morning, of a white fish seven feet long by a small boy.

In holiday mood, the arriving men and some of their accompanying families swung ashore. Those men and women had been traveling for days from their advanced area of operations on the Guaporé River. Some of their colleagues not long before had been caught by hostile Indians. In the pioneer tradition they are fearless, and gay at times. Such a time was this. They became serious when they told of losing a raft of twenty-three rubber balls representing months of hard work. They suspected it had been stolen to be smuggled eventually across the border into Argentina. The hard-pressed Argentines are offering almost any price to get rubber away from the monopoly held by the United States over most of South America's wartime production.

Meanwhile Mr. Munro and I were waiting for the Catalina that was to take us up the Guaporé. Since his original radiogram from Cochabamba to Manáos, more than a week had passed. No ship came, nor were there messages of any kind in response to numerous additional radiograms. That gives some notion of communications difficulties in the Amazon Basin. Where the blame lies would take more than a congressional investigation to uncover. It is standard practice in much of the South American interior for telegrams to take weeks before arrival. Sometimes they don't arrive at all. Mr. Munro had urgent business back in Cochabamba. A large pile of supplies for advanced posts had been readied under canvas on the river bank for loading into the plane.

We waited.

In the interval I had ample opportunities to see RDC "with its hair down," as Mr. Munro remarked one day. A Yankee far from his present Boston home, he is as frank as New England baked beans. He invited the Colonel in command of the local garrison, and the town's few leading citizens, to a modest party. In the afternoon we went together across the river to Guajará-mirim in Brazil to buy sandwich spreads or other delicacies. The crossing was made in the largest dugout canoe I ever have seen. It was driven by a temperamental outboard motor that had a way of stopping. We were above the rapids. Gouged from a single log, the canoe at its widest mid-section would almost have accommodated a jeep.

As we stepped on Brazilian soil, Mr. Munro began to ask questions about three piles of rubber balls that were spread on the bank and at points toward the railway station. This is the upstream end of the Madeira-Mamoré Railway that runs for some 200 miles around a series of cataracts. The chief of Bolivian RDC operations wanted to know in his quick, emphatic way, whether this valuable rubber was being guarded. No watchman was in sight. From the near-by customs shack we were sent to the police. It developed that the Bolivian agent who was being paid to take care of the rubber wasn't fulfilling his contract. Having just lost twenty-three balls during the voyage of the *RDC I*, Mr. Munro was not impressed by assurances that no one would touch the rubber. He took immediate steps.

There is no point in piling up more examples of inefficiency. They thrust themselves before any observer. More pertinent is the question: Are critics ready and willing to come down into these backward, infested areas and do a better job?

Not all the sinkings of ships in this global war result from

Nazi or Japanese torpedoes, bombs, and shellfire. Many a valiant hull has gone down in the South American battle of wild-rubber production. One untamed river, the Chaparé, hides its javelin-roots of twisting tree stumps beneath the muddy surface. It clogs its channels with fallen trunks until boats become egg-shells in a rock crusher. The Chaparé in seven months sank launches and cargo valued at nearly 8,000,000 *bolivianos*, or $160,000. Yet this river forms the most direct route between the main artery of the Mamoré River and the Bolivian highlands. In turn, the Mamoré flows to the Madeira and on to the Amazon. A man who knows, from experience, about the Chaparé and other rivers on the Bolivian rubber front, described to me a single incident that shows the odds in these remote logistics of rubber. He is Wade Stiles of Coconut Grove, Florida, currently in charge of field transport, mostly by river, for the Bolivian RDC.

"One of our largest boats hit a log in the Chaparé and went down," Mr. Stiles said. "She caught on a sandbar and we were able to start salvage operations. It took months to plug the holes. Finally, cased with concrete and pumped out, she floated. Our emergency construction crew forgot how hard they had worked, in the momentary satisfaction of seeing their success. Twenty minutes later, as they watched, she hit another log and went down—to stay."

The hazard of submerged logs occurs throughout the Amazon system. Once in a while a brief note appears in Brazilian newspapers stating simply that such and such a river steamer was lost. It may even be one of the larger ships operating between Belém and Manáos on the main river. More often than not the undisclosed reason will be one of the submerged logs. The Chaparé is particularly subject to fallen trees. Its banks cave easily. Over a period of years the debris has accumulated. Yet this river commands the most logical route from Cochabamba, the metropolis of the eastern Andes at 8400 feet elevation, and the Beni region of Bolivia where the best rubber grows. Cochabamba has rail and highway connections—barring time out for landslides and washouts—with the mining center at Oruro.

From Oruro the routes level out to the capital, La Paz. These cities are in the *altiplano* at some 13,000 feet elevation, and are surrounded by peaks up to 22,000 feet.

To reach the low-lying Beni from Cochabamba, a traveler can fly, but that is inordinately expensive even compared with other airplane tickets. *Lloyd Aéreo Boliviano* has a monopoly. Bolivians must pay 2395 *bolivianos* for this flight of just over three hours. In United States money that comes to $55. Naturally only the privileged in a land such as Bolivia can make the trip except at great sacrifice.

The plane swings north and flies close to mountain ridges that force us up at times to 19,000 feet. Across the same barrier winds the road that connects Cochabamba with approaches to the Chaparé River. This road climbs to 14,500 feet before plunging down to San Antonio in the jungle. That far the road is not too bad, as South America mountain passings go. Beyond San Antonio are twenty miles of mud where even a jeep may be bogged on the way to Todos Santos at the Chaparé. RDC has tried hard to obtain agreement of the Bolivians to spend rubber development money on this road, and on clearing logs out of the Chaparé River. Not only have the Bolivians held back, but some doubt is expressed about their motives. It is customary, when Bolivians let contracts, to earmark about 25 per cent for political patronage. RDC bookkeeping is said to rule out this kind of wastage.

Even if the Chaparé should be cleared once, there is a question whether the Bolivians would be willing, in later years, to remove additional logs. Upkeep is one of the most disturbing phases of Good-Neighbor spending in South America. United States taxpayers ask at least a substantial sign that their sacrifices in wartime will be matched by South American willingness to maintain improvements after they have been established. This of course implies that the original spending is wise and commands South American respect as well as collaboration.

So far as overland transport to the Bolivian rubber country is concerned, the Cochabamba-Chaparé route offers highest returns for lowest investment, according to Mr. Stiles. He told me that this twenty-mile road is the most important in Bolivia.

It would open the Beni, not only for immediate rubber work, but to help Bolivia in an inevitable shift from almost sole reliance on minerals to a more diversified farm income. Apart from this road-river line, overland transport to the Beni is extremely difficult. Trucks make the run to the Mamoré River, but it is a long, rough passage.

Seen from the air, this part of Bolivia overpowers by its empty spaces. Our pilot swooped low to allow Bolivian Army officers on board a close look at land configurations. Tropical birds rose in slow, graceful flight as we dipped over lagoons. The land is formed in islands of trees outlined by the high-water mark of recurring floods. Cattle tracks here and there cross the open savannas or swamps. A few huts appear at tremendous distances from each other. These are the only signs of habitation most of the way to Riberalta. Gradually the islands of trees merge until, in the transition that forms the rim of the inner Amazon Basin, magnificent tropical forest fills the horizon.

There, scattered in a density of from one to four to the acre—seldom more—rise the world's finest rubber trees, straight silver shafts in the jungled twilight. Riberalta serves as an RDC clearinghouse not only for the western part of Bolivia's Beni region, but for Peru's province of Madre de Dios. In a jagged arc on the north and west lies the Brazilian Territory of Acre. The Acre, Beni, and adjacent plateaus of Brazil's Mato Grosso are acknowledged as the home of the world's most resilient, longest-lasting rubber. *Acre fina* is the yardstick against which all rubber coming out of South America is measured for quality and for price. On this area and its continuation northwest into the Javarí River region of Brazil and Peru, rest hopes for both wartime and postwar rubber in Amazonia.

Coming down from the Bolivian highlands, I found gloom heavy over the Beni due to torrential rains that had overstayed their time and drowned prospects of increased production. Dr. Oswaldo Vaca Diez, latest scion of a pioneer Beni family, told me many tappers had been able to work only one day in four. RDC officials set the average at two days in three, or a one-third loss. The House of Suarez told me their output had held even with the last gathering season, but no more. These results were the more disappointing since Douglas H. Allen, then President of RDC, had talked six months before in terms of doubling production during 1944. The year's total had not yet been tallied, but in this region it got off to a slow start. Nowhere did I hear anything but weather blamed. Within a half year the flow of tappers' supplies had caught up with demand. This is an entry on the balance side of RDC's ledger.

Some intimate details were disclosed to me about early stages of the rubber battle as it was fought between the United States and Argentina. Dr. Vaca Diez had an Argentine contract early in 1942 to deliver forty tons of rubber to La Quiaca, railway frontier town between Bolivia and Argentina. The rubber would have to come up the Chaparé, over that quagmire road, across the Andes, and along the *altiplano*. Transport and production difficulties prevented delivery. The export permit of Dr. Vaca Diez had expired. At this point the Argentines proposed taking over and arranging a new permit at La Paz. By then, RDC was in the field. It short-circuited Argentina and bought the rubber, which was still piled up at Cachuela Esperanza on the Beni.

RDC officials emphasize that their operations in Bolivia and Brazil not only are distinct, but separate and widely divergent. Brazil, under the supplementary rubber agreement with the United States that was announced February 8, 1944, agreed to take over on June 30 many of the responsibilities formerly assumed by RDC. In contrast, Bolivia's rubber operations are almost entirely under RDC. For the United States to curtail either spending of money or the provision of supplies and personnel in Bolivia would mean reduction of rubber production to that extent. In Cochabamba the Bolivian Rubber Development Corporation maintains its headquarters between La Paz and the rubber forests. The manager and his staff shuttle back and forth between headquarters in Cochabamba and the plains.

As Bolivia considers development of its eastern valleys and lowlands, in the immediate foreground stands rubber, the best rubber in the world, waiting only to be gathered. Yet Bolivia's storehouse of *Hevea brasiliensis* in magnificent tropical forests is not easily unlocked. To start with, anyone has only to approach the rubber country from any direction to grasp quickly the difficulties of transport. Pioneer British firms kept up their struggle against the odds of distance from 1908 to 1932. The Anglo-Bolivian Rubber Company experimented with an overland route by oxcart or mule from the Beni to Concepción, San Ignacio, and overland to faraway Montevideo in Uruguay. It didn't pay. The only other practical outlet is the long riverway down the Mamoré, Madeira, and Amazon to Belém. This route measures 1500 to 2000 miles, depending on where the rubber is first gathered. Transportation is costly and not always available. The British, as well as Bolivian firms such as the House of Suarez, turned away from rubber toward other crops, chiefly Brazil nuts or *castanhas*. Into this declining rubber area that had been abandoned in some parts stepped RDC a little less than three years before this writing. Not the least of Bolivia's rubber problems is its almost complete dependence on Brazil for importation of supplies, and exportation of rubber. Except for rubber smuggled across the Argentine border, or sold in legitimate trade up to the amount of 250 tons that are reserved to Bolivia for this purpose, the traffic is all downriver into Brazil. RDC officials in Bolivia told me that machinery they desperately needed had been piled on wharves at Belém for months. They showed photographs as proof.

The Brazilian Madeira-Mamoré Railway is a bottleneck. I saw balls of rubber that had become cracked and weathered by lying in the sun and rain several months before being moved over this slender single track in the wilderness. Sometimes the railway is held up by shortages of ships reaching Pôrto Velho at its downstream terminus to take the rubber to Manáos and Belém.

I had a vivid reminder of transport and communications gaps, as days passed and no message arrived regarding the Catalina ordered by Mr. Munro. He decided to give it up, and helped me catch a *Panair do Brasil* flying boat that landed unexpectedly early one morning on an RDC charter flight to the Brazilian side. So I reached Manáos again in the center of the Amazon Basin to make my final observations of the wild-rubber program in Brazil. The Good-Neighbor purse had just closed in Washington with a bang that still echoed throughout the Amazon Basin. A principal reason was that Brazil had over-drawn it original rubber development fund of $5,000,000. This fund took care of long-range productive measures beyond the more immediate operating costs of gathering rubber. Brazil is committed under the new rubber agreement to provide its own development fund of Cr$10,000,000. That imposing amount of currency comes down to $500,000 at prevailing U. S. exchange. By this action the United States has given tangible expression to two conclusions of master significance for the future of the Good-Neighbor Policy and of South American rubber. They are:

1. An early and definite curb on spending or lending in South America beyond urgent war necessities and sound finance.

2. A vote of no confidence in the future of Amazonian wild rubber until far more encouraging results have been obtained.

These winds of policy are unmistakable throughout the new dispositions that had begun to affect the rubber program when I reached Manáos.

RDC had spent a total of nearly $60,000,000 in the Amazon Basin between March 3, 1942, and December 31, 1943. Most of this went to Brazil. The figure, according to former President Allen, covers not only the purchase price of rubber, but all costs of capital outlay including items on which a cash return is expected. RDC spending does not stop under the supplementary agreement with Brazil, but it is curtailed and headed in the direction of termination as rapidly as possible. Until December 31, 1946, RDC has contracted to aid individual producers and perform certain indispensable services. Talking these things over with managers of RDC activities in Brazil I obtained this sum-mary: RDC plans, as long as is necessary, to maintain its staff of field technicians. Shipping priorities will be arranged from the United States to meet vital needs of Brazilian rubber produc-tion and export. Also, river services will be maintained that benefit Brazil. When RDC needs to use ships of SNAPP, or

Serviços de Navegacão da Amazonia e de Administracão do Pôrto do Pará, the Brazilian official monopoly line, operating costs will be paid. Tappers' supplies will be brought in from the United States at cost, but not subsidized as heretofore. These supplies will be sold direct to *seringualistas,* instead of passing through the hands of other middlemen. The Aviation Division, although no longer needed in Brazil as much as in Colombia, Bolivia, and Peru, will be maintained. On other phases of the rubber program, RDC will work with the *Banco de Credito da Borracha,* or Brazilian Bank of Rubber Credit, and the established merchants.

Apart from these activities, which are subject to curtailment as time goes on, RDC is specifically exempted since June 30, 1944, from all payments, subsidies, and contributions except those already incurred. To remove all ambiguity at key points, RDC wrote into the agreement that food would no longer be supplied at fixed prices. This superseded an accord of April 3, 1943, with the *Superintendencia de Abastecimento do Vale Amazonico,* or SAVA. Also, coal will not be sold to SNAPP at less than cost, as had been proposed, nor freight rates paid that are higher than established levels.

RDC listed development works which are considered essential to success of the program, as terms of the new agreement. Brazil assumes responsibility for these. Mentioned by name are road building in southern Mato Grosso and a labor subsidy in the same region. New *estradas,* the paths connecting rubber trees, are to be built, and additional workers brought to the Amazon Basin. For this development work, Brazil is to draw on profits of the *Banco de Credito da Borracha* from rubber on hand at the beginning of the price premium in February, 1944, and from the premium itself, amounting to 33 1/3 per cent on every pound of rubber bought by the United States.

The price premium represents a middle-ground solution for insistent demands of Amazonian merchants. Instead of a flat and larger increase, the premium is temporary. It is designed to offset increased wages, living costs, and other expenses incurred by rubber gatherers. The agreement states categorically that primary producers—including the lowly *seringueiro*—are to receive a fair share of the increase from 45 to 60 cents a pound *f.o.b.* Belém. Also, the premium is made tax-exempt. It terminates on March 31, 1946, unless renewed a second time.

Several provisions protect the RDC. In one clause Brazil agrees to keep export and internal prices of rubber on the same basis. Tires and tubes sold to the United States are not to go up in price because of the premium. Finally, Brazil agrees to provide favorable exchange rates for RDC.

This all adds up to a shift of emphasis in the rubber program from early enthusiasms to a more reserved attitude on both sides. At many points RDC appears intent on defending itself. At other points Brazil reasserts control over its own affairs that temporarily had been shared with RDC. Why these changes have come is a question that will throw light, when answered, on long-range issues of Brazilian relations with the United States. Not to be overlooked is the underlying influence of difficulties inherent in Amazonian rubber. During those first hours of menace to their cherished independence in the lengthening shadow of Pearl Harbor, the United States and Brazil deferred less pressing questions. The United States desperately needed rubber. Brazil had it. So was born the Brazilian wild-rubber program. It set the model for similar activities in the fifteen other rubber-producing nations of the Western Hemisphere. The wartime necessity for wild rubber remains urgent, but the Governments of the United States and of Brazil have entered a whole new phase in their dealings on this emergency program. The Combined Raw Materials Board at Washington declared in a public statement that natural rubber is still one of the most critical of all strategic materials. RDC reported that reserves of natural rubber in the United States declined from 139,594 tons on January 1, 1944, to 92,371 tons on September 30, despite importation of 72,427 tons during the first eight months of that year. The use of 119,650 tons in nine months testifies to indispensable war functions of natural rubber. Synthetics do not serve for all heavy-duty purposes. The longer the war lasts in the Orient, the more urgent becomes the need of Latin America's wild rubber.

For this reason, RDC is still charged with carrying through every activity that is vital for producing rubber. The significant change has come in RDC's interpretation of what is vital. At the beginning, under the Rubber Reserve Company before that pioneer venture had been replaced by the present RDC organization, a grandiose program for Amazonian development took form. Going far beyond measures that were clearly needed to speed rubber output, this program aimed at a wide range of social and economic reforms. Radio stations and airports were blueprinted to cover the Amazon Basin. Education and sanitation were part of a move designed to awaken slumbering Amazonia and give it a long-range impetus. Anyone who has been in the basin would agree that all of these things are worthy objectives when properly approached. Hard-headed Brazilians who know how to gather rubber in a hurry looked on the fancy New Deal trappings and said:

"Cut out all this nonsense. Give us a price that makes it worth our while to work rubber, and we will do the rest."

What many of them meant was that they could energize a semifeudal economy in which big profits go to the bosses and merchants, while the *seringueiro* treads his jungle paths on bare subsistence wages, or lower.

The kind of gouging practiced by some of the Amazonian merchants is disclosed in an incident that occurred at Manáos within a few blocks of the RDC office.

A high RDC official needed five flashlight batteries. He called in a secretary and asked her to order them. Being new—the turnover in RDC personnel is terrific—she went away and prepared a cash voucher. She should have typed a requisition to the corporation's own warehouse. The boy sent to make the purchase returned with five batteries, and a receipted bill for 80 *cruzeiros*, or $4, U. S. That came to 80 cents U. S. for each of the small flashlight batteries. Interested, to say the least, RDC officials referred back to the price at which those same batteries had been sold to the merchant down the street. It turned out to be one tenth of the gouge price, or a normal 8 cents U. S. How long this had been going on at a 900 per cent profit was not known. Presumably from the first, although the merchant had signed a contract agreeing not to sell for more than 15 per cent net profit. Confronted with the evidence, this Amazonian merchant joked about it.

Commenting on this incident, the RDC manager said that enforcement of contract provisions in Amazonia is almost impossible. When such violations can occur in a metropolis such as Manáos, it is easy to imagine the economic serfdom practiced on remote rivers where *seringueiros* and their families depend entirely on grasping merchants for food and rubber-gathering equipment.

To the credit of United States aims in Amazonia it can be entered that Washington wanted to slash through this jungle maze of modern peonage. On Washington's early debit ledger must be entered an unrealistic view of Amazonia. After all, the basin is Brazilian except for a few fringes in neighboring countries. When the North American Good Neighbor appeared to be moving in and taking over most of the house and family, it is understandable that Brazilians were alarmed. For Brazil has its own program to stimulate Amazonian development. Dr. Vargas himself came to Manáos in 1940 during a 10,000-mile trip that took him also to Pôrto Velho on the Madeira River. He proposed a conference of Amazonian powers. Later he set in motion a typically Brazilian series of projects. Although relegated to the background by the war, these projects are long-range. When the wartime rubber crusade began, Brazil was willing to collaborate, but carefully kept its own rights to the fore. The original agreement of March 3, 1942, placed responsibility for maximum rubber production on Brazil, not on the United States. The fullest assistance was to be provided by Washington with wartime dollars, materials, shipping, and technicians. During those days of expansive Good-Neighboring in the friendly warmth soon after Brazil had broken diplomatic relations with the Axis, it was easy to become overenthusiastic. People of high position who didn't know enough about Amazonian conditions put in circulation exaggerated figures. Brazilian officials promised that 100,000 workers would be moved into the basin, and that 50,000 tons of rubber would be gathered the first year.

It would be unfair to judge actual rubber results against such misinformed propaganda. The only valid yardstick is to ask what has been accomplished in terms of overcoming obstacles which were apparent from the first to anyone who knew Amazonia and its rubber history.

To clarify the approaches to an assessment of this wartime campaign, it is essential to lay down traffic lanes. They are:

1. How much rubber might Brazil have produced by its own unaided efforts, assuming merely a profitable price and normal trade facilities?

2. How much rubber can rightly be credited to United States expenditures in Brazil itself, as well as provision of supplies and ships through choked channels of wartime trade?

Under the first point, it is plain that Brazil could not have maintained the volume of its prewar rubber production, much less increased it, without some form of assistance from the United States. Ships, tools, even food, had to come in large measure from outside Brazil. Normal trade facilities simply didn't exist in the dark wake of Pearl Harbor. The United States in any event would have had to assign shipping from the common pool to carry supplies to Brazil, and bring back the rubber. Wartime industries also had to make machetes, shotguns, tapping knives, cups, and all the other essentials of rubber production. Even so, this might have been done *f.o.b.* the mouth of the Amazon, so to speak. That would have left the distribution of supplies and the delivery of rubber entirely in Brazilian hands. From the incident of the flashlight batteries, and the widespread theft of canned food that goes on even before the boxes reach Manáos, most United States taxpayers would conclude that they need some control over what happens to their money and supplies. Some boxes arrive with the cans inside, neatly emptied of their contents. It is the responsibility of the Brazilian Government to police their own boats, but repeated RDC complaints have not stopped these leakages. Actually RDC has followed a mid-course, with emphasis shifting rapidly of late toward letting Brazilians do the job. Someone who knows the voracious instincts of many Amazonian mercantile barons referred to this as: "Throwing the *seringueiros* back to the wolves." This remark is typical of bitterness engendered among many idealistic North Americans who came to the Amazon with high and patriotic hopes, only to be disillusioned. Leaving aside these by-products of the rubber program, what about RDC's productive record in Brazil?

Figures are not available for a final conclusion. RDC advised me that it is impossible to separate the figures for Amazonian countries to give those for Brazil alone. This statement leaves the balance sheet for the whole Amazon Basin as the only RDC public accounting on Brazil, but that country covers most of the Amazon Basin, and is the outlet for nearly all its rubber, including the most remote yields of Bolivia, Peru, and Colombia.

In his defense of RDC before the Gillette Committee of the United States Senate on December 9, 1943, Mr. Allen gave estimates which he later confirmed as substantially borne out by events. His figures are:

1. Rubber imported by the United States from the Amazon Basin, April, 1942, to December 31, 1943, totaled 23,700 long tons.

2. Total disbursements in Amazonian operations, including cost of rubber purchased, plus development expenditures, capital investments, loans, operating and administrative expenses of RDC, and all other applicable disbursements for the same period, totaled $59,710,477.

3. Cost per pound of rubber, on the basis of the above figures, is $1.12. When capital investments are amortized over the entire program ending December 31, 1946, this pound-cost comes down. Mr. Allen said he hoped to finish with an average cost of 75 cents a pound, for everything.

The conspicuous point is that RDC takes credit for all the rubber coming from Amazonia. Yet even in the lowest two years of unaided production, 1932 and 1933, Amazonia turned out 16,340 metric tons. Just before this war, the 1938 and 1939 total came to 29,320 metric tons, as recorded by the statistical service of Carlos and Luiz Frazão at Belém.

Reducing this figure to 21 months for comparison with the RDC period, and further allowing for differences in the ton-measurement, we have 25,219 long tons. This is giving RDC the fairest possible basis of comparison with what the Amazonian countries might have done with nothing more than a profitable price and the provision of supplies through normal channels of business and shipping. RDC's figure must in turn be increased somewhat to include rubber produced but not exported to the United States either as crude or as tires and tubes. Brazil is allowed 10,000 tons a year for its own rubber industries. Mr. Allen reported that some 3000 tons of manufactured rubber came from Brazil in 1943. It is reliably stated that Brazil has not always had its full quota. So a rough estimate is about 14,000 tons to be added to RDC's total for 21 months, or a gross total of 37,700 long tons. Other rubber that may have been produced and not yet brought in from upper rivers must affect later accounts. RDC's Amazonian net thus comes down to 14,611 long tons, over and above the comparable 21 months of 1938-39.

On this basis, which is impartially acceptable as contrasted with Mr. Allen's claim to credit for all Amazonian rubber imported—the cost per pound goes up to $2.14. Amortized on the same percentages used by Mr. Allen, this would indicate a final cost of $1.71 a pound for Amazonian rubber, washed, dried, and delivered. This is not $500 a pound, or even $50, as RDC's more reckless critics have charged, including Senator Butler of Nebraska.

RDC bookkeeping has ceased to separate Amazonian rubber costs from those of the hemisphere as a whole. Import figures are still given. The latest available total is 38,177 long tons, carrying the total analyzed above forward through August 31, 1944. Because of increasing imports and declining development expenses, it is estimated that the comparable cost for Amazonian rubber has dropped from Mr. Allen's $1.12 per pound to 75.2 cents.

In figuring pound-costs of wartime natural rubber, a factor not to be left out of account is purchase by the United States of preclusive rights to all rubber gathered in Latin America, beyond minimum necessities of the producing countries. Francis Adams Truslow, who succeeeded Mr. Allen as RDC President, told me that if the Latin-American Governments had not abandoned their rights to sell rubber to the highest bidder, they could have made from $1 to $4 more per pound. Multiplied over Amazonian rubber alone, this means that Brazil has practiced Good-Neighborliness to the extent of a direct financial loss of between $66,000,000 and $264,000,000.

Latest average RDC pound-costs in the various areas of its imports are given as 43.74 cents between April 1, 1942, and August 31, 1944. This figure includes rubber from Ceylon, India, and other regions where RDC has not assumed responsibilities for stimulating production. In Liberia, where RDC operates to aid plantation output, the cost came down to 27.79 cents per pound. For all of Latin America, the figure is given as 68.02 cents.

Considering the wartime emergency, the price is low—provided all costs have been entered. Financial history may settle that someday.

Prominent among charges deciding Amazonian costs are those of the *Banco de Credito da Borracha*. A direct levy of Cr$1,10 a kilo was being made for bank expenses at the time of my visit. A 12 per cent dividend was allowed. Any profit over and above this amount goes into a reserve fund for rubber development. Washing and drying the raw rubber are done by commercial firms under contract with the bank, which has this large source of revenue under its control. The bank has a twenty-year charter and its president is named by the President of Brazil. Its board of directors consists of three Brazilians and two North Americans. The capital has been increased to $7,500,000, divided 60 per cent to the Brazilian Government and 40 per cent to the United States Government. Loans for rubber production and for agricultural production related to rubber are made at 7 per cent for one, two, or three years. This interest rate is well below the prevailing commercial rate of 12 per cent in Brazil.

While some of the large producers go their way without asking credit from the bank, its loan funds are quickly depleted. There has been a tendency for misuse of funds by farmers interested in getting their land cleared. They say they want to start a rubber plantation, but under existing conditions, the net result would simply be new cattle pastures, since the time is not ripe for successful rubber plantations in Amazonia.

For rubber workers, actual and potential, the immediate question is how much they can earn, and what they will have to pay for food, clothing, and tools. Their rate of income from each kilo of rubber is fixed. To earn more, they either must improve quality, or increase quantity. For many, this offers some hope; for others, the conditions under which they work are unfavorable to advancement. One constantly hears that the *seringueiro* generally is not interested in getting more than a bare subsistence. Workers from Ceará and other parts of the Brazilian Northeast are more energetic than those in the Amazon Basin. With income fixed or at least limited, the *seringueiro* must pay rising prices. For every kilo of *xarque*, the standard sun-dried meat, he pays more than he gets for more than a kilo of rubber. *Xarque* often comes to 60 cents a kilo in U. S. currency. Cutting knives, other tools, lanterns, kerosene, shoes, clothing—all are high. To meet this situation, the Brazilian Government has held back the worst inflation, and RDC for some time sent in goods at lower prices. On the Ford plantations, *xarque* is sold for 30 cents a kilo. Despite these and similar efforts, inflation creeps ahead.

A force making for price rises is this: The *seringualista* earns such a small profit on rubber that he regards it merely as a means of exchange. His profit comes from the goods he sells to the *seringueiros*. In the organization of Amazonian commerce and labor, at the top stand the *casas de aviadores*, the typical houses of capitalists and merchants. Each casa has its *seringua-listas* who distribute supplies to *seringueiros* in the jungle, and take their rubber in return. The result of this semifeudal economy is that *seringueiros* become dependent on the *seringua-lista* and often go deeply in debt to him. It is the company-store technique familiar in coal mines of the United States and elsewhere.

Labor relations in rubber districts of Bolivia differ because these districts are more remote from governmental control than even Brazilian Amazonas. Large landholders such as the Suarez family recruit rubber laborers through contractors. When they want men already employed by some other large producer, such as Seiler, they must pay the worker's debt first. This debt totals in most cases from $20 to $100 U. S. Often a bonus is exacted for each worker obtained in this market where labor is practically bought and sold. Throughout Amazonia, the men who actually endure the toil and dangers of the jungle find themselves at the bottom of the heap. *Seringualistas* as I saw them in Belém flash diamond rings. Tightfisted merchants wage their hard and ceaseless quest for profit and security in an economic flux as unstable as the shifting bottom of the Amazon itself.

These are primary reasons for low rubber production which largely is due to lack of labor incentive. In both the wartime and postwar outlook for natural rubber, how to bring more manpower into action remains the key to results in Amazonia. This also is the case in arid regions of Brazil's Northeast. Everywhere from Belém near the Amazon's mouth to the richest rubber areas of Bolivia and back to the drought-stricken zone where both laborers and rubber are gathered, the demand is the same: "Give us manpower and we can do this job." Manpower cannot be found by the twist of a hydrant or the pasting of posters on mud walls of huts in village streets, as those responsible for enlisting rubber tappers know from experience. In the State of Ceará exists the greatest single reservoir of available manpower for rubber gathering as well as for other possible development of the Amazon Basin. Yet when I traveled in Amazonia and into rubber-producing districts of the Northeast, I found many spots parched for *braços* to do the work.

Transport difficulties loom large. Officials in Rio de Janeiro, when explaining why so few men had been sent to the Amazon, stressed the human factor. To persuade a man to leave his home and go into unknown hazards is the first and indispensable act of recruitment. Compulsion has not been introduced. The rubber workers are volunteers.

A clearer picture of the labor situation emerges in the home of a potential rubber gatherer in the arid Northeast. The home itself is simple, and, by North American standards, uninviting. It has only two bare rooms. The floor is dirt. Through the open doorway and single window may be seen, fringed at the top by dry palm fronds of the thatched roof, a field dried to the roots and beyond by three years of drought. Anything that could better the lot of the family would be welcome. The only water for the whole village comes from two holes in the sand of the dried river bottom. One is rimmed by a square wooden box. In the other, staves of a small keg hold back the sand. Into these small pools the villagers dip their gourd ladles and fill earthen jars which the women carry on their heads. It is a period of migration. Through the village has come word of the call for *braços* to bring in rubber. Men from Fortaleza, capital of Ceará, have brought posters and pamphlets telling Brazilians of their patriotic duty to send rubber across the seas. Tanks and airplanes of the United Nations have been pictured as rolling forward to victory on treads and tires that could be made possible by men from this village.

A family has two alternatives. It can migrate on its own as a unit, joining other families and using any available means of transport. Or it could, at the time I was in the rubber area, avail itself of official Brazilian migration services. To obtain the fullest official aid, the family head would have to sign a contract. He would agree to place himself at the disposition of the rubber program for two years. His wages in return would be Cr$6,00 a day, or about 30 cents U. S., while traveling, and Cr$10,00 while working. The family would receive from Cr$7,00 to Cr$11,00 a day. In Brazil the legal minimum wage at that time was Cr$6,00. At the end of the two-year period, return transportation to their home would be provided. If sickness or other circumstance should require an earlier return, this also would be provided free. The main route followed by migrating workers is over various roads to the railhead at Teresina on the western border of Ceará, and by rail to São Luiz do Maranhão. Boats complete the journey to Belém and into the Amazon River system.

Uncertainty over the outlook for Brazilian rubber, I found, was exerting a powerful brake on production. In distant parts of the Amazon Basin a similar concern was shown. One group of small Bolivian producers went so far as to send a request to regional RDC officials, asking for a letter of assurance that their contracts would hold good all the way to December 31, 1946! The request was presented verbally through a spokesman in my presence, and I took a small part in the incident by helping with the Spanish interpreting.

In the future of Amazonian rubber, a hopeful factor is the growing demand of South America's own rubber industry. Even before the war emergency, this industry had given a healthy stimulus to Amazonian rubber production. From 21,900 tons in 1898, when Far Eastern competition began, Amazonia rose to a peak of 42,410 tons in 1912, and then fell gradually for a decade. The low price of plantation rubber from Malaya and the Netherlands East Indies, in combination with other factors including the cleanness of plantation rubber and its more uniform quality, sent Amazonian rubber to a low of 6550 tons in 1932.

By that time, Brazil's rubber factories were important buyers in the market at Belém. This aided a rather quick comeback to 9790 tons in 1933. Also, Nazi Germany began amassing rubber against the coming war, and Amazonian production rose steadily. By 1940, it had reached 17,480 tons, or not quite half of the boom-time peak. The increase since then has been substantial in annual totals, but not spectacular.

At São Paulo, I visited modern plants where Brazilian rubber is being fashioned into thousands of commercial items, from erasers and hot-water bottles to large truck tires. The *Orion* factory lists some 10,000 distinct rubber items. *Theodore Putz & Companhia, Limitada,* is credited with beginning the fabrication of rubber in São Paulo, about 1911. *Orion* started a half century ago making combs and other items from horn. In 1923 *Orion* went into rubber, and now is rated as the largest single producer of its kind in South America. In the more massive uses of rubber, Goodyear and Firestone are turning out tires in ultramodern plants. Their great molds open automatically like the shells of giant clams. Workmen wielding long iron bars pry the hot casings out and roll them away, just as others do in Akron. São Paulo's rubber factories are using as much rubber as possible of kinds not ordinarily exported to the United States. This leaves more of the standard *Hevea brasiliensis* for war uses. I saw *maniçoba* and *mangabeira* rubber being washed and processed. There is still some argument among specialists over the qualities of these rubbers. *Hevea* remains the best. Among other qualities, it dries rapidly, and so speeds the manufacturing process.

Under Brazilian national law, each group of firms comprising a distinct element of industry must form a syndicate. There are corresponding syndicates of workers. Both groups are organized under auspices of the Government, which supervises their relations and holds the final power of decision in labor or industrial disputes. This is essentially a fascist conception of economic relations. The report of the Syndicate of Rubber Manufacturers in São Paulo was placed in my hands. Its printed list of members included forty-eight firms. Indicating the rapid growth being experienced in São Paulo's rubber industry, another nine members had been written in by hand, evidently having entered after the report was in print.

An impressive plant included in the list is *Pirelli,* makers of wire and electric cable. Webs of copper as fine as hair were being drawn. The air was filled with the whirring of ingenious machines that braid wire around cables used by the Brazilian Navy, and for export. At the apex of *Pirelli's* present achievement stand great machines that complete the lead casing on underwater cables three inches in diameter. Some time after that visit to *Pirelli*, when on the way to Belém, I saw a wooden spool about three feet high of the kind used for shipping cable. It was at a United States air base defending the South Atlantic coast against U-boats. The name stenciled on that spool was *Pirelli*. Brazil's industry is coming of age, and has directly strengthened the United Nations war effort.

Brazilians are concerned over the role of synthetic rubber in the postwar world. The outlook is serious, for synthetics will undoubtedly retain some part of the rubber market. Yet it would be writing a lien on the future for petroleum supplies to be converted into rubber when natural rubber can be grown. Petroleum pools form only during millions of years. Synthetics from alcohol avoid this difficulty, but are more expensive so far. Plantations of the Far East can be counted on to supply increasing amounts of natural rubber after a shorter or longer period of readjustment when Japan's grip has been broken.

The great question for Brazil thus becomes: Can Amazonian rubber compete in the postwar world with synthetics and Oriental natural rubber in combination?

As we have seen, part of the answer lies in Brazil's own rubber industries. It is inconceivable that this nationalistic country would import rubber rather than bend every effort to produce its own. A short-range answer lies in demands that will continue at least until Far Eastern rubber again flows freely across the Pacific. On the long range, the United States never again wants to be caught with indispensable rubber supplies bottled up in some distant part of the world across fragile lines of communication. Whether this desire will be strong enough to sustain Amazonian rubber production through difficult years of development ahead, remains to be seen. Also, the United States may seek political and other solutions abroad, in combination with provision of a safe Amazonian rubber supply.

Still farther ahead is the possibility of large plantations on the Amazon. Let no one mistake, that is a very long-range proposition. It will cost millions on millions, and years of patient, undiscourageable toil. The experts say it can be done. Although

Ford technicians claim to have won their battle against a destructive leaf fungus, long and arduous effort lies ahead.

Beyond the powerful Ford efforts being made at Belterra, the development of Amazonian rubber plantations rests on the Brazilian *Instituto Agronômico do Norte* outside Belém. Plantations never have received an adequate test in Bolivia's rubber highlands. Some Bolivians would like to see it done, but the cost runs into millions. Dr. Felisberto Camargo, as Director of the *Agronômico,* has worked closely with Belterra. At the *Agronômico's* experimental plantation on the outskirts of Belém, one of Dr. Camargo's assistants told how it feels to tackle this jungle. He said there were only a handful of technically trained research botanists, varying in number from five to eight.

"We are a slender reed jabbing the wilderness," he said. The jungle itself crowded in on the *Instituto* clearings as he spoke. Out of a forest path came a *seringueiro* holding a gourd container with a few pints of white latex. His small contribution was poured into the experimental vats.

What it means to develop plantation rubber in this region was graphically driven home to me as I rode through the Ford holdings on a plateau 576 feet above sea level along the Tapajóz River. Whole groves of fine young rubber trees had been topped, and stood as bare trunks awaiting the next slow step in their process of developing a high-yield, blight-resistant strain. Archibald Johnston, Director-Manager of the *Companhia Ford Industrial do Brasil,* and his technical assistants, did not emphasize their difficulties. Yet the charred trunks of great trees still choking fields that had been planted as soon as there were spots for the individual rubber saplings, are reminders that clearing the Amazonian jungle is in itself a gigantic task. Mr. Johnston and his assistants are soberly confident, but without overflowing enthusiasm. They have battled Amazonia too long for that. The successful trees I saw, their leaves glistening and green as they should be, confront the Amazonian jungle as forerunners of millions of scions being prepared for other advance bases. Someone close to the development of plantation rubber in the Amazon

Basin told me that anyone except Henry Ford would have surrendered long ago.

Restoration of Amazonian rubber to a commanding place in world markets would do more than any other single factor now in sight to develop South America's great basin. Other riches of the tropical forest are gradually being brought into use. Whenever the master key is found to unlock this diffused storehouse, the harvest could be phenomenal because there is so much of the forest. To date, Amazonia's exuberance pays few dividends in proportion to the area it occupies. A costly characteristic is the diversity of vegetation. Rubber, hardwoods, and other trees occur as isolated individuals instead of solid stands. Exploiting such a forest requires operations over large areas against a heavy overload of profitless materials.

Along the rim where the outer valley steps down to lowlands, many rapids foam. Hydroelectric power could be developed if such large capital outlays ever were made profitable. Pending such future prospects, evidently far ahead, the Amazon Basin appears likely to go on developing slowly. Its pallid inhabitants slip as shadows through the forest.

So the world's last gigantic frontier shouts that only strong pioneers, armed with knowledge and the most powerful of modern devices, can count on wresting from Amazonia more than a bare subsistence.

Frontiers: Brazilian Northeast

Discovery of minerals has given new strength to Brazil's Northeast. Tantalite, so vital to the war effort that it was being flown to the United States when I came through the area late in 1943, is one of the recent mineral discoveries. Rutile, used for arc welding, is another product lately found in the State of Ceará and now moving northward with increasing volume.

To accommodate these and other essential exports that funnel from the interior into Fortaleza, an expansion of shipping facilities in the harbor is moving forward rapidly. Dr. Francisco de Menezes Pimentel, Federal Interventor for the State of Ceará, took evident satisfaction in telling how the Northeast has awakened in recent years.

"For a long time after its early period of development, the Northeast was almost abandoned when Brazil's center of gravity shifted southward," Dr. de Menezes Pimentel said as we talked in the reception room off the patio of the unpretentious Executive Palace. "During the past decade this region has been rediscovered. President Vargas has shown special interest in this part of Brazil, as well as in Amazonas. The Federal Government at Rio de Janeiro and the State Government here are now collaborating fully, with the result that in ten years production has been doubled."

The harbor is being enlarged by construction of a new breakwater. The Interventor said that 1100 meters in the total of 1400 meters had been completed at that time. The new quays will measure 800 meters, of which more than half were completed.

An encouraging result of mineral discoveries in Ceará is that people formerly dependent on agriculture now have another possibility of employment and so may remain in their homes instead of migrating during periodic droughts. Dr. de Menezes Pimentel also told about improvements in transport and the construction of small dams. These measures are slowly improving a situation that remains grave. Far from being able to offer food to a war-hungered world, Brazil's Northeast is grappling with multiple problems in the endeavor to feed itself. The picture is one of overflowing bounty in sections of the well-watered coastal zone and parched want in much of the interior.

Geographically, the Northeast is Brazil's territory most accessible to Europe and the United States, with the exception of Amazonia. Because of this geographical advantage and the discovery of indispensable minerals, leaders foresee a strong upsurge both during the war and afterward.

Especially enthusiastic along this line is Dr. José Guimaraes

Duque, an official of the Brazilian Government in charge of irrigation projects. He sees in Ceará two resources of exceptional value—manpower and natural wealth. Ceará has farm land as well as minerals. Some of Brazil's best soil is said to be in this area. As in California and other semiarid regions, irrigation holds the key.

Generally in South America where rainfall is heavy, the soil tends to be leached of its humus and productive elements. That has not occurred in the Northeast. Some lands have turned alkaline, as in many similar terrains, but other areas await only water and organized development to help meet the Northeast's dominant necessity—effective measures against drought.

Some of the more enterprising Brazilians foresee vast irrigation and power projects by development of Paulo Afonso Waterfalls. Ever since its discovery this natural marvel has fired the imagination of builders, yet to date the actual development is nearly nil. The tourist possibilities remain almost as neglected as the industrial and agricultural possibilities of this impressive natural resource. Although a great potential source of hydroelectric power, Paulo Afonso so far gives light only to the remote town of Pedra, and turns the looms of its one small textile mill. Paulo Afonso Waterfalls could generate 1,500,000 horsepower, according to preliminary estimates. The existing turbine house, perched on a shelf halfway down the perpendicular wall of resounding rock, has a top capacity of only one-tenth that horsepower.

The reasons for Paulo Afonso's retarded development are tied in with the sweep of events in a large segment of Brazil—the strategic Northeast and the São Francisco Valley. Traveling widely in the area, I met Brazilian and United States engineers hard at work in remote towns whose dust, for years beyond the memory of their inhabitants, had not been whipped up by anything except wind. The whole feeling of what is going on in this part of Brazil seemed to be shouted by two whirling and wide-awake windmills over the town of Sento Sé in the São Francisco Valley above the falls. Mounted on the roofs of two houses, they were driving generators for private radios. Clearly legible on the

vanes were the words: *Silvertone 6-Volt de Luxe Air Chargers.*
They generate a combined 12 volts within reach of 1,500,000
potential horsepower!

What might have occurred in the São Francisco Valley if its
natural outlet had not been choked off by the falls is not easily
answered. During the reign of Dom Pedro II this foresighted
Emperor sought to unlock the São Francisco Valley by building
a railway around the falls. That was in 1879, and the town of
Pedra began as a railway station stop. The rails are still there,
rusting away. Only once a week does a train crawl the whole
distance of seventy miles each way from Piranhas, below the falls,
to Itaparica, upstream. Another train makes the round trip from
Piranhas to Pedra once a week.

How far the São Francisco River falls short of being a main
artery for the broad valley it drains may be read in actions of
the textile mill at Pedra. My introduction to the strange story
of this pioneer mill came when I reached Rio Branco on the
railway in Pernambuco State. Seeking to reach Paulo Afonso, my
first try had been through Garanhuns, at one time the railhead
for excursions to the falls. Turned back by slow and uncertain
transport, I was sent to Rio Branco on advice that many trucks
make the trip to Pedra near the falls. This information proved
correct. The very night of arrival I was able to book an upper
berth on top of a load of cotton bales. Eventually Pedra was
reached on another truck, also loaded with raw cotton. There is
an important economic factor behind that jolting ride over 120
miles of pitted track. It is that Pedra's diminutive cotton industry lives with its back turned on the São Francisco River,
except for the drinking water and power that are drawn a
distance of six miles.

José Menezes, factory manager of the *Companhia Agro Fabril
Mercantil*, explains that the bad road to Rio Branco is still the
fastest transport available. Yet Pedra lies on Dom Pedro's railway. The sea is only 150 miles away by rail and the lower river,
offering a sea haul 200 miles shorter to Rio than the ship route
from Recife. Also, the São Francisco River runs literally at

Pedra's doorstep. Senhor Menezes finds the São Francisco route slow and uncertain. The river delta silts up badly and does not form a substantial seaport. This bottleneck at the natural outlet of the São Francisco Valley does not entirely explain its retarded growth. The bottleneck could be broken by adequate rail and highway service over the relatively short distance from the falls to the sea. Long piers could be built to reach water deep enough for large ships. Such costly works first require profitable reasons, as the pressure of resources needed by the outside world, the building of productive centers along the river, and the influx of population.

This process is actually beginning under war demands for quartz crystal, fibers, vegetable oils, and other products of immediate and long-range value. How far the development will go in the postwar period is one of Brazil's many engrossing questions in a future studded with interesting prospects. Climate has much to do with the slow pace, especially along the lower São Francisco. The zone of periodic droughts has its driest area about halfway between the falls and Joazeiro.

So it is that, instead of new power projects at Paulo Afonso, a turbine rated at 2500 horsepower was being hauled away during my visit, after lying unused for twenty-five years waiting a demand for increased power. The demand never came. The southern State of Rio Grande do Sul bought the equipment to provide energy for the city of São Leopoldo. Across the freshly painted orange turbine had been stenciled in large letters a national slogan of the hour: *Tudo pelo Brasil*. That is, "All by Brazil," an appeal for national awakening and more self-reliance.

For Brazil and for Rio Grande, the slogan pays immediate dividends. For the Northeast, this single dramatic incident underlines the fact that the watchword is still waiting—waiting for some galvanizing action that will draw together the power, the irrigation, the mineral and agricultural resources of Brazil's Cinderella region.

Closely related to the semiarid Northeast is the upper São

Francisco Valley, often described as one of South America's beckoning frontiers. I approached the valley by way of Joazeiro, railhead of the port at São Salvador, capital of Bahia. Between Joazeiro and Pirapora, the São Francisco River rolls smoothly for the most part through a broad, flat valley flanked by intermittent ridges and mesas. Pirapora is nearly 1200 miles from the delta where this river pours its silt-laden waters into the blue Atlantic just below the easternmost bulge of Brazil. Joazeiro is only 350 miles from the river's mouth and 200 miles above Paulo Afonso Waterfalls. That leaves something under 900 miles for the upper valley, where it is served by regular steamer transport.

Lyrical descriptions have been written of the São Francisco Valley and its economic promise. The region has possibilities, but so far it is largely a deserted land, not a fresh one. Even Roman Catholic church buildings have fallen into disrepair and decay in many of the towns.

The first two thirds of my trip bisected the State of Bahia. At times I met mining engineers and rubber workers. Even in this dry section, *maniçoba* and some other types of rubber trees grow. Quartz crystal and castor beans to make airplane oil are other important materials. These activities have suddenly startled the region from a slumber that began when the first great wave of pioneering here subsided. During the period of dominance by the Northeast in Brazilian Government, much of the population was crowded into the coastal zone. Slave-trading was centered at São Salvador. Food production had to be increased. Pioneers pushed into the São Francisco Valley. They founded cities and built churches.

Why this development has not lasted is a question of interest to modern pioneers. In the lower reaches of the valley it is evident that drought exerts the same kind of deterrent effect it does in the Northeast. Also, the river is a magnificent means of communication, but it is handicapped by rapids, in addition to having access to the sea entirely cut off for river boats by Paulo Afonso Waterfalls downstream from Joazeiro. Adequate means of land transport could be developed in the valley, if there were economic reasons for doing so. Possibly the new emphasis on minerals may be the key.

Until such prospects open, at the end of Bahia State in the town of Carinhanha the frustrations of this region pile up under the sultry air. Into the suspended animation of the place we ship travelers burst as meteors, even though we walk slowly in the heat. At the end of the main street a small chapel stands dejectedly. Its altar not long ago had fallen to the deserted and broken floor. Outside against the wall a resident sits in the scanty shade. Asked why the stores have almost no fruits or fresh vegetables, he raises eyes weary with watching a hard horizon, and replies that everything like that has to be brought in from a distance. Dry as it is, this day has had the benefit of recent rains. In the droughts, Carinhanha must be fed from more fertile lands.

On the outside wall of the cement market building which was erected during some past spurt of civic initiative in Carinhanha appears this sign, as I translated it from the Portuguese:

VISIT THE HOUSE OF SÃO JOSÉ DE OLIVEIRA LISBOA, CORRESPONDENT OF THE BANK OF BRAZIL, COMMER- CIAL AND INDUSTRIAL BANK OF MINAS GERAIS, GERMAN TRANSATLANTIC BANK, AND OTHER IMPORTANT FIRMS OF THE COUNTRY. WE SELL AT LOWEST PRICES FARM EQUIPMENT, IRON GOODS, HATS, SHOES, AND VARIOUS OTHER ARTICLES. WE MAINTAIN PERMANENT DEPOSITS OF COFFEE, SALT, KEROSENE, CAUSTIC SODA, GUNS, MATCHES, AND OTHER MERCHANDISE OF GREAT UTIL- ITY IN THIS REGION. VISIT THE HOUSE OF SÃO JOSÉ. YOU WILL CERTAINLY PROFIT. IN SANTO ANTONIO STREET.

With North American advertising zip, a venerable gentleman behind long white whiskers is pointing at this sign from one side and saying:

BY AGE AND EXPERIENCE I HAVE LEARNED IT PAYS TO

DEAL WITH SÃO JOSÉ DE OLIVEIRA LISBOA, AND SO I
COUNSEL MY FRIENDS TO FOLLOW MY EXAMPLE.

There—with skins of jaguars and large snakes as some of the
active items of trade in this frontier warehouse—is a measure of
economic advancement in the depths of the São Francisco Valley.

Carinhanha, most remote city of Bahia and the low point of
the São Francisco voyage, fell behind as I entered the better-
watered lands of Minas Gerais. There new *fazendas,* or farms,
are being started. The lean and competent proprietor of one,
whose high button shoes do not go with the easy saddle swing
of his stride, says he could "grow anything" in this soil. Such
improving prospects of the São Francisco lead on to the sparkling
town of Januaria, a gem gleaming in the wilderness, neglected
and feeling neglected but still keeping up its standards. The
contrast with Carinhanha is startlingly pleasant. Here is culture,
civic initiative, clean food and plenty of it, wholesome milk,
a sports club, and informed conversation under shady trees as
the Sunday afternoon promenade begins.

Januaria shows what can be done when the human resources
equal or exceed other resources. The main complaint of leading
citizens is that the State capital, Belo Horizonte, neglects
Januaria. State politicians, they say, view anything in the São
Francisco Valley as somewhere off near the end of the world. An
apparent need in Januaria is more paving to clean up stagnant
puddles in some streets. A local shovel brigade could drain the
worst pestilence holes.

In the region from Januaria southward there are said to be
substantial farming possibilities. Neither drought nor excessive
rain exists.

"Transport, transport—give us transport," is the cry of farmers and businessmen who want to go places, fast.

Minas Gerais, however, remains noted chiefly for its minerals.
This State forms the transition from Brazil's Northeast to the
highlands that extend from behind Rio de Janeiro through Mato
Grosso on the southern rim of the Amazon Basin.

Frontiers: Brazilian Highlands

Cauê Peak, Brazil's Iron Mountain in the State of Minas Gerais, thrusts 69 per cent pure metal into the sky. The rock itself is almost iron. When I broke a piece from the lichened gray surface, its inner side sparkled in my hand. On the mountainside, eroded ravines show rust where rains of untold years have beaten down on the iron roof of this natural storehouse. Cauê is one of many resources that open for Brazil possibilities of becoming a great industrial nation. Most of these possibilities exist on the Brazilian highlands along an arc from the State of Minas Gerais south and west into the State of Paraná and the massive plateau of Mato Grosso.

São Paulo is queen city of the highlands. Capital of a State bearing the same name, São Paulo with its 1,325,000 population is the most industrialized, best educated, most intelligent, democratic and progressive community in Brazil. São Paulo sends its civilizing influence into Goiaz and Mato Grosso.

Along these highlands Brazil has concentrated the bulk of its industries, population, and transport. Second to São Paulo in industrialization, and first in mineral wealth, is Minas Gerais. The name itself means General Mines. Itabira Mine, on the slopes of Cauê Peak, is set in the midst of forbidding mountains. Its remoteness explains why iron ore of such richness, combined with low phosphorus content so that smelting is expedited, should have been left until now for its first large-scale development. I saw what a transport handicap these mountains constitute for Brazil as I reached the railhead at Pirapora on the São Francisco River and went from there into mining communities of Minas Gerais. The mountains are not high, certainly not in comparison with the Andes. In the State of Espírito Santo, Mt. Bandeira, highest of the peaks, attains 9462 feet. This is considerably above the average. The plateaus that swing inland are seldom more than 3000 feet above sea level. Even so, the abruptness of coastal escarpments, and the jumbled confusion of peaks, are obstacles. The main rail line of the *Central do Brasil* between Rio de Janeiro and São Paulo bores through one tunnel after another until the upper level has been reached. There is urgent necessity to enlarge the carrying capacity of this line between iron mines and the new $65,000,000 steel mill at Volta Redonda, but the cost is tremendous.

It is the same with road building. On slopes where granite is overlaid by deep deposits of loose earth, highways must be cut in broad slashes between red banks. Landslides, a hazard also in the Andes and other ranges of South America where rains are torrential, must constantly be guarded against by Brazilian engineers. The overlaid gneiss formation, as at Rio, continues to erode down to bare granite. When I visited Itabira's Iron Mountain, the driver from the mine who met me at the main railway line took satisfaction in telling how many trucks had rolled down the mountains with landslides. He stopped the car in the middle of a particularly unstable spot and pointed down into the gorge. It must have been nearly 2000 feet to the river.

"One went down here just a few weeks ago."

"Would you mind telling me about that after we've crossed this slide?"

It is a wild road, yet all the ore ever brought out from Itabira, until the new railway was started, had to come this way. When South America's great resources are listed, some of these costly factors should always be taken into account.

Whole cities have been relocated because of the mountains. Accessibility was the primary motive for moving the capital of Minas Gerais from Ouro Preto to Belo Horizonte, or Beautiful Horizon. The city is pleasant, clean, set among green mountains at an altitude of 2500 feet, where the breeze can be refreshing even in midsummer. Selected as a capital site and laid out by skilled city planners, Belo Horizonte is more suitable for modern industry than the colonial capital of Ouro Preto, or Black Gold.

Ouro Preto dreams on its heights. Colonial architecture overhangs cobbled streets so steep that just walking from home to office is a good start on a day's work. The railway to this former remote capital winds through narrow gorges, crossing clear streams that sing in depths where dense foliage hides all but their sound. In days of colonial mining the capital was located near the main producing veins. Above the city may be seen old mine entrances. Like rabbit holes along a bank, they pit the high ridges. For all its atmosphere of colonial charm, Ouro Preto has begun to feel modernity. A new hotel, designed by an architect of the United States, streaks its unbroken balcony lines and pale blue exterior along a hill overlooking some of the most Spanish façades. Until only yesterday, as Brazilian history goes, Ouro Preto held its political position. Then, in 1897, the capital was moved bodily to Belo Horizonte. The new capital lies on the main rail line from Rio de Janeiro to Pirapora.

My trip to the Iron Mountain began in Belo Horizonte. The original itinerary had called for an approach through the Valley of the Rio Doce from the port of Vitória. While I was in Rio de Janeiro a series of landslides broke the railway line between Vitória and Itabira. Not only did this make it impossible for an individual traveler to reach Itabira from its own seaport, but shipments of iron ore could not move. Returning inland from Rio de Janeiro to Belo Horizonte, I took the train toward Nova Era, junction of the new Itabira railway. Soon we reached the first of several iron smelters. Pig iron was stacked in fenced enclosures where the hand of modern industry has begun to transform these mountains.

Fuel is the principal problem. Brazil has coal, but it either is of low grade or located far from developed industries. The main mines in use are in the southern coastal States of Santa Catarina and Rio Grande do Sul. The coal must be brought 700 miles by sea and then transshipped to overloaded rail lines that cross the mountains. Oil has been discovered in Bahia State, but is not yet produced on a commercial scale. Of sixteen wells drilled near the city of São Salvador, thirteen struck oil. They have been capped.

Brazil hesitates to let foreign capital develop its oil, and so far lacks technical skills of its own. Brazil seeks to keep its national economy as far as possible from being dominated by alien influences. One incident illustrates an extreme aspect of this trend. Monsanto Chemical Company of St. Louis in the

United States started a plant at Bahia. Working through its São Paulo office, the firm spent $425,000, and then could not obtain materials to complete the plant. While material shortages are easily attributable to the war, this incident was seen by observers in Brazil as due to economic nationalism of the kind that is delaying production of Bahia's oil.

When the oil finally begins to flow from Bahia, it will have to be transported 1000 miles by sea to reach southern mines and industrial areas. Meanwhile, much of Brazil's smelting is done with charcoal. Along the rail line are many charcoal pits. Brazil is abundantly supplied with wood, although the supply near the mines has already been seriously depleted. Ranging farther afield for wood throws an additional burden on transport.

These elements in Brazil's industrial outlook became more evident as I neared Itabira. The automobile trip from Nova Era to the mine turned out to be exciting. Heavy rains had deluged the Valley of the Rio Doce. Our road clung precariously on shelves of mud above flooded streams. It was easy to see why whole mountains of iron could remain untouched behind the barrier of Brazil's coastal ranges. Evidence of mineral wealth sparkled as we passed. Mica flakes glistened in eroded banks. Along the stream beds, flashing like diamond points, were countless crystals of iron and other minerals. The road climbed steadily. We looked down into granite gorges. Walls fifty feet high had been blasted to make way for the new railway built with United States money. At other places the line crossed fills 75 to 100 feet deep. The hastily deposited earth had been washed away in part, leaving the new rails sagging in mid-air.

The young Brazilian sent from the mine to meet me had been regaling me with information, much of which I later learned was inaccurate. As we reached the upper levels he pointed out Cauê Peak, 4300 feet high. From that distance it resembled any other mountain. The top appeared to be bare rock, but that rock is almost pure iron. An adjacent mountain rolls with less spectacular lines, but also is solid ore. Brazil has other deposits not so exposed, yet equally rich. First in iron ore among countries of the world, Brazil has 22 per cent of known reserves, and much of its estimated 15,000,000,000 tons is high grade. Anything below 50 per cent is not considered in Brazil to be worth mining at present. Piles of ore began to appear as we neared Itabira. Breakdown of the railway left mounting stocks that should have been moving toward Britain to make up for high-grade ores not then available from Sweden. As we crossed the railway in sight of the town below, a characteristic sign showed that North Americans had been on the job. BROOKLYN was daubed on a board, and an arrow pointed toward a shack in the ore yard. The road swung past a high cleared space where the railway ends. On the station appeared the name Presidente Vargas. Of all the cities in Brazil, new and old, that might have been given this name, it fell to a small but vital railway terminus. Itabira clings to its traditional name which means, in a native tongue, shining rock. The town lies in a deep valley near the top of Cauê Peak. Streets are paved with iron cobblestones. The central thoroughfare climbs at an angle that made our car stall several times.

Itabira is the focal point in a wartime development involving Brazil, the United States, and Great Britain. The aim was to provide the Allies, especially Britain, with high-grade iron ore. Beyond the war, Brazil stood to gain access to some of its richest iron for an expanding steel industry. An agreement was reached by the three powers. British interests had long been working to develop the Valley of the Rio Doce. They built the *Estrada de Ferro Vitória a Minas*, a railway of less than standard gauge. Under the tripartite agreement of 1942, Brazil received the railway and iron ore deposit. A new corporation, the *Companhia Vale do Rio Doce, S. A.*, was formed. Common stock in the amount of $5,500,000 is owned by the Brazilian Government. Another $4,500,000 in 6 per cent preferred stock has been sold to Brazilians. The Export-Import Bank of Washington advanced $14,000,000 to be repaid with iron ore over a period of twenty-five years. Warren Lee Pierson, President of the Export-Import Bank, must have been looking the other way when the accord provided that interest notes, if not covered by payments in ore, were to be returned and canceled. Mr. Pierson told me late in

1944 that this provision was being amended. It could have been an open invitation not to pay. The loan was for rehabilitation of the railway, extension of the rails from Nova Era to the mine, and installation of machinery.

Planned ore capacity at Itabira is 1,500,000 tons a year. Britain and the United States are to share equally in exports from the mine. Under the contract, Brazil must pay a penalty on any shipment that falls below 68 per cent iron in the ore, or rises higher than .020 phosphorus content. The United States and Britain have a right to reject any cargo that falls below 67 per cent. In the United States, ore of 45 per cent is considered rich, and the dividing line between Bessemer and non-Bessemer processing is a phosphorus content of .045. During my visit to Itabira, production had hardly begun. Ore removed in road work on slopes of Cauê Peak helped to provide the current total of 5000 tons a month. With six miles of the new railway washed out in one stretch, no shipments were moving to Vitória. Ore previously exported had gone entirely to Britain. While the United States has abundant iron reserves, the high-grade Brazilian ore is desirable for mixing with lower grades. In this way the United States plans to save its own richer veins against future needs.

In several respects the Rio Doce accord has not come up to expectations. When I came into Belo Horizonte late in 1943, I was told that the Rio Doce project would have to be written off as a war measure. All possibility of placing sufficient ore in England to speed victory had already disappeared. The reasons were not only technical but political. Engineers complained that on the Brazilian side politics had been given precedence over production. Dr. Vargas had appointed as President of the company Dr. Israel Pinheiro, formerly Secretary of Agriculture in the State of Minas Gerais. North American technicians might not have minded being subject to the final authority of a political appointee, if he had kept politics out of management. In conformity with prevailing dictatorial methods in Brazil, all power was concentrated in a few hands. Dr. Pinheiro insisted on full control over personnel. No one could be employed or discharged without his detailed approval. He held the balance of power among the four Directors, two of whom were Brazilian, and two, North American. The Brazilians at the time were Gen. Horta Barbosa and Major Punaro Bley. Robert K. West represented the Export-Import Bank. Bernard Blanchard was Director of Finances.

That was the organization resulting from changes made in September, 1943. C. Alven Lorensen, on loan from Bethlehem Steel Corporation, previously had been a Director in charge of engineering and development work at the mine. I met him at his home in Belo Horizonte as he and the family were packing to come home. Mild-mannered and self-controlled, he told me about his reasons for leaving. He had begun the work and stayed with it until political interference became unbearable. The 1943 reorganization, he said, had ruled that no Director could be in charge of an operating department. He felt this was aimed against himself. The President of the company had been undercutting him for some time through a *Presidencia* established near the mine.

Dr. Pinheiro spent most of his time in Rio de Janeiro. The day I arrived by road he came in by air for one of his infrequent visits to the mine. The *Presidencia* acted as a separate entity and in effect took over the construction work. Delays occurred which nonpolitical engineers found beyond explanation. An air compressor of 160 cubic feet capacity had been bought a year before my visit, with three drills. This and other equipment had not arrived. All mining was by hand after blasting. The British had left one old air compressor. When repaired, it proved of some use. Trucks were hauling ore, but there were no steam-shovels or other heavy equipment. Wooden sheds stood where extensive machine shops are planned.

Since the Rio Doce project has ceased to be a war measure, its success or failure will depend on how Brazil carries through. Technical men told me that Brazil might be able to compete with high-grade iron ore from Sweden, Russia, Australia, and Africa, provided the wasteful hand of politics is removed from the Rio Doce Company. There is an opportunity for a two-way traffic of ships taking ore to the United States and returning loaded with coal. Brazil's own growing steel industry will be needing more ore as well as fuel. Mr. Lorensen displayed to me no anger over the way his hands had been tied by politicians. He said there simply was no use trying to mine ore when the controlling managers were more interested in favoritism than in efficiency.

Cauê with its exposed hematite offers an engineer's dream from the mining standpoint. I was driven up the road that spirals around the peak through solid ore. The mountain will be blown apart, top first. Ore will be trucked down the road until both peak and road have disappeared. Open-pit mining may then go on indefinitely. Drillings indicate that the outcropping is merely the exposed point of a deep ore bed. The same kind of iron has been found in the saddle between Cauê and its adjoining peak. The latter is owned by Brazilian Iron and Steel Company. A long conveyor belt is to carry ore from Cauê Peak into crushers and other processing machinery above the town of Itabira. Eventually, when the railway to Vitória has been stabilized, the aim is to produce 5,000,000 tons a year. Cauê's greatest merit is the ore's low phosphorus content. Mr. Lorensen told me he is not sure this advantage will hold for all of Cauê's ore. He found evidences of increasing phosphorus. The terms of the original Rio Doce agreement are strict on this point. Some of the engineers felt there might be difficulty in meeting them, or at least a narrow margin to spare.

On the way out of Itabira I traveled another road, by bus to the railway at Santa Barbara. We came to a rickety wooden bridge that had been washed out. The new concrete span was incomplete. Our driver jockeyed his way across on planks. Even so, this route passed through far more accessible terrain than the upper Rio Doce. So I returned to Belo Horizonte, metropolis of Brazil's most highly developed mining region.

Mica, quartz crystal, and numerous other minerals were being mined to speed the war toward victory. Engineers who have come from other parts of the world remarked that mining is on a surprisingly small scale in Minas Gerais. My own impressions fell short of what I had expected to find. Many of the minerals are scattered in small beds that make hand-mining more profitable than machine-mining. North American engineers tried to introduce steamshovels and found that mica was better extracted by hand. At Sete Lagoas I visited one of the most famous quartz crystal mines. It consisted of an open pit about as long as a city block, with men using picks and shovels. There were tractors and trucks. One tractor was stuck in the mud. Despite the rudimentary aspect of this operation, it has sent many a ton of crystal north to perform indispensable war functions in delicate instruments. During my visit the wartime program of mineral procurement was already being curtailed. The general feeling, as expressed to me, was one of disillusionment rather than enthusiasm.

Even so, Brazil has minerals in such variety and quantity that a tremendous industry can thrive here, under proper management. Bauxite of excellent quality in large quantities near the surface and easy to mine, provides a base for large-scale aircraft production. Manganese, chrome, nickel, cobalt, rutile, tin, wolframite and scheelite, beryllium, bismuth, corundum, carbonado or black diamond—so the list goes. Brazil is the only important world source known for quartz crystal, an invaluable material in modern electronics. High-grade tantalite is found only in Brazil. Brazil shares with Bengal, India, in supplying fine sheet mica. The minerals museum in Belo Horizonte marshals gigantic block crystals and the most delicate of ores resembling petrified snowflakes dyed in vividly refracted colors.

Waterpower possibilities exist, and in some areas may take the place of other motive sources. São Paulo and Rio de Janeiro have shown the way. Brazil's waterpower, however, is limited near natural industrial areas. Some of the main falls and cascades are in remote parts of the Amazon Basin. Outstanding possibilities center at Paulo Afonso in the mineral-rich Northeast, and in the Guairá-Iguassú region of Paraná State.

The opening of Brazil's Steel Age is signalized by the Volta Redonda project. At the site I found work progressing rapidly on the extensive mill buildings and installations, as well as a new town to house the staff. A modern hotel replete with outdoor swimming pool and spacious entry halls commands views of the mill and its surrounding countryside. Coffee trees had been growing on the rolling hills not long before. The Paraíba River rolls pleasantly through the valley, supplying water for the mill through impressive intake pipes already installed. Foundations for the principal furnace buildings tapered into the distance. It is a vast undertaking, freighted with significance for South America. Success would give the continent its first heavy steel industry, capable of converting the Iron Mountain into steel shapes hitherto imported from older industrial nations. Already in another mill Brazil has rolled its first rails. Bridges and railways in time will be fabricated here to open new sections of the interior.

Activity at Volta Redonda was proceeding to the expressed satisfaction of engineers from the United States, in marked contrast with the disappointment voiced to me at Itabira. Brazil is keeping as much as possible of the work in its own hands at both sites. Of the present $65,000,000 capital, an original $25,000,000 came from the Export-Import Bank of Washington, buttressed later by an additional $20,000,000. It was surprising, in view of the elaborate and apparently definitive character of this undertaking, to hear some doubt voiced as to whether it will pay dividends. Again the geographical handicap of misplaced mountains along Brazil's central coast makes difficulties. Coal must be brought from the south by sea, and iron ore from the north by sea or rail. In either case the final haul to the mill is thrown on overworked and inadequate railways. Coming into and going out of Volta Redonda on the main line between Rio and São Paulo, I experienced the travel shortage in unforgettable ways. Not once during the all-night ride to São Paulo did I set foot inside the car. Jammed on the platform, we swayed on together through the darkness. Behind us on the door in enduring bronze appeared this sign, disregarded by common consent: PASSENGERS NOT PERMITTED TO RIDE ON PLATFORM.

A possible solution for coal and ore is the strengthening of short railways to the coast. These must climb sharply to cross the escarpment. One runs to the small port of Angra dós Reis. These are some of the costly factors that give Brazil an uphill road toward producing its own steel shapes for less than they could be imported. Unquestionably South America's Steel Age will come, and Volta Redonda is a pioneer.

The mountainous parts of Minas Gerais are on the east. Westward, the highlands flatten toward Goiaz and Mato Grosso. Goiaz, like Minas Gerais, has a new capital. It is reached from Rio de Janeiro or São Paulo. The railway goes as far as Anápolis, and is being extended to Goiânia, the new capital. The road connecting Goiânia with the outside world is still somewhat of an adventure. Bridges have not been built at a few points where, in rainy weather, a bus has to take swimming lessons. Goiânia's location in the State of which it is the capital throws considerable light on geography in this part of Brazil. From the city to the southern border is 100 miles. To the northern border is 800 miles. Those northern expanses follow down the Araguaia and Tocantins Rivers into the eastern border zone of the Amazon Basin. The Tocantins comes into the Pará and is connected with the main Amazon system just above Belém. Most of Goiaz is in the tropical belt. The southern plateau where Goiânia is located belongs to the more temperate heights. On the bus from Anápolis to Goiânia, a Brazilian waxes enthusiastic about resources being poured out for the United Nations.

"One block of quartz crystal," he tells several listeners as the small bus jolts and wrenches over the unfinished road, "was so large it had to be cut in sections before it could be brought out of the jungle. It weighed 500 tons."

There may have been such a find, but if so, the engineers at Sete Lagoas in the State of Minas Gerais, as well as those in Goiaz, neglected to tell me about it. They did describe a thirty-ton block found at São Luiz do Tocantins. In this remarkable piece the pure crystal amounted to one ton. The rest was inferior, and much of it useless. The Brazilian in the bus continues to regale his listeners with stories of the natural wealth in Goiaz. He is genuinely amazed at recent discoveries. A few hundred tons of exaggeration could be forgiven him under the circumstances. The war has awakened Brazilians generally to many of their own resources that had been there all the while.

Goiânia is a capital still under construction. Wide avenues are being paved. The central stem radiates from the Executive Palace in the grand manner, flanked by two other avenues as spokes of the wheel. The capital was conceived by the present Interventor, Dr. Pedro Ludovico Teixeira. He is a Federal dictator appointed to administer a formerly self-governing State as though it were a province. Like other Interventors, he was named by Dr. Vargas, as there are no public elections of any kind in Brazil at this writing. The old capital, bearing the same name as the State, or Goiaz, lies on lower ground, and is more shut in. While not as inaccessible as Ouro Preto in the State of Minas Gerais, it did not please the modern Interventor. Some ten years ago he succeeded in carrying his project through to the planning stage. On March 8, 1937, the act legally authorizing transfer of the capital was signed. Various properties were bought on the plateau. At an elevation of 2400 feet, Goiânia commands extensive views with ranges of moderate height in the distance. In seven years much has been done toward providing the framework for a capital befitting one of Brazil's rich and little-developed states. Young trees already cast a few cool spots of shade over stone benches along the parked avenue. Store buildings, public utilities, and a hotel retain their newness against the encroaching mud and carelessness of a pioneer countryside not used to such luxury and refinement.

On the way I had seen with unpleasant directness how primitive the region is in many respects. A mason and his assistants were mixing mortar to build a partition wall inside a house. The whole thing was of adobe type, and the workmanship quite smooth. Yet for mortar these masons were mixing ordinary cow dung, sand and water. They said the smell wore off after a while inside those rooms. There should be no necessity for such poverty in building, but sanitary engineers of the United States tell me they have had to allow natives to use the same methods at times to have buildings put up quickly. Brazil does not lack material.

It lacks, as one Brazilian said with emphasis, the organization to make better use of its resources.

Although Goiaz is still largely undeveloped, it is one of Brazil's most promising frontiers. I met enthusiastic young Brazilians who have set up homes there. They tell of nickel mines, of quartz crystal, of cobalt, and other mineral resources. They also are interested in projects to increase diversity. They want a balanced economy made possible by agriculture that keeps pace with mining and industry. Nickel deposits in Goiaz are officially stated to be among the world's richest. At Anápolis I saw quartz crystals in quantity. Brazilian buyers said the largest then in stock, about the size of a football, were only average. It pays to gather them as small as eggs, or even less than that, when they are Grade A. Crystal occurs also in the neighboring States of Mato Grosso on the west, and Minas Gerais on the east. Bahia along the São Francisco River has crystal.

When Brazilians talk of their Wild Western pioneer State of Mato Grosso, they easily slip into lyrical language.

"Such vegetation, *senhor*," one of them said to me. "The Mato Grosso is a paradise!"

It seemed discourteous to ask if he had been there. Also, at the time my own observations had not proceeded far enough to raise serious questions about his remark. This mammoth State is more than twice as large as Texas. All of Mexico tops Mato Grosso's 570,138 square miles by only a third—193,806 square miles. Mato Grosso undoubtedly has size, but after skirting it and talking with people who had seen enough of it to reach fairly definitive conclusions, I reluctantly had to revise downward my own sight-unseen enthusiasms. As elsewhere in South America, the unknown often lures with attractions beyond what you find when you arrive. A realistic approach to Mato Grosso must be undertaken from at least two directions if it is to be reasonably complete. This great State could be divided into many parts of distinctive character, but in broad lines it falls into two contrasting lands.

Along the western borders of Mato Grosso from the Apa

River at the Paraguayan frontier north to Pôrto Velho on the Madeira River, the two great zones merge. On the south are open lands adorned by clumps of palms with clean straight trunks and a top rounded as though made of windmill blades whirling in several directions at once. This is opposite the Paraguayan *Chaco* before it takes on, far to the north, a more jungled aspect. The Paraguay River bisects both Paraguay and the central part of Mato Grosso. Along its banks lie untamed savannas and swamps where jaguar hunters have a field day. A Brazilian Army Captain on a frontier post showed me a dozen huge skins he had collected in the past few months. As we walked back from his quarters to the steamer, he turned a large flashlight down toward the river bank. In the dark his beam picked up brilliant spots of light—the eyes of *jacarés*.

"Don't go down there at night," he warned me.

In his small zoo he had some of the most brilliant and unusual macaws I have ever seen. He also had a jaguar cub.

Another time, on the train from São Paulo to Pôrto Esperança at the Paraguay River near Corumbá, commercial center of Mato Grosso, I noticed a young woman, evidently North American, with two small children. She was in the seat across the aisle. Her dress and manner were decidedly those of someone who lived out of doors most of the time. As North Americans—the only two within hundreds of miles—we exchanged greetings. She turned out to be the former Edith Bray of Philadelphia, and now the wife of Sasha Siemel, famous jaguar hunter who once took Theodore Roosevelt into Mato Grosso. The hunter himself was waiting at the appointed station with some of his men. A Latvian of close-cropped graying beard, massive chest and the easy strength of movement that goes with his occupation, he rode on the train for a while until the family reached its destination.

The Siemels have a houseboat and roam up and down the rivers of Mato Grosso. Gradually the roaming is giving way to a house and garden. Sasha Siemel, who sallies forth at times armed only with a pointed stick to meet jaguars, has a domestic side of his character. On the train with the two flaxen-haired jungle babies, Dora and Sandra, he was a marvelous daddy, as gentle and kindly as he was powerfully self-controlled and confidence-inspiring.

Evidences of encroaching wildness do not need to be sought in Mato Grosso. Yet colonization has been moving ahead. One reason Sasha Siemel is an honored member of the frontier community is that he and other hunters work to protect Mato Grosso's cattle herds. Their hunting is an economic necessity, not a sport. At times they make sport of it, as when they take parties of outside hunters into the savannas. There the jaguars are concentrated.

Moving northward through Mato Grosso I next encountered the *pantanal*, a low-lying plain in the center of South America that floods during part of the year. In the *pantanal* are hummocks where the grass stays above water in normal times. Other parts are covered entirely. Cattle range the *pantanal* even when it is under water. They find some of their best grazing in the swamps. Here, as elsewhere in the interior, the cattle sometimes bear on their hides a high-water mark, showing how far they have stood under the muddy surface.

This kind of cattle-raising can be risky, for an immense drainage basin pours its floods down into the *pantanal*.

The next aspect of Mato Grosso—still within the southern half—is the plateau. It forms part of a series of highlands that divide the eastern portion of the Amazon Basin from the Atlantic Ocean. The central section of these plateaus and mountains begins in the State of Minas Gerais, crosses Goiaz State, and swings widely across Mato Grosso in a northwesterly direction. Along that line occurs the major division to which reference was made earlier. Mato Grosso is cut in two on the low watershed almost as with a knife. Dense forests of the Amazon Basin push southward until they meet conditions of elevation and climate that no longer favor them. South of this variable line the country is more open. It has occasional stands of tropical trees in damp gullies. Once in a while a forest manages to cover extensive areas. The rest is given over to scrub growth and some grasslands. Scattered palms, anthills deserted and grass-grown to form cities of mounds some three feet high, rivers broken with rocks and unsuited to large-scale navigation—these are other aspects of the southern Mato Grosso highlands.

Across the divide, on headwaters of the Xingú and other Amazonian rivers, conditions in Mato Grosso do not differ essentially from those prevailing along the basin's extensive periphery. The eastern end of this region is believed to offer greatest prospects of profitable development for some time to come. It is there that the Brazilian Government lately sent its Xingú Expedition, previously mentioned. Unless unusual conditions combine to set this section apart, the expedition is likely to find leached soils. This is so wherever soil technicians have examined varied lands in similar segments of the Amazonian highlands. Far to the west along the Guaporé, Mamoré, and Madeira Rivers, farming has been held back in Mato Grosso by distance from market and the difficulties of tropical agriculture. Microscopic clearings in the immensity of tropical forest do little more than feed the few local inhabitants after a fashion. Food actually has to be imported. Along drier southern plateaus of Minas Gerais, Goiaz, and Mato Grosso, the principal land use is for cattle raising. There are some sheep.

The effect on me of journeying across this plateau was cumulative and disillusioning. Here, if anywhere in the central land mass of Brazil, climate and elevation should favor large-scale increases in population. Mineral wealth also provides a potential backbone for industry. Yet from the mountains of Minas Gerais where farming is not generally possible, the westward lands turn out to be poorer than most people expect. A young Brazilian returning to his home in Minas Gerais after studying at a farm school in the United States was on the bus. Noticing the scrub vegetation and scarcity of corn or other crops, I asked him if there were some better soils not in view.

"No, *senhor*." He waved a hand at the horizon. "It is poor soil, most of it."

There are some better portions of Goiaz, but also much scrub land. As for the southern plateau of Mato Grosso, observers who have access to the farm facts are not optimistic of expanding production greatly. They say that some of this grassland will not support more than one head of cattle on two acres of land. While that is a good cattle ratio, it does not indicate hopeful prospects for general agriculture, or for expanded cattle production. It would be hasty to generalize about a region as large as Mato Grosso, but there appears solid evidence for dismissing the most rosy talk frequently heard.

The most important factor is the type of political and industrial management that finally sets forth to develop Mato Grosso. Despite numerous handicaps, the land has many possibilities. South of Corumbá in the Urucum Mountains, are iron and magnesium deposits in close proximity and large quantities. They are near the Paraguay River, a splendid waterway. Unfortunately, the river runs away from Brazil and offers no direct outlet to the sea for that country. The Paraguay does, however, supply inland water transport for the central valley of Mato Grosso south of the Amazon divide. Boats from the Atlantic at Montevideo can reach Cuiabá, capital of the State, 260 miles north of Corumbá as the crow flies. The river meanders to such an extent that the boat trip may take a week. Beyond Cuiabá there are projects for a barge canal, and roads, to cross the low divide and connect with rivers of the Amazon Basin. One long track through the jungle now reaches Pôrto Velho on the Madeira River.

In climate, the highlands are pleasant. Their resources are substantial. With right management they should develop new Pittsburghs and Magnitogorsks, Birminghams and São Paulos. It is refreshing to see what has been done with the eastern end of these plateaus by intelligent pioneers in the State of São Paulo. Coming into São Paulo from any of its neighboring areas, a traveler is struck by evidences of advancement. Part of the explanation is written in a purple-red soil known as *terra roxa,* pronounced terr'-rah ro'-shah. This soil is the foundation for Brazil's coffee plantations. In it thrive also figs, oranges, lemons, cotton, and numerous other specialized farm products. The *terra roxa,* however, is a limited resource both in extent and in durability. It is not to be confused with the ordinary rust-red earth seen so commonly in South America. *Terra roxa* occurs in fingers rather than over vast areas. It does not cover all of São Paulo. Also, being on the verge of the tropics, it does not stand intensive cultivation as well as do Temperate-Zone soils. Department of Agriculture technicians who have studied São Paulo report that new lands are constantly being farmed, and older ones turned to cattle grazing. Possibly this explains why cattle are the chief farm resource on fringes of São Paulo and inland through Mato Grosso. There is a limit to this process, however, since South America's need is not more cattle, but more diversified farming. In the cattle industry, better quality is required. Strains of the zebu and gayal types from India are helping to solve this problem with cattle adapted to tropical conditions.

One of the most promising areas on the Brazilian highlands is the State of Paraná. Fingers of *terra roxa* reach into it from São Paulo. Yet, before the Paraná River has been reached, the purple earth gives way to sandy and less fertile soils. Paraná has timber of many varieties, including the famous Paraná pine. In the great waterfalls of Guairá and Iguassú are possibilities of tremendous hydroelectric plants. Minerals exist in Paraná. Climate is agreeable in the mid-zone between tropics and the temperate *pampa*. Some of South America's most magnificent forests are found in Paraná. Deep humus and a more moderate rainfall than in the tropics offer a basis for diversified agriculture at many points.

Unquestionably there are pioneer possibilities on Brazil's plateaus, even though the most enthusiastic estimates must be reduced in presence of the land itself. Many Brazilians freely acknowledge that the success of São Paulo is due to the type of immigrants who settled there. Italians, Germans, Poles, and others of advanced technical ability came from Europe. They naturally gravitated to the more temperate highlands. Japanese also chose this region for their characteristic farming. I have visited some of their *fazendas* that brought a bit of old Japan into Brazil. Even the carp were swimming in shallow artificial pools overhung by broad elephant ears of taro, starchy root-food of the Orient. Some of the Japanese were sent to Brazil as spies, but most of them were simply seeking new lands. They have left their mark on the highlands. Some 200,000 of them live in and around São Paulo.

The pattern of Brazilian development probably will continue from the coast to the plateaus, and from there, gradually, into the Amazon Basin. Joãa Alberto Lins de Barros, as Brazil's Co-ordinator of Economic Mobilization, told me that Brazil has so much undeveloped land there is no point going into the low-lying areas for a long time. The Xingú Expedition was one of his ardent enthusiasms. He said he hoped to survey a road along the highlands that lead to Santarém on the Amazon. This would pass the Ford rubber plantation at Belterra. The Co-ordinator flew to the Xingú for week ends. He took delight in telling about the refrigerator he had installed at his camp. During his revolutionary days he once marched through Xingú country. Dropping northward from the Mato Grosso plateau, it is the home of hostile tribes, including the Chavantes. There the English explorer Fawcett disappeared in 1925. In an effort to open the Xingú for settlement, Brazil has sent two parties from Leopoldina on the Araguaia River. Their aim is to meet in wild country between the Xingú and Tapajóz Rivers, and eventually reach Santarém.

South America's future will be greatly shaped by what is done, or not done, to develop these central highlands, several times the area of Texas, from Brazil's Minas Gerais to Mato Grosso and on to the Bolivian territory of Santa Cruz.

Frontiers: Chaco and Pampa

In Asunción, Paraguay, after I had come south along the entire length of the *Chaco*, it was my good fortune to spend several days with someone who knows pioneer possibilities of the *Gran Chaco* firsthand. He is Jacob A. Braun, purchasing agent and one of the business managers of the Mennonite colony known as *Colonia Mennonita*. It is located inland from Puerto Casado. A rail line runs from the river to the center of the *Chaco* at Minas-cué. The colony is reached by road southward from the rail terminus.

Mr. Braun and I shared a crude penthouse on the roof of one of Asunción's smaller hotels. It was part of my program for roughing-my-way through South America to see some of the things that never appear in the best hotels. He is racially German, but professes to be anti-Nazi. The Mennonites are pacifists and came to Paraguay seeking refuge from wars. They chose the heart of the *Chaco* as early as 1875. The colony has increased until there are 2400 residents in 420 families. Cotton is a principal crop. Mr. Braun told me they do well, and have imported machinery to speed the work. By frugality and hard labor, they have established a remote home. Unlike some other colonies, this one is extremely self-reliant. The *Chaco* is by no means a get-rich-quick area, judging from their experience. Other settlements have dwindled and disappeared when their members lacked the religious fervor to keep them striving against social, economic, and political hardships.

The groundwork of Paraguay's political and social earthquakes is based in its lack of outstanding resources. Nearly everything the country produces is also produced by larger neighbors at points closer to available markets. There are no tin mines, copper mines, nitrate fields, or rare minerals to match those of Bolivia, Chile, Argentina, and Brazil. Coming down the Paraguay River I saw lime kilns at intervals. The rock is burned and the lime shoveled into battered iron barrels that roll down steep banks into cargo holds of river steamers. Lime forms one of the few nonagricultural industries. Even so, there is no prospect of a large-scale cement development. Cement and other industrial products are mostly imported from Argentina or Brazil.

Paraguay accordingly is thrown back on its farm resources. Here again the land does not differ greatly from surrounding areas. The nearest potential importers—Argentina, Brazil, Uruguay, and Bolivia—can grow the same kind of crops. Peanuts are a Paraguayan specialty. In Asunción's warehouses I saw mountains of them. Peanuts, too, can be grown elsewhere. Hardwoods of excellent quality are cut. Some of them are so heavy they will not float. So a characteristic sight of the Paraguayan countryside is the log-hauling cart with two huge wheels higher than a man's head. Yet this is an expensive method of transport. Central America, far closer to world markets, produces fine woods.

United States Ambassador Wesley Frost, since retired at statutory age, felt that a key to solution of Paraguay's central economic problem is to discover specialized products of small weight and high money value. There are several promising herbs. One is named, in Guaraní, *caahee*. It is a sweet that replaces sugar. Each vowel is pronounced separately: ca-a-he-e. Dyestuffs, perfumes, flavors, fibers, vegetable oils—these are possible outlets for Paraguay. At present $1,000,000 of Good-Neighbor money is being devoted to developing such industries.

Charles E. Kellogg, Soil Survey Chief in the United States Department of Agriculture, told me in Washington he wants to go to the *Chaco* and study its soils. Mr. Kellogg feels he might find some answers to South America's generally poor soil outlook. One point he makes is that no soil should be dismissed merely with the comment that it is poor, nor other soils unqualifiedly described as rich. The term he advances is *soil response to management*. Somehow the *Chaco* attracts Mr. Kellogg. Possibly one day he will make that trip and contribute importantly to South America's development. Such help is needed in the central mid-zone between Amazonian borderlands and the richest soils of all South America in the Argentine *pampa*.

On northern borders of the *Chaco* the land rises toward Santa Cruz in Bolivia, containing some of the rich soil areas in South America. Grapefruit grows to extraordinary sizes and is delicious. The main handicap of this region is its distance from markets. The Andes cut it off on the west. Some of the wildest country of the continent separates the city of Santa Cruz from Corumbá in Brazil. During my stay in Corumbá a band of out-

laws was terrorizing the country. They had their lair in swampy
country west of the city. In flight all the way across Santa Cruz
I saw a panorama of mesas and plains. Parts of this remote
region hold promise for the future, when South America has
developed more accessible lands. Adjoining Bolivia's Santa Cruz
region on the south is not only the Paraguayan *Chaco,* but the
Argentine *Chaco,* merging with the *pampa.*

Argentina is conscious of having conquered most of its own
land. One of the first things told to me in Argentina seven years
ago was that the whole country is fenced. With the kind of
persistent dreaming that causes many sensible people to brush
aside such statements about South America because the illusion
of vast open frontiers lingers, I mentally pigeonholed the remark as some pessimistic quirk. Now I have seen enough of
Argentina to accept that 1938 statement at face value. Argentina, to put it bluntly, feels land-poor and population-poor.

Mendoza is a vantage point from which to grasp some of
Argentina's unexpected reasoning along territorial lines. A city
at the foot of the Andes, Mendoza is famed for its fruits, grapes,
and other specialized farm products. The secret is irrigation.
Outside the pleasantly shaded streets and the orderly plantations,
semidesert conditions prevail. Barren mountains of great height
overhang the city.

Mendoza already is drawing heavily on its once abundant
water supply. Since irrigation is limited within easy reach of the
Andes, the more distant *pampa* must depend on rains that do not
always suffice. The underlying pressure in Argentina of a
technically advanced people on a land they have fenced, explains
recurrent expansionist tendencies, especially among fascist-
inclined Army officers who at this writing constitute the Argentine Government. Land poverty is felt even though Argentina possesses the largest fertile and arable lands in South
America. The picture is drawn into focus by starting at the
north and coming down through Argentina to the *pampa.* Although most of Argentina spreads over the great plains of the
pampa and adjoining lowlands, the northwest corner goes up
with Bolivia to plateaus 15,000 feet high. Chile at that three-

cornered junction of nations also has a slice of the *altiplano*. This part of Argentina offers almost nothing in agriculture. Indians tend herds of llamas. There are sheep. In midsummer I have seen potato plants curled up at the edges with frost. Below barren ridges of the eastern Andes, lower forested slopes lead to the Garden of Argentina in Tucumán Province. This garden, incidentally, has been one of the hotbeds of Nazi agitation in Argentina. Tucumán is a truly pleasant change after the harsh *altiplano*. Sugar cane thrives. Flowers abound. Gently sloping fields and others as level as a table offer a good basis for subtropical agriculture. To the east extends Argentina's portion of the *Gran Chaco*. The *Chaco* so far has not developed any agricultural gold strikes, but there are those who believe it has possibilities.

In the northeast corner of Argentina, the finger of Misiones Territory is among the more promising of South America's farm and forest areas. It escapes the worst leaching action of tropical rains, and in places has built up a substantial humus. Misiones is only a sliver of land in Argentina's total area, with some 14,000 square miles to the nation's 1,112,743 square miles.

The central land-mass of Argentina radiates from Buenos Aires and washes up against the Andes on the west. Buenos Aires Province enjoys the cream of soils not only in Argentina, but in South America. Nowhere else do naturally fertile soils cover such large areas, although a few pockets of soil in other South American countries may at times excel temperate Argentina's best. Traveling away from Buenos Aires, I saw a rapid decline in the visible profits of land-use. Parts of the central area, notably Santiago del Estero, have poor soils and scrub land that result in poverty of the people. There are few compensating resources. Elsewhere, irrigation has produced lush areas of specialized fruits and vegetables in hot regions otherwise too dry for profitable production.

A point to note about Argentina's mint of land resources is that some of the world's best exploiting genius—Spanish, British, Italian, German, North American—has long been at work here to coin its wealth. Argentina's land-use in its richest promise is either a present fact or a question of more intensive cultivation. At this point an important social factor enters. Many fertile soils in Buenos Aires Province could be turned to specialized production such as turkey-raising, instead of being kept for cattle, corn, or wheat, the big three of Argentine farm income. Many large landholders of the cattle aristocracy refuse to see their lands broken up. It is an old Latin-American pattern, dating back to royal grants of colonial times.

In central Argentina there can undoubtedly be economic expansion, but frontier days long ago yielded before advances by a modern nation of increasing industrial power. From now on the opportunities lie in more productive use of developed land, for there simply isn't any open frontier left.

Frontiers: Land's-End

All that remains in this search for South American frontiers is the cornucopia of land that narrows to Cape Horn. Significantly, this cornucopia spills its riches northward toward Buenos Aires Province and the central valley of Chile. Land's-end declines in fertility as it diminishes in width. The broad rich fields near Buenos Aires give way to smaller fruit areas in Rio Negro Territory. Below that, instead of being a pioneer farm region, Argentine Patagonia for at least a decade has reached capacity in its one outstanding farm product—sheep.

On plains of Patagonia the most significant mineral resource so far discovered is oil. Coastal Comodoro Rivadavia is center of the industry. This is fortunate, since one of Argentina's greatest lacks in the *Chaco* and *pampa* is wood even for elementary needs such as cooking and heating. Chile has forests, as well as coal, on its lands across the Andes from Patagonia. Chile also is hopefully exploring for oil.

Argentina's southern plains, throughout most of their expanse, offer only bunch grass that spreads to the horizon from sea to mountains. There are low hills. Even sheep are few in the immense landscape, although they add up to many of Argentina's 50,900,000 head. Patagonia holds open few if any pioneer gates of the kind imagined when people talk about South America's great possibilities. Long-time residents see nothing ahead except sheep, unless and until more oil, minerals, or other new resources are found and utilized.

Chilean Punta Arenas is the metropolis of a region that counts its wealth chiefly in wool, frozen mutton and other products from sheep. Punta Arenas so thrived in days before the Panama Canal that the city has not materially increased its population since then. With some 30,000 residents, Punta Arenas has paved streets, piers, docks, warehouses, parks, hotels of metropolitan atmosphere even if small, an urbanity and progressiveness not anticipated in such remote parts. It is hard in such a city to realize that this point of land jabs toward the Antarctic Sea and Little America a full 1200 miles south of Africa's Cape of Good Hope, and 500 miles south of New Zealand. Punta Arenas lies at 53 degrees 9 minutes 53 seconds South Latitude.

There are 2,600,000 sheep in this part of Chile, producing 22,000,000 pounds of wool a year. Of that output in 1943, 14,000,000 pounds were exported to the United States. Such has been the growth since 1855, when 34 woolly noses were counted here! By 1903 there were 1,830,000 sheep. One report has it that in 1928 there were 3,500,000. Agreement is general among sheep ranchers that capacity of the land has been reached for some ten years now. Of late years successful results have been achieved by shifting from Romney Marsh sheep to Corriedale. Although smaller, the Corriedale line has denser wool and better meat. Quality is such that Argentina and Chile have no trouble competing in world markets.

That this part of the world has reached saturation in sheep raising is proved by recent unfortunate experiences. Former President Aguirre Cerda of Chile, carrying through a social program for increasing small landholdings, used governmental power to break up some large ranch areas in Tierra del Fuego. Some of the distributed lands fell into the hands of political favorites. Impatient for quick profits—a failing admitted by thinkers among Latin Americans as a handicap to long-range development—the new sheep ranchers increased their flocks. They either did not know, or shoved aside, the fact that this land on the whole does not support more than one sheep for each five acres the year around. In Iowa the figures are reversed, with five sheep to an acre on good bluegrass pasture. New Zealand has one sheep to an acre. Overloaded lands in Tierra del Fuego were eaten to the roots of the *coirón* grass. When sheep could no longer make a go of it, goats were turned loose. Result: Blowing sand under a wind that quickly turns pastures into a dust bowl.

Fortunately, such haste and waste are so far limited to relatively small areas. The main pastures are still controlled by experienced men, including many a canny Scot. They know that dry lands of the kind being ruined in Tierra del Fuego should be grazed only in the rainy season, for Chilean Magallanes, like Argentine Patagonia, is a fenced and at times overworked preserve.

I used to stand at Puerto Montt and look south, projecting the fertile valleys and giant trees of that region into what I had been told was a pioneer field for settlement. It was disillusioning to enter the rain-drenched rocky islands where moss simulates fertility but nothing else would grow. Midway in the soggy passages as our ship came north from Magellan's Strait we stopped to pick up the product of this region's sole industry—mussels. Hurriedly rowing toward the ship from a headland where they shelter under a few tents and shanties, the men had diving helmets stowed under thwarts. When they harvest they go down in diving suits and break the mussels from the rock. Puerto Montt is the seat of this industry. No serious attempt has been made to maintain more than shelters in the channels. It is too dismal, too lacking in soil and sunshine, for human habitation except to extract such resources as it may offer. So far that means mussels, a lucrative trade giving employment to a comparative handful of men. Mineral wealth is not anticipated in this rock formation.

On the fourth day we begin to emerge into more cheerful

latitudes. By the fifth day we approach the pleasant island of Chiloé. Its rounded hills of fertile soil are stitched in a quilt of potato patches. On the mainland, conditions also have improved. Rains diminish, and forests that have marched north on mountain ridges, back from the drenched coast, reach their prime. In that restricted area of southern Chile there still are pioneer possibilities. New settlers, however, will find that hardy Germans have long before selected the best lands. Their forebears colonized this part of South America in the mid-nineteenth century. Geese march along country lanes past houses stamped with the blunt roof lines of German architecture. A fog of smoke hung over southern Chile during my last trip. Fires set to clear the land had blazed out of control. Skeletons of forests are a melancholy aspect of the landscape until slow processes of cultivation have replaced them with mellow and fruitful fields. So this pioneer region merges with Chile's central valley.

*   *   *   *

It is evident from the foregoing survey that South American frontiers are far more limited than is generally supposed. Most of the wide-open spaces are so because they do not attract settlers. The few beckoning frontiers are hedged about with geographic and political difficulties that will have to be overcome before pioneers can pour in to build new cities, new industries, new cultures.

Immigration Prospects

Southern Chile is an unusual vantage point for asking a question about South America that is uppermost with many people: How many more inhabitants could South America support, and how many of these will be admitted as immigrants from abroad?

Until new resources are discovered, and new industries built around them, neither Argentina nor Chile can absorb many new settlers in any of the lands from Cape Horn north to the most southerly line usually reached by tourists, the justly-famed lake district between Puerto Varas, Chile, and Bariloche in Argentina. This is sheep country, and the average manpower needed on sheep ranches runs about 50 men to 100,000 sheep. That helps explain why there are only some 150,000 people, at the most, living south of Bahía Blanca near the southern tip of Argentina's Buenos Aires Province. A standard South American joke is that if Argentina had as many human inhabitants as it has animals in its herds, the country would be almost as important as some excessively proud Argentines think it is already! With only 13,700,000 people, Argentina has 31,500,000 beef cattle, 50,900,000 sheep, 8,260,000 horses, 5,700,000 hogs, and 4,760,-000 goats. The animal total comes to 101,120,000—a sizable populace if it could be matched head for head by taxpaying citizens. Chile in its southern sheep lands has the same kind of relationship between human and animal populations.

Reviewing the continent's most highly developed industrial areas, as well as its open frontiers, I find a reasonable expectation that South America can absorb millions of new settlers, provided intelligent steps are taken to attract them and enable them to succeed. I find no basis for the extravagant statement, frequently heard, that South America could support hundreds of millions more than its present estimated 94,000,000. Such increases are possible, but not probable. To sustain even 200,000,-000 people, South America would have to undergo drastic changes in basic economy as well as in political and social structure.

For the most part, South America is in the phase of a naturally increasing population, rather than a static or decreasing one. Recent nationalist phobias of many governments have closed ports of entry to all except a few select immigrants. The result has been to check the rapid growth that resulted from an influx of extremely valuable artisans, day laborers, and intellectuals. Part of the stoppage came from nationalistic governments abroad. Italy and Germany banned emigration to keep their manpower geared to war preparations.

Thinking South Americans freely admit that the continent needs new settlers and new initiative. The natural handicaps

are such that only the most advanced peoples can ever overcome them. The present residents of South America possess
many admirable qualities, chiefly in the realm of abstract culture. They do not incline naturally, except in the case of rare
individuals, to the kind of practical idealism and technical
curiosity that build vast industrial and political structures. Admittedly the geographic barriers are high in South America.
For that very reason, the architects and craftsmen who are
to galvanize these slumbering possibilities into actuality must
be superlatively endowed.

Several South Americans have told me they consider the
greatest single lien on the continent's future to be the impatience of most industrialists, financiers, landowners, and governments, for quick profits. They grasp for wealth today, the
easier the better, and do not often enough allow for the future.
In this respect they are less foresighted than the Incas, whose
stone-walled terraces are still monuments to soil conservation
in the Andes.

Granted that South America needs immigrants, what are
prospects they will want to come, or will be accepted? The
second part of the question is more important than the first,
since the supply of refugees in the world is greater than South
America, or any other region, cares to absorb. The era of un-
restricted immigration passed long ago. In my travels I found
South American Governments open to special kinds of immigrants, and firmly set against others. They want farmers, day
laborers, pioneers able to develop stubborn terrain. They do
not want small storekeepers or other commercial types who
gravitate to the cities and gradually take over business. That
is the main complaint heard against admission of Jewish refugees.

Concrete plans for postwar immigration have largely been
kept secret, even when formulated. Brazil has been particularly
active in preparations to deal with the question. That country
is so intent on Brazilianizing national economy that the alien
faces a hard road. I have talked with non-Axis Europeans who
had been in Brazil many years, and were in process of becoming
citizens. They found themselves restricted in many directions.

Their feelings indicate that Brazil will have to moderate its nationalism before the desired influx of builders from abroad can be attracted. Similar conditions exist in other countries.

Small colonies of refugees have lately been founded. They include the *Simón Bolívar* Spanish Colony near Quito in Ecuador, and the successful Jewish agricultural colony of *Buena Tierra* sixty miles east of La Paz, Bolivia, in the Yungas, at an altitude of 8000 feet.

So it is that indications of a large-scale migratory movement are not strong at this writing. This is another way of saying that South America's frontiers will probably continue to develop slowly, with the people already there seeking technical assistance from outside but trying to keep control and profits more largely in their own hands. The history of foreign capital in South America makes this attitude understandable. On the other hand, no pioneer region can be brought to its full production without venture capital and venture colonists. Both reasonably expect to be welcomed and given assurances of a progressive future, to the mutual benefit of guest and host. That indispensable condition for South American advancement remains too largely unrealized. Foreign capital, immigrants, and particularly the South American Governments, will determine the answer. Nothing short of mutual give and take can bring forth solutions.

OUTLOOK FOR OPPRESSED MILLIONS

THE HUMAN EQUATION not only in the Amazon and Andes, but in many parts of South America away from the cosmopolitan centers, is generally negative. This fact goes far toward explaining the backwardness of those regions. Whether the land or the people are ultimately responsible is not the important question, except in so far as the answer might indicate solutions.

The South American setting is difficult at its best. After seeing all of its typical regions over a period of years, I can think of only a few that attract with unmarred satisfaction. Many of the natural advantages could be used far more satisfactorily, and some of the disadvantages lessened, by a population equal to the task.

The largest single group of submerged and oppressed millions is located along the upper Andes, where some 7,000,000 Indians live in modern serfdom.

Whether the Andean Indian is capable of education and improvement is a controversial issue. Some mine operators tell of making sincere and strenuous efforts to raise the living standards of their workers. While progress occurs, the inertia and counter-influences are heavy. Social workers of heroic and self-sacrificing stature have here a field of labor for centuries to come. First they must break through the most encrusted resistance of all—that of a ruling caste which insists the Indians are incapable of emancipation. Looking at the native Andean peoples one is made aware that somewhere along the line they have either lost, or never developed, most of the standards that underlie Christian civilization. Immorality with resultant venereal disease, and heavy drinking are not even resisted, except when wholesome influences from outside come in. Yet in the faces of the best of these original South Americans I have frequently seen promise.

They are often physical masterpieces, as rugged as the mountains, as smooth and lustrous of skin as the copper they mine. These millions constitute the mass of the population in Ecuador, Peru, and Bolivia. City-dwellers are only as a fringe of white lace on the copper ingots.

For anyone who seeks wealth in terms of giving light and freedom to this enslaved and darkened segment of humanity, South America's Andes call. This is without question one of the greatest challenges in South America. Those who climb the mountains to meet it need fortitude and the backing of powerful supporters. Some South Americans already are in the field with their helpers from abroad. The sun of human freedom at length must shine where a ball of fire in the sky has long been worshiped, and where no religious or social agency yet in the field has done more than hold a lighted match to the entrance of deep social caverns.

Another and quite different set of social problems exists in Brazil's drought zone of the Northeast. A wise and sympathetic friend of Brazilians in that area said to me: "These people have everything—they need everything."

The first part of the statement is open to some reservations. The second part is evident to the most casual observer. Until the drought has been at least measurably conquered in its recurring effects on food production and on general employment, the Northeast could hardly be said to have everything. Between droughts the region thrives, although even then the fixed habits of food use—or misuse—are a handicap. The Northeast offers a significant case study in efforts to alleviate the lot of 3,000,000 people oppressed by natural conditions even more than by human despotism.

"*Tem não,*" or "There isn't any," is the response to inquiries at many roadside stores for fresh fruits, vegetables, eggs, milk, wheat bread, butter, canned goods—almost anything a hungry buyer wants. Meat, however, is generally abundant, and is often available even in the worst of the "*Tem não*" districts. The result is a monotonous, unbalanced diet during the periods of drought. Between droughts the situation improves, for the soil gives forth richly in much of this area when it is touched by water.

In Salgueiro, a parched town on the highway connecting the States of Pernambuco and Bahia, I saw the food battle in process. On the glare-lighted rear wall of the bare entry lobby in a main street pension hung a proclamation of orders to the populace in what the poster called the *Battle of Alimentation.* General Newton Calvacanti, military commander in charge, signed the proclamation as Co-ordinator of the Battle of Food Production in the Northeast. The General emphasized a twofold need—more food, and wiser use of existing food. Helping Brazil in this undertaking of great social significance is the United States Office of the Co-ordinator of Inter-American Affairs.

The situation is urgent. One who lives in this region among these people for only a short time parts company with romantic notions that Brazil as a whole is bursting with plenty. Brazil is rich in food, but not uniformly so. Some of the most acute food problems center in the Northeast. It would be difficult to find a comparably large area anywhere in the world where human feeding is more backward or more disastrous to public well-being. During seven years in travels throughout Latin America I have encountered worse food conditions only in completely Indian or colored communities. Yet the Northeast interior is predominantly white.

The Brazilian Government and the Co-ordinator's office in Washington were striking simultaneously against both flanks of the food battle line. Plans of the campaign for increasing food production were necessarily long-range. So is the campaign of public education for better food use, although both campaigns have important short-range objectives now on the line of march. In Fortaleza, State of Ceará, sixty girls were being chosen for a training course of one year in a Nutrition School to be built by the *Comissão Brasileiro-Americano.* Two girls were to be given eight months of training in Rio de Janeiro. The sponsoring *Comissão,* or Commission, was maintained by the Brazilian Division of Development in the National Department of Vegetal Production, and the North American Co-ordinator's Office.

Three fourths of the money was North American. Brazil provided equipment as well as more than half of the personnel. It is a small beginning for sixty girls instructed in better food uses to march against generations of unsanitary habits among at least 3,000,000 persons. Yet another sixty can come, and more, until the Northeast no longer fills its plates with a sawdust of dried *mandioca* and a few greasy chunks of meat prepared under conditions best not described.

In cities such as Fortaleza, and on fringes of the interior where better and more diversified food has displaced the dishes of poverty and habit, *mandioca* already has been reduced to its proper place as an occasional part of a well-balanced meal. I talked with persons who are themselves so close to this social transition that they express pleasure at having advanced beyond it. *Mandioca* is a fibrous root and has distinct food value. Usually known in English as manioc, it is widely used under various names throughout tropical regions of Latin America. Some measure of the bad effects of its overuse can be seen in this: A cupful of the dried and ground root placed in water will swell to five or six times its original volume. These people eat two or more cupfuls, when they can get it, with every meal. The young children and even babies are given it. So ingrained is the *mandioca* habit through long dependence on this easily available food, that persons accustomed to it do not savor even a good meal without spreading some of this sawdust over it. I have seen them in hotels or on boats—cultured people—pause as though not satisfied with their plate. They reach for the large *mandioca* shaker as others might reach for salt and pepper. Weaning the people away from poverty-stricken diets that are as unbalanced as the grease and grits of the North American South requires first of all the availability of fruits, vegetables, fresh milk, well-prepared meats, and diversified cereals. Development of such foods in the Northeast is hindered by the hesitation of private capital to invest until more security is provided against ruin in years of drought.

The first large-scale efforts to solve this underlying problem do not run back as far as the recorded droughts of greatest intensity. There was a devastating one in 1877, another in 1888, one in 1915, a smaller one in 1919, another in 1930-32, and the latest which began in 1942 and was in its third year during my trip. While many observers deny the existence of a regular cycle, some sets of figures show a drought roughly every eleven years. The Government of the Brazilian Republic established in 1908 the *Inspetoría Federal de Obras Contra as Sêcas*, charged with solving, or at least ameliorating, effects of the droughts. With varying intensity the work has continued to date. The Inspector General when I last visited Brazil was Dr. Vinicius de Berredo, with headquarters at Rio de Janeiro. Work of the *Inspetoría* is to study soils, give technical assistance to farmers in plans of irrigation, increase knowledge of plants, control insect pests that abound in the Northeast, promote education, and provide transport. Relatively little of a tangible nature was done until the late 1920's and early 1930's. Small and medium dams were built at first, wells were sunk, and roads improved.

No superficial examination of a map could convey a clear picture of difficulties that have to be surmounted. The map shows a few railways. Hopeful red lines indicate highways. So much for the map. When I went into the interior and rode on the ponderous milkshake machines called trucks in these parts, I began to get the idea. In fairness to Brazil's heroic and pioneering enterprise against great odds, it must be added quickly that there are some fine trunk highways of good graded gravel, and that others are being pushed ahead as rapidly as resources permit. On both sides, the dry Northeast is flanked by food-producing areas, or potential bread baskets. Maranhão State on the east is well watered and has some good soil. The coast also is capable of producing more food than it needs locally. Transport is inadequate, and so the Brazilian Government is pushing ahead with its road program.

Irrigation within the drought area has long been a major reliance. Two main handicaps occur in the Northeast—a porous subsoil that makes necessary expensive paved irrigation ditches, and a water table reached in many places only by wells of from

60 to 150 feet deep. The difficulty of transporting water explains in part why so many dams have been largely unused for irrigation. The deep water table explains why wells are not the answer, due to the cost of lifting water to the surface.

Ambitious irrigation projects have surged to the fore. At Orós on the Jaguaribe River in Ceará State, work actually was begun on a dam to be at that time the third largest in the world. The Orós reservoir was dramatized for Brazilians by the fact it would hold more water than Guanabara Bay at Rio de Janeiro. Work at Orós, as well as at other sites of big dams, came to a standstill several years ago, largely due to exhaustion of capital. Much of the early effort has resulted in forming stagnant pools. Regular use of the water for irrigation has yet to become general even around dams already built. Capitalization of new dams is proceeding in smaller ways. There are two types of co-operative plans. In one, the Brazilian National Government pays 75 per cent of the cost, and the State pays 25 per cent. The dam then belongs to the State. Under the other plan the National Government pays half, and individual farmers or groups of farmers pay the other half. These dams belong to the farmers. More than 200 dams have been built by farmers. The Government lists 68 of its own having capacities of more than 1,000,000 cubic meters. Four others of this size are under construction.

Paralleling the dam program is the road program, for transport of food and the rapid movement of populations from areas hardest hit by drought. The *Inspetoría* has built more than 3000 miles of first-class gravel and dirt roads, with concrete bridges and culverts. There are many more miles of second-class roads. These roads are kept up by the *Inspetoría*. On the main trunk lines, the way is generally broad and satisfactory. Trucks maintain the interior's communications, not only for freight, but for passengers. Few are the bus lines under war conditions. Eight agricultural posts are maintained in the Northeast, extending to the banks of the São Francisco River.

Irrigation officials report that the people are receptive to new ideas. Generally the workers are more receptive than their employers. People crowd around the dams. In April, 1938, it was reported that the reservoirs held 700,000,000 cubic meters of water. Reckoning 30,000 cubic meters of water as an average needed to irrigate one hectare for a year, this would provide for 23,300 hectares. A hectare is not quite 2½ acres. Less than 5000 hectares were irrigated late in 1943, according to governmental officials in charge. To remedy this situation, engineers are laying out networks of irrigation canals on their drafting boards, but large-scale capital does not appear to speed the work. Until larger measures are possible, relief officials are concentrating on better use of existing dams, foods, and other natural resources.

The regional headquarters of the Co-ordinator's Office for Ceará, Piauí, and Maranhão is located in Fortaleza. Director Sanford B. Fenne told me of his plans for one large model farm in each State. Smaller projects are to deal with irrigation, truck farming, and cattle. There is to be a training school for farm boys. Victory Gardens have been promoted by Dr. Fenne with good results. Many of these have to be planted in boxes of soil raised on stilts and protected against ants. Several varieties of ants operate here, including one that specializes in digging tunnels along the rows and carrying away planted seeds before they can sprout. Small loans are made to farmers. Dr. Fenne reported that 930 farmers had received a total of $53,111. Seed distribution is also an important phase of the work. A public restaurant is planned in Fortaleza, to be operated in conjunction with the Nutrition School for Girls, previously mentioned. The lot has been purchased. In this area, the Co-ordinator's Office puts cultural and information services at the end of its line of activities, after public health, sanitation, food, and nutrition. Part of its work is to supply United States armed forces in the area with some of their food requirements, giving due regard to needs of the local market.

Special attention is being directed to increasing food production in naturally watered areas. Outstanding is Guaramiranga in the mountains about sixty miles south of Fortaleza. At 2600 feet elevation, Guaramiranga catches high moist winds and is green, its valleys resembling the valleys of Virginia. Soil is good. Potatoes can be grown and cattle thrive. Even parched wild growth is being combed for its food possibilities. Dr. José Guimaraes Duque, in charge of irrigation for the *Inspetoría*, has located a new source for flour and food oil from beans of the *favela* tree. Millions of the trees grow wild in the Northeast. They belong in the family of the castor bean. Rich in food value, the bean makes cake for animal fodder with 66 per cent protein; its bread flour is palatable and nourishing.

So far, impounded rains in small reservoirs are the main means for increasing food production. In 1942 there were 4665 hectares under the irrigation program, producing 23,000,000 pounds of agricultural products. During 1943 the irrigated areas rose to 4907 hectares, and food moved up toward the 30,000,-000-pound mark. Reduced to tons, that still is a small figure—15,000 tons in a region where the needy population divides this amount into less than a pound of relief food per person during a whole month. That drives home the magnitude of the Northeast's food problem. Brazilian officials say it cannot be solved by the area alone, and offers a serious challenge to Brazil itself.

Elementary education could save people of the Northeast much suffering. During my voyage on the *Octavio Carneiro* for seventeen days on the São Francisco River, a baby in one of the migrating families en route from the drought region of Ceará State to new homes in Goiaz State, regularly had its plate set on the floor outside the men's primitive latrine. Baby's hands alternated between the filthy deck and food on the plate.

In view of the unsanitary conditions and the sickness rate on that boat, it is no wonder this baby looked like one of those photographed in Spain after the ravages of Franco's civil war. This was in first class. What went on in the steerage was equally visible and more heartbreaking. These people could be saved so much by such a little cleanliness! As a prominent Brazilian woman said to me later in Rio: "A cake of soap would make all the difference."

Of course many first-class passengers on the *Octavio Carneiro* were not of that needy sort, but there were several families of them. To see them suffer when even the strong laborers and heads of families took to their hammocks with entirely needless diseases, was to grasp some of the social work to be done in Brazil.

Argentina, too, has its dark spots. Back in 1938 it was surprising to me to see the sudden drop from the luxury of Buenos Aires to the poverty of small towns.

Chile's peons are terribly enslaved by liquor on which they squander not only their scanty earnings but their future.

Right through the continent a friendly observer sees millions oppressed by a harsh environment and by even harsher economic and social customs. In recent years there have been numerous efforts to solve some of the underlying problems through legislation. It is frequently stated that social laws of South America are among the most advanced in the world. On paper, yes. In practice, serious reservations must be entered.

South America's greatest need is a change of attitude among the ruling classes. Colonial and feudal traditions cling. They retard all branches of society. Money will not buy for South America the things it most needs, whether the money comes from inside or outside the continent. Well-regulated loans and constructive projects of Good-Neighbor assistance have been of benefit to the degree that they help South America to help itself. Rutted habits must be broken. Outsiders can help, or try to help, but I keep coming back to the basic fact that people make a country.

Even the oppressed millions could do far more to improve themselves. Through an unfortunate series of social, religious, geographic, and political circumstances, South America has not risen even to the stature it could attain without addition of a single new element to the populace or resources. Into backward and darkened areas both of the land and of human thinking, wholesome currents are flowing. Already South America responds to these salutary influences, including democracy, purer forms of religion, just plain cleanliness, and initiative in learning how to apply modern techniques to stubborn natural obstacles, instead of accepting their limitations for centuries.

As those forward-looking forces spread with progressive momentum, the outlook for South America's oppressed millions will brighten. Fascism and all retrogressive systems may clamor for undeserved place and power, but in South America as in the whole earth, humanity's advocates will win, for they are inspired and sustained by the constructive powers of the universe.

A FEW DEFINITIONS

NOTHING IS MORE like sawdust in the breakfast cereal bowl than to have a writer use political terms, especially during a period of ideological conflict, as though everyone knows exactly what he means. The following definitions could hardly satisfy every reader, but at least they pin me down. I pledged myself to use the defined terms as precisely as I could, and never to bandy them about loosely. South Americans especially will want to know the sense in which terms such as *fascist, totalitarian,* or *authoritarian* are applied to any phases of public administration in their countries.

Democracy: Self-government by the people through regular legal processes with established safeguards of their individual rights, responsibilities, and sovereign power.

Dictatorship: A system of government in which there are no political mechanisms for exercise by the people of their democratic rights. One man or a small group seizes and wields supreme authority.

Totalitarian: A term descriptive of a dictatorship overlaid by mystical concepts such as nationalism, racialism, aggressive conquest in the name of these or similar fetishes, and the attempt to impose such concepts on private as well as public life. In a totalitarian state the individual is subordinated by force to carry out the will of a ruthless minority in possession of the instruments of national power. The press becomes a medium for ideological propaganda. Religious and other liberties are attacked when they interfere with totalitarian ambitions. Secret police responsible only to the dictatorship become terrorist agents.

Authoritarian: Dictatorial with overtones of totalitarianism

319

in public affairs, but stopping short of totalitarian controls over individuals and the home.

Fascist: In popular usage, a generic term for totalitarian dictatorship. In this book it appears with a small f to indicate the general outlook and practice of antidemocratic forces, when these go beyond traditional South American dictatorship and are spearheaded by modern devices. Such devices include: 1. Public opinion control. 2. Domination of industry and its conversion to production for wars of aggression. 3. Violation by a powerful minority of individual rights. With a capital F, Fascist and Fascism refer to the system developed in Italy under Mussolini, including rule through a single political party.

Nazism: The special form of ruthless totalitarianism developed in Germany under Hitler. Includes rule through a monopolistic political party and various extragovernmental agencies such as Storm Troopers and the Gestapo secret police. These became elements in the national forces when the Nazis established full control. The national economy is bent to ends of foreign conquest.

Communism: In philosophy, the system of socialism advanced by Karl Marx. In politics, a system of totalitarianism applying communist ideology and ruling through a theoretical dictatorship of the proletariat. In economics, communism demands collective ownership of natural resources and productive capital, with communal sharing of the product in a classless society. The term is not used in this book as a tar brush for everyone with leftist tendencies any more than all extreme rightists are called fascist, unless these definitions apply.

ADVENTURES IN PHOTOGRAPHY

SOME OF MY experiences with a camera in South America may prove useful, and at times amusing, apart from the main purpose of this book. I have carried a wide range of equipment including a snapshot Kodak, Rolleiflex, Contax, and three types of motion picture machines. Black and white has been indispensable for reproductions with my news stories, but in the presence of South American color I have abandoned black and white except for utility and an occasional shot better rendered in that medium.

During my 1942 trip I assembled en route a traveling laboratory to develop my own 35 mm. black-and-white negatives. It was a move of necessity, due to the loss of irreplaceable scenes. Away from the large cities there are few competent developing centers, unless some exceptional individual is met who has a private darkroom.

Jay Kershner, a Danish photographer of talent, was responsible for starting my portable developing kit. I had come as far as Rio de Janeiro with disappointing results that had to be corrected to safeguard the rest of a long trip. Mr. Kershner advised buying a Kodak Dayload Tank. We went to the store and he soon had the counter loaded with bottles and gadgets, including a glass funnel, graduated beaker, and quart bottles of chemicals.

"And how do you expect me to carry all that in my airplane bag?" I asked.

"Maybe we can cut it down."

We cut, and the resultant laboratory in embryo began with the tank in a box 9 inches by 7 by 4. A small white porcelain rectangular pan, an unbreakable funnel, rubber hose fitted with a hydrant nipple in two sizes, a glass beaker of 150 cc. capacity,

321

small packages of Kodak Fine Grain DK-20 Developer as well as Single Powder Hardener and Fixer, a special thermometer to fit the tank, a squeegee to speed drying of the film and four clips to hang it in any available closet, were the essentials.

That night in my bathroom at the Copacabana Palace Hotel Mr. Kershner set up the laboratory. His first roll turned out magnificently. I set off for southern Brazil the next day with the new equipment dispersed among socks and shirts.

My first independent effort came in Pôrto Alegre. Mind you, I never before had developed a film of any kind. I went through all the motions, brought in buckets of ice as Mr. Kershner had done, but couldn't control the temperature evenly enough in the midsummer heat. At 2 a.m. I gave it up. The next morning I went to a hardware store and emerged with a length of ¼ inch brass pipe, more rubber hose, and a new wrinkle—a water filter only 5 inches long and 1½ inches in diameter. The pipe was shaped by a local blacksmith into a coil 6 inches long and 3 inches wide, with three layers of pipe all around. This was a device to control the temperature of water for washing after it passed through the filter and before it entered the tank.

Buttressed by these new gadgets, that night the laboratory began to function. With two or three ice cubes I could hold the intake water at an even 18 degrees Centigrade, the recommended norm. The small filter worked admirably. Its fiber case and white filter unit weighed only a few ounces. Chemicals were mixed with filtered water and cooled in the hotel icebox, using bottles that did not need to be carried with me. A small aluminum pan took care of heating water to 52 degrees Centigrade for mixing the developer.

Possibly I poured into that first development more care than ever since. At any rate, Roll No. 1 is the best in my collection. Small refinements have since been made in the laboratory, and it no longer mingles with my shaving kit. At the end of that trip I had a lightweight fiber box made. It is only a little larger than a briefcase.

Developing en route has enabled me to keep a close check on my light meters, cameras, and settings. When black-and-white exposures are coming through successfully, it is reasonably sure that color exposures are all right. This is important on a long trip when not a single result in color stills or movies can be seen before return to the United States. The greatest utility of the tank is that it can be used in broad daylight. With it negatives can quickly be obtained to cut from the roll and send home air mail with the story they illustrate. Naturally no printing is attempted en route.

I have used muddy water of the Iguassú, Beni, and other rivers. The filter makes it sparkling clean whenever there is enough pipe pressure to push the water through. Some of the Amazonian rivers clog the filter in twenty minutes. It is quickly restored with water and a small brush.

Peruvian customs officials and police had a field day of suspicions when I arrived at the Lima airport with this laboratory in my suitcase. They let me go once, and then brought me back from the taxi. That time they spread my chemicals and coils and tubing on the counter and thought they had uncovered a Nazi spy. My credentials quickly satisfied the chief inspector, but it took a long time to reassemble the luggage.

Also, my cameras usually are the means of placing me honorably in the hands of the Vargas secret police in Brazil. It started in 1938, and was still going on during the last trip. As I approached the Itabira Iron Mountain by train, we came to a handsome new industrial center with cement buildings under curved roofs that resembled airplane hangars. I had a permit to take photographs anywhere in Brazil, provided they were not in military zones. The permit was signed by Amilcar Dutra de Menezes, Director-General of the *Departamento de Imprensa e Propaganda*, or DIP. Seeing no military installations in the vicinity, I started to take a picture. Before I could snap the shutter a secret policeman emerged from the crowd on the station platform and took me by the arm. The train was about to leave, with my luggage on board. Even though I had not taken that scene, he insisted on having the film. The roll was almost entirely exposed and included irreplaceable shots from the São Francisco Valley. I sought to reason with him. He not only compelled me to open the camera and give him the entire roll, but refused to give me the metal roller that fitted my Contax. The train was moving when he permitted me to board. I had a feeling that was not the end of the incident.

Sure enough, I was met at the station in Nova Era by several plain-clothes police. They whisked me into a car and drove to headquarters. In that remote mountain town it was a relief when the young man who had been sent from the mine to the station to meet me arrived at police headquarters. He quickly cleared me, and we started in his car toward Itabira.

*   *   *   *

Rio de Janeiro is a photographer's dream, and despair.

Senhorita Rio, I have found, can be a playful and temperamental beauty on occasion. She entered my photographic parlor, or, rather, I entered hers, on a morning when never in all my visits had her skies been so blue, her sea so sparkling, or her skyline more distinct. I started the day as such a day indicates, by joining the sea-loving *Cariocas* for an early morning dip in the breakers at Copacabana Beach. This is done without a long ride from the city. *Cariocas* walk from their homes to beaches of the bay or ocean side. For those living farther away, bus services are numerous and prompt.

From the beach, I look up at Sugar Loaf, and catch a glimpse of the Corcovado. These and other high peaks lure me with the prospect of magnificent color photos, taken in this crystalline air. Accordingly the swim ends sooner than otherwise, and I arrange the day's affairs so I can arrive on the summit of Corcovado at the best photographic time, or early afternoon. There is a cog railway to the top, leaving at two and grinding up the last few steep yards about three.

That is the perfect moment. The sun is sloping westward behind Corcovado. Sugar Loaf, looking rather small from this rock twice its own height, is drenched in sunlight. Facing Sugar Loaf I look down on the city, the bay, and the open sea. It is a view to make any amateur photographer excited as he checks his lens, calculates the light, and tries various compositions in the view finder. There are those who have said, and with considerable justice, that the season itself might change before this particular amateur photograher would be ready to click the shutter. Be that as it may, not more than fifteen minutes could have passed after my first arrival at the top of Corcovado when I became aware that strange transformations were occurring around this point of granite. Corcovado thrusts its sheer spire 2100 feet above the city, nearly in the center of Rio's most highly developed districts. From this height I watch the sky. Not at one point, but all over it, a subtle change takes place, as though an embryonic cloud had burst forth suddenly from every aërial molecule. While I watch, great white plumes form in the wind that whips steadily from the sea across Corcovado.

Those white clouds will add interest to the shot, I think, the while poising to shoot. Before the shutter can be clicked, where is Rio? She has hidden playfully behind a veil. I am enveloped in sudden shadows as a cloud catches momentarily on the point of Corcovado. So I wait, or move to a new vantage spot for another view. There is a large lagoon almost directly below to the right. It is flanked by rounded granite ridges and divided from the sea only by a narrow strip of land. The Botanical Garden and Hippodrome are spread between this lagoon and the base of Corcovado. Or I try for a back-lighted shot of Gavea, with its flat top overhanging sheer cliffs, masterful and unflinching in outline. I shoot and shoot, aware all the while that Rio is partially escaping the lens. There she is, running in and out of sight, versatile and lovely, but as exasperating as a tease of a sister.

So I come down from the mountain at length, resolved to try again, and earlier. I make the trip by car and run up the final stone steps two at a time until it becomes evident that the sky is so immovably blue it couldn't possibly change in the next hour. I slow down to catch breath. The wind from the sea does not linger. Today it blows from a different quarter, and brings sooner its patented, invisible, instantly expansible and pervasive wisps of cloud. Again I shoot, and another day I come, seeking that perfect combination of sea and air and sun that will mirror to others, through the camera's lens, this Rio as I have seen her. Possibly it is the awareness of how limited a picture can be given by any camera that makes the upper air seem at times perverse. Long-time residents tell me there are seasons when it is usually clear all day. I wonder if they went to the summit of Corcovado or Tijuca on those days. For even when the upper air is playing pranks, sunshine radiates, strong and clear, on Rio's streets, with only occasional passing shadows. The clouds seem to form on the summits themselves, concealing more than their size warrants.

Rio can be just like that, but be it recorded that for me the perfect day came, after another half-dozen tries spread over three weeks. Rio did her part, magnificently. Yet after several years of photographing the elusive *Senhorita* of Guanabara Bay, I am far from satisfied with results. Artists in oils must feel, as a photographer does, that Rio cannot be seen in all her glory through any limited art form.

*   *   *   *

Highest of Rio's many granite peaks, sheer and rounded above tropical forests—all within city limits—is Tijuca. Seen from in front of Itamarity Palace where the 1942 consultations of American Foreign Ministers were held, Tijuca terminates in a diminutive Sugar Loaf set atop the main ridge of this mountain reserve that fills the center of Rio and drops precipitately into the sea. On previous visits my photographic jaunts had taken me to the lower elevations—Sugar Loaf, Vista Chinesa, Alto da Boa Vista, and Corcovado. This time someone remarked that the place to take pictures of Rio was Tijuca. Also, that the time was afternoon. So, on a day when the afternoon was relatively free, I set forth. There had been heavy rains. The car had to leave me short of road's end. On foot the going was easy, and I reached the top by way of a woods path that ends in steps cut on the wall of granite for the last hundred feet or so.

Tijuca fulfilled expectations with a lingering persuasiveness that led on to sunset and the prospect of seeing stars kindle land and sky simultaneously. I recalled that other night view of Rio, from Corcovado, and knew this broader setting must be even more splendid. There was, of course, the question of getting down the mountain. One of the left-behinds on this sudden flying trip had been the handy fountain-pen-size flashlight, and another had not been picked up en route. Without a flashlight, could I follow the trail? It was plain, broad, lined with cut banks, but zigzagged a bit. The final decision was to start down while there still was some overtone of the sunset, just after the city lights had come on and the first stars appeared.

Everything came through as anticipated, and in the reflected city lights which cast shadows behind me, so strong is Rio's illumination even at this height, I started down the plain trail. It was as easy as I had expected until those last pale embers faded in the sky. Then I learned what darkness can mean on Tijuca. Something about the slopes of this mountain gathers the darkness in as a cloak. The plain trail was there. I could feel it underfoot, but trail and feet might as well have been in another world so far as seeing them was concerned.

Numerous thoughts, and numerous devices, filled the silence as glowworms came out in the spicy dampness. The first concrete woods lore I adopted was to wave a thin branch from side to side. As long as it hit nothing, the trail must be there, for trees crowded in on both sides. That was fine until I stepped into a hole. After the forward-waving-wand had fallen short, I hit upon the device of keeping always in contact with the cut bank. There was the unmistakable evidence of human hands that had gone before. While the bank was with me, I was on the trail.

Never have I felt such darkness. It was not oppressive, but velvety and all-concealing, balmy and alive with perfumes and warm sounds of the tropical night. The first test of woodsmanship came when the trail seemed literally to have vanished. I knew it was there. Just after stepping in the small hole I had adopted the rule—applicable elsewhere than in the dark woods, of never lifting one foot from a firm position until the other has been planted in a position equally firm. So I explored in every direction, and after a half hour unraveled this tricky turn in the trail. Passing two such tests I came out into the open space where, in daylight on the way to the top, I had admired a single great tree, standing almost alone. It reminded me of the Jeffrey Pine on Sentinel Dome in Yosemite, but was larger and not so bent by the wind. Before that descent ended near midnight, I passed at least three turns where there seemed nothing to do but sit down and wait for day. Always a glowworm would wink, or a firefly pass, or a star break through the roof of leaves. Giant tree ferns formed a filigree of black lace. Often the city lights came into full view, giving momentary impetus to the journey.

So I emerged in the clearing at Bom Retiro, with its stream of singing water, cool and cheerful.

The next day I bought a flashlight. Months later it came in handy when I climbed a Chilean volcano at night to be set for early morning pictures.

*   *   *   *

Light conditions in South America present a constant challenge to the photographer. In the jungle at Iguassú Waterfalls I have tried on two separate trips to bridge the gap between highlights and shadows. Foaming water in the sun and jungle green are beyond the range of Kodachrome color film. So are many other spectacular effects in South America. My best results at Iguassú came in full sun at an angle that reduced shadow areas in the jungle to a minimum. Even then, color is sacrificed somewhat at both ends of the scale. I have studied the best books I can find on color photography, but evidently color film will have to improve before justice can be done to tropical South America.

In the Temperate Zone of Argentina, Chile, Paraguay, Uruguay, and southern Brazil, a standard light meter gives good results in color, although the strong light makes heavy shadows that must be kept to a minimum.

*   *   *   *

In humid areas, both film and chemicals require special care. Weather in the Amazon Basin can quickly wash out photographic negatives unless they are developed and fixed without delay. That is another advantage of the traveling laboratory. I never set off for South America without films marked Tropical Packed. All films are developed as rapidly as possible.

During my last trip in and out of the Amazon Basin, I carried special containers for chemicals. An enthusiastic experimenter in charge of the laboratories of United Drug Company in Boston supplied treated paper boxes sealed with wax around the metal pressure-lids. On earlier trips I had been bothered by caking of chemicals in humid areas, even when the glass bottles were supposed to be moisture-proof. This time there was none, thanks to J. Wallace Reddie and his prim laboratory assistant, Miss Ora Ashley, whom he calls Ash. Her quiet New England efficiency safeguarded my chemicals through months in the Amazonian jungle.

INDEX

For maximum accessibility, every significant detail has been singled out and organized under broad headings. Topics and locations cross each other to form the pattern. *Fascist education in Argentina* occurs under FASCISM—**Argentine: Education**. *Brazil's Amazonian frontiers* occur under FRONTIERS—**Amazonian: Brazilian**. Stated cross references provide direction finders where needed.

ACONCAGUA, MT., 147-8

Acre Territory, Brazil, 35, 252

Adams, Hugh T., Lieut., j.g., U.S.N.R., 14

AFRICA, 9, 26, 48, 89, 143, 146, 190-1, 218, 235, 285, 303

AGRICULTURE, 56, 99-100, 144, 161-8, 172-4, 185, 188, 190-6, 212, 228-32, 238-9, 241-3, 252, 264, 272-3, 276-8, 291, 294-307, 310-6

Amazonian: 185, 188, 238-9, 241-3, 264

Andean: *Altiplano,* 231; southern Andes, 232; stone-walled terraces, 230, 307

Argentine: 231-2, 298-307; the "big three," 302

Bolivian: 99-100, 231, 252, 298-9

Brazilian: 298-9; diversified, 291, 295-6; Goiaz, 291; Mato Grosso, 294-6; Minas Gerais, 294; Northeast, 190-6, 272-3, 276-7, 310-6; São Francisco Valley, 278; São Paulo State, 295-7

Chaco: 212, 297-301

Chilean: 231-2; central valley, 161-8

Diversified: 295-6

Ecuadorean: 228-9, 231

Paraguayan: 212, 297-9

Peruvian: 229-31

Potentials: Andean, 232

Subtropical: 301

Tropical: 172-3, 185, 188, 190-6, 228-31, 238-9, 241-3; difficulties, 294

AGRICULTURE—(*Continued*)

Uruguayan: 298-9

U.S.A. Department of: 144, 228, 231, 238-9, 296, 299

Venezuelan: 228

See also: AMAZON BASIN; ANDES; ANIMAL HUSBANDRY; BANANAS; Brazil Nuts; Castor Beans; *CHACO;* CLIMATE; CACAO; COFFEE; COLONIZATION; CORN; COTTON; DROUGHT; ECONOMICS; Fibers; FLOODS; FLOWERS; FOODS; FORESTS; FRUITS; GEOGRAPHY—Handicaps; GRASSLANDS; HERBS; HIDES; INSECTS; IRRIGATION; JUNGLES; LABOR; MARSHES; Olives; Peanuts; PLAINS; PLATEAUS; RAINS; RICE; RIVERS; SOILS; SUGAR; TRANSPORT; VEGETABLE; OILS; WHEAT; WINDS.

AGUIRRE CERDA, DR. PEDRO, former President of Chile, 303

ALAGOAS STATE, Brazil, 195

Alcoholic Drinks, 227, 309, 317

Allen, Douglas H., former President of RDC, 253, 255, 261-3

ALTIPLANO, Andean plateau, 38, 89-91, 98-101, 146, 150-4, 158-61, 226, 231, 251, 253, 300-1; Illustrations Pages G-I; *páramos,* or lofty moors, 161, 231

ALUMINUM, See BAUXITE.

Berredo, Dr. Vinicius de, 313
Beryllium, 287
Bethlehem Steel Corporation, 285
Bingham, Hiram, 232
BIRDS, 160, 192, 203, 218-9, 252;
Brazilian Northeast, 196; macaws,
246, 292; parrots, 192, 196, 200-3,
209
Bismuth, Bolivian, 100; Brazilian, 287
Blanchard, Bernard, 285
Bley, Major Punaro, 285
Blumenau, Brazil, 208
BOGOTÁ, Capital of Colombia, 154,
158, 227
BOLIVIA, xi-xii, 9, 17, 19, 21, 25-6,
30, 36-8, 40, 81, 83, 87, 89-103,
106, 110-11, 113, 129, 131, 144,
226-7, 231, 233-55, 259, 261-3, 265,
267, 270-1, 297-301, 310; pro-
Nazis, 9
See also: BENI RIVER AND RE-
GION; BOLIVIAN REVOLU-
TIONARY JUNTA; CHACO;
PATIÑO, SIMÓN I.; SANTA
CRUZ DEPARTMENT; Bolivian
subheads under AGRICULTURE,
AMAZON BASIN, ANDES,
CULTURE, DIPLOMACY, ECO-
NOMICS, FRONTIERS, GEOG-
RAPHY, INTER-AMERICAN
RELATIONS, PEOPLES, POLI-
TICS, PRESS, RESOURCES, SO-
CIAL CONDITIONS, SOCIAL
LEGISLATION, TRANSPORT,
UNITED NATIONS, WAR.
BOLIVIAN POLITICS, 97, 251
Parties: 96; MNR, or National
Revolutionary Movement, 96-7;
PIR, or Left Revolutionary Party,
96-7
BOLIVIAN REVOLUTIONARY
JUNTA, 9, 93-5, 129; Cabinet, 97;
coup d'état of Dec. 20, 1943, 9, 79,
91, 93, 100; diplomatic recognition,
25-6; political terrorism, 111; recog-
nized, 98; social motivation, 96-7;
social propaganda, 97
Braun, Jocob A., 297-8

BRAZIL, ix, xi-xii, xiv, 3-9, 14-7,
19-22, 26-31, 34-78, 81, 84-5, 88,
104-8, 112, 118-21, 126, 128-39,
144-5, 243, 298-9, 328; Colonial
period, 68-70, 74, 192; area, 35, 67,
204; Maritime, Air, and Frontier
Police, 35; National Brazilian Acad-
emy of Letters, 133
See also: ARANHA; BRAZILIAN
EMPIRE; BRAZILIAN NORTH-
EAST; BRAZILIAN REPUBLIC;
BRAZILIAN STATES AND
TERRITORIES; VARGAS and
VARGAS REGIME; Brazilian
subheads under AGRICULTURE,
AMAZON BASIN, ANTI-
SEMITISM, CULTURE, DIPLO-
MACY, ECONOMICS, FRON-
TIERS, GEOGRAPHY, INTER-
AMERICAN RELATIONS,
PEOPLES, POLITICS, PRESS,
RESOURCES, SECRET POLICE,
SOCIAL CONDITIONS, SOCIAL
LEGISLATION, TRANSPORT,
UNITED NATIONS, WAR.
Brazil nuts, 239, 254
BRAZILIAN EMPIRE, 68-70
Braganza dynasty: 69-70; Dom
Pedro I, 69; Dom Pedro II, 49,
69-70, 76, 206, 274
Independence in Grito de Ypi-
ranga: 69
BRAZILIAN NORTHEAST, 69-70,
190-203, 264-7, 271-8, 287, 310-7
Droughts: 190-2, 194-7, 202, 266,
272-7, 310-4
Harbor construction: 271-2
Industries: 196
Textile mill at Pedra, 273-5
See also: AGRICULTURE; BIRDS;
CLIMATE — Duality; DESERTS
—Semideserts; FLOWERS—
flowering trees; IRRIGATION;
JUNGLES; MIGRATION; RE-
SOURCES; TRANSPORT.
BRAZILIAN POLITICS, 70, 276,
278, 281, 295
See also: BRAZILIAN EMPIRE;
BRAZILIAN REPUBLIC; VAR-